THE
JOSIAH
MANIFESTO

JONATHAN CAHN

**FRONT
LINE**

THE JOSIAH MANIFESTO by Jonathan Cahn
Published by FrontLine, an imprint of Charisma Media
600 Rinehart Road, Lake Mary, Florida 32746

Scripture quotations marked TLV are taken from the Tree of Life Translation of the Bible. Copyright © 2015 by The Messianic Jewish Family Bible Society.

While the author has made every effort to provide accurate, up-to-date source information at the time of publication, statistics and other data are constantly updated. Neither the publisher nor the author assumes any responsibility for errors or for changes that occur after publication. Further, the publisher and author do not have any control over and do not assume any responsibility for third-party websites or their content.

Visit the author's website at jonathancahn.com and booksbyjonathancahn.com.

Cataloging-in-Publication Data is on file with the Library of Congress.
International Standard Book Number: 978-1-63641-332-7
E-book ISBN: 978-1-63641-333-4

23 24 25 26 27 C 9 8 7 6 5 4 3 2 1

Printed in the United States of America

Most Charisma Media products are available at special quantity discounts for bulk purchase for sales promotions, premiums, fund-raising, and educational needs. For details, call us at (407) 333-0600 or visit our website at www.charismamedia.com.

CONTENTS

PART V: THE JUBILEAN REDEMPTION

PART VI: THE APPOINTED DAYS

PART VII: CHILD OF THE NILE

PART VIII: DAY OF THE TURNING

PART IX: THE BROKEN ALTAR

MANIFESTO

Part I

BEGINNINGS

Chapter 1

THE PRESENT DARKNESS

ADARKNESS HAS COME upon the world.

It is an ancient darkness and yet new in its manifesting. It is, at the time of this writing, permeating our media, our entertainments, our marketplaces, our schools, our corporations, our public squares, our governments, our culture, our lives. It is setting in motion the transformation of our society, the overturning of ancient foundations, and the destroying of age-old standards of morality, values, perception, and faith.

It is an unrelenting darkness, one that seeks not only to exist and grow but to exercise total dominion, to force all it touches into submission, to subjugate language, to alter perception, and to bend reality into its image. It is a darkness that requires every tongue to confess its name and every knee to bow down in its homage. As for those who would defy or resist its conquest, it seeks to assimilate and transform them or else destroy them, even to destroy their will to resist it. It is a totalitarian darkness. It cannot rest until all lights are extinguished.

In other books, I have written of this darkness, of its progression, of its consequences, its judgment, and the mysteries that lie behind it and that foretell its future. I have often been asked, "Is there hope?" "What can we do?" and, "How then should we live?"

There *is* hope. And there is a template that holds the keys and provides a guide as to how to live and prevail in light of this present and coming darkness. More than any book I've yet written, *The Josiah Manifesto* will reveal in detail and clarity that answer, that template, and that guide.

It will answer other questions as well...

> Could the events of modern times, even of recent years, be the outplaying of mysteries going back two and a half thousand years?
>
> Could these mysteries have ordained the exact timing of a recent calamity that dramatically altered our lives?
>
> Could they reveal the template of an event that overtook the United States Capitol?

Could they lie behind the rise and fall of a South American dictator?

Could they have altered the makeup and rulings of the Supreme Court?

Could a three-thousand-year-old calendar of appointed days provide the secret to the most dramatic year in living memory?

Could a child, a river, and a princess provide the key to a critical altering of America's course?

Could an ancient instrument sounded in biblical times to mark the rise of kings, the fall of cities, the changing of times and epochs, and the power of God have ushered in a historic change with regard to American civilization?

Could an array of Middle Eastern mysteries going back to the days of the Pharaohs have converged on Washington, DC, to touch America in a single hour, in a single moment?

Is America heading for judgment and calamity? Is the world?

Is there hope?

Have we been given a chance for redemption in the midst of judgment?

Is it possible that there exists a key, a blueprint, a revelation, an answer as to where we are, as to what the future holds, and as to how one can stand, in light of all that is to come, and prevail?

In order to find the answers, we must set out on a journey of prophetic mysteries. The journey will lead us to two islands, one in the Caribbean, the other in the Pacific, and to two ancient kings, one who remains a mystery, the other, a revelation. It will involve a mystery of times, a plague, two gates, two Supreme Court justices, a god of darkness, a calendar of sacred days, a night of signs, an ancient evil, a prophetic foreshadowing, more than one prophet, a multitude of leaders, an appointed word, a child and a river, a sacred assembly, a vision, an altar, a redemption, and an ancient instrument through which the power of God was manifested.

In my books I generally avoid making mention of myself. In that respect, *The Josiah Manifesto* will be different. I will appear in some of the mysteries to be opened, the reason being that I could not reveal them without bearing witness to what I saw and heard firsthand.

The Josiah Manifesto will go into realms I have never before gone into. Some of the mysteries will begin where others left off, as in those of *The Harbinger II*, *The Paradigm*, *The Oracle*, and *The Return of the Gods*. Their revelations will thus be furthered or brought to their conclusions. I will need to set the stage for those who have never read or heard of them and to refresh those who have. *The Josiah Manifesto* will take them to their next stage and level and will reveal what I've long held back from revealing as well as that which came after. And so there will be mysteries that in the past were launched that will now come in for a landing.

We will embark on a journey. The journey will open up a tapestry of mysteries, each interwoven with the others. At first appearance, they may not seem directly related to one another. And it may not be obvious where they are all heading. Each will be a puzzle piece of a still larger mystery in which they will all be joined together.

In most of my books, the overall context in which the mysteries appear could be discerned earlier on. But in this one, one mystery and context will lead to another and another. But as the revelation progresses, each piece will begin converging with the others and ultimately into one specific time and place. This, in turn, will open the door to the final revelation. That final revelation will, in turn, provide the answer, the key, the blueprint, and the manifesto.

We now begin the journey in an ancient valley out of which came the destruction of a nation.

Chapter 2

THE VALLEY

THE KING GAZED out into the valley. From the days of his childhood, he had heard of its many infamies and horrors.

The Most Unholy of Places

It lay just outside the walls of the holy city, but it was the most unholy of places. As he surveyed its expanse, he could see the heaps of stone that dotted its landscape. He could smell the charred remains and the smoldering ashes that covered its soil. It was a cursed valley.

Up to that moment, he would have had no reason to approach it and every reason to avoid it. It was the antithesis of everything he believed and was. His heart was pure, consecrated to God, undefiled. But the valley was the epitome of impurity, defilement, and unholiness. As he stared into its expanse, his heart could be filled only with revulsion, if not horror.

His people had been warned of it from the beginning. They had been separated from the surrounding nations for the purposes of God. But they had done as they had been warned never to do. They became as the peoples that surrounded them. They turned to other gods, to the gods of the valley. And there in the valley stood their idols along the heaps of stone. There they gathered to partake in the dark rites and rituals required of their new deities.

Strange Sacrifices

It was into that valley they brought their children. It was there by the altars of stone that they initiated their little ones into dark ceremonies. And there on those altars they lifted them up as sacrifices. They murdered their sons and daughters. They caused their children to pass through the fire. They slaughtered their most innocent. They inverted the most basic and natural instincts of life, that of parenthood, into a demonic pagan mania of death. Fathers became the executioners of their sons, and mothers, the murderers of their daughters.

The king had heard of the valley's evils since childhood. His own ancestors had partaken of them. In that valley, his grandfather had murdered his own son. Had he sacrificed another of his sons, the young king would never have been born.

But he had gone against the ways of his grandfather and father, turning to God from his youth and committing to following the ways of God with all his heart and strength. He knew exactly what the valley was—the most glaring witness of his nation's departure from God, its lowest depths, and the ultimate embodiment of its fall.

The Voices of the Children

And he knew that it was more than that. The valley held not only the darkest evils of his nation's past but the fate of its future. No nation can knowingly kill thousands of its most innocent and, in the end, escape the judgment of God. The voices of the children killed in that valley cried out for judgment.

He had no illusions as to the stakes involved—they were nothing less than his nation's destruction. And yet, despite what he knew, he could hope against hope for a different outcome. If he could bring the darkness of that valley to an end, then perhaps there was hope, perhaps there could be mercy, and perhaps the judgment could be averted or forestalled.

Of Life and Death

The valley had been, for the nation's children, the arbiter between life and death. Now it would be the arbiter of the nation's life or death. The king's descent into the valley would be central in his mission to turn the nation away from darkness and back to God—an undertaking of repentance embarked on in the hope of redemption.

Is it possible that the same ancient valley of darkness could hold the key to another nation's future—America's? And could the king and the act he would perform in that valley reveal the key to America's redemption and a blueprint for God's people?

———————————

To find the answer, we must move to the next puzzle piece of the mystery—an ancient ordinance of redemption and restoration and its manifestation on an island in the Caribbean.

Part II

ISLAND OF MYSTERIES

Chapter 3

THE YOVEL

THE MYSTERY GOES back to an ancient ordinance given to Israel at Mount Sinai, the law that ordained the observance of what would be called the *Yovel*.

The Seventh Sabbath

Every seventh day was a holy day, the *Shabbat* or *Sabbath*. Every seventh year was a holy year called the *Shemitah* or *Sabbath Year*. But the seventh Shemitah ushered in the most dramatic of years, the Yovel—the Jubilee.

> And you shall count seven sabbaths of years for yourself, seven times seven years; and the time of the seven sabbaths of years shall be to you forty-nine years. Then you shall cause the trumpet of the Jubilee to sound on the tenth day of the seventh month; on the Day of Atonement you shall make the trumpet to sound throughout all your land. And you shall consecrate the fiftieth year, and proclaim liberty throughout *all* the land to all its inhabitants. It shall be a Jubilee for you...[1]

Year of the Ram's Horn

The word *Jubilee* comes from the Hebrew *Yovel*, which is, itself, linked to blasting of the ram's horn. It was the sounding of the shofar, or ram's horn, that would mark the completion of the forty-nine years and usher in the fiftieth—thus the year of the Yovel, or Jubilee. The sound of the ram's horn evoked the power of God. The Jubilee was the year of God's power—and blessings.

Year of Return and Reconciliation

The Jubilee was the year of return.

> ...and each of you shall return to his possession...[2]

If one had lost one's possession, in the year of Jubilee, one was to return to it.

...and each of you shall return to his family.[3]

In the year of Jubilee, if one was separated from one's family, one was to return to them. So the Jubilee was both the year of return and reconciliation.

The Sabbath of Sabbaths

...you shall neither sow nor reap what grows of its own
accord, nor gather the grapes of your untended vine.[4]

The Jubilee was a Sabbath of Sabbaths. And as the Sabbath involved rest, so in the year of Jubilee, no one was to labor in the fields or vineyards. The land was to rest, as were those working the land. The Jubilee was a year of cessation.

Year of Restoration

The Jubilee was the year of restoration.

...what was sold shall remain in the hand of him who bought
it until the Year of Jubilee; and in the Jubilee it shall be
released, and he shall return to his possession.[5]

If one had been forced to give up part of one's possession, one's field, one's plot of land, or one's ancestral inheritance, in the year of Jubilee one's land would be released to go back to the one who had lost it, the original owner. In the year of Jubilee the land would return to the owner and the owner to the land.

Year of Release and Freedom

Engraved on the American icon, the Liberty Bell, are the words "Proclaim liberty throughout all the land unto all the inhabitants thereof."[6] The words come from Leviticus 25, the Jubilean ordinance. The Jubilee was the year of liberty.

And if one of your brethren who dwells by you becomes
poor, and sells himself...And if he is not redeemed in these
years, then he shall be released in the Year of Jubilee.[7]

If one had fallen on hard times to the point that one had sold oneself into servitude, then in the year of Jubilee, one would be set free. In the year of Jubilee, slaves were set free, prisoners were released, and those in bondage were liberated. It was the time of release and freedom.

A Mass Nullification

When the shofar sounded to inaugurate the Jubilee, everything changed. What was lost was restored. What was separated was reconciled. The prisoners were set free. And the exiled came home. It was a mass nullification. That which was done was undone. Everything was reversed. Everything was inverted. Everything came full circle. Everything returned to the beginning, to its original place and state.

Could this most unique of years transcend the bounds of ancient times and its Middle Eastern context? Could it touch the modern world? Could it have ordained and determined some of the most critical events of recent times? Could it have altered the course of America and the world?

For the answer and the next piece of the mystery, we must journey to an island of palm trees, sugar cane, salsa music, and old American cars—a beautiful tropical island under the weight of a brutal curse.

Chapter 4

THE STRANGER IN THE LIVING ROOM

IT WAS A secret meeting. The man was a stranger to me, but he had requested my presence.

A Secret Meeting

I was driven to a house in northern New Jersey in which the man was staying on his visit to America. We met in the living room. He was short, elderly, bald, and stocky. His name was Samuel. He spoke to me through a translator. He had come to America with a mission—to ask me if I would come to his homeland. It was an island in the Caribbean, one unlike any other in the region or, for that matter, the world.

A Cursed Island

The island, he said, was cursed. Those of its inhabitants who believed in and followed God lived under an iron hand of oppression and persecution, not to mention extreme poverty. But there was hope. A change was coming—and thus his mission and his invitation.

The island was Cuba, the only Communist nation in the Western Hemisphere. In January 1959, Fidel Castro and his army of revolutionaries entered the city of Havana to set up a revolutionary government to rule the island. The beginning of his reign was greeted by many with great optimism and hope. But that would quickly fade.

The air of freedom soon dissipated into an era of arrests and imprisonments, indoctrination into Communist ideology, the crushing of all dissent, and the execution of those who were now viewed as enemies of the state. Many sought to flee the island. Many lost their homes and possessions. A persecution was launched against Christians. Churches were closed; pastors were exiled, imprisoned, or sent to reeducation camps. Christians were driven underground. Under Castro's reign Cuba became a land of impoverishment, hopelessness, totalitarian repression, and paralysis.

The Changing

But there had been a change, he said. After decades of oppression Castro had agreed to allow a measure of religious freedom. It would take the form of a monthlong evangelical celebration. During that time, Christians would be free to worship in a series of mass public events to be held throughout the island and broadcast on Cuban television. The last event would take place in Havana, in Revolution Square.

Samuel was one of those given charge to organize the celebration. "I came on behalf of the Christians of Cuba. We want you to come and inaugurate the month of celebrations by sounding the ram's horn at the first event. We want you to minister throughout the island." I prayed about it and said yes.

"You Will Be Given Access"

A week before leaving for Cuba, a man showed up at Beth Israel, the congregation I lead in northern New Jersey. He asked to speak to me after the worship service. He had come from Cuba. He was a pastor. He had been arrested on account of his faith and ministry and was sent to one of Castro's prison camps. After his release, the door had opened for him to come to America. That morning, he ended up at Beth Israel. It was the service in which I had asked the congregation to pray for my upcoming journey to Cuba.

After giving me advice on what to do and not do on the journey, he said, "You will be given access to go where others have not gone. The doors will open before you. And you will enter the king's palace."

The Jubilee Is Coming

When I prayed as to what I should share with the people of Cuba, I was led to the message of the Jubilee. On one hand, it would be the most contrary of messages to proclaim on an island under the rule of a totalitarian government, a message of freedom, restoration, reconciliation, and liberation, the reversing and undoing of bondage. And so to those who had known only oppression, I would proclaim freedom. To those who had lost their lands and possessions, I would proclaim restoration. To those who had been separated from their loved ones, I would proclaim reconciliation. And to those who lived their lives as captive of brutal totalitarian regime, I would proclaim release.

The sharing of such a message in such a context was dangerous. But I had no doubt that the Jubilee was the message I had to bring them. The entire celebration would be ushered in with the sounding of the ram's horn, the same instrument by which the Jubilee was ushered in. I sent word to the leaders who had invited me to minister, letting them know that I would focus on the Jubilee. I thought of the phrase *"The Jubilee comes!"* It wasn't long before many of the believers in Cuba were referring to the celebration as *El Jubileo*, the Jubilee. And as the event drew near, three Spanish words began appearing everywhere on the island on churches, on houses, on walls and fences, even on taxi cabs, *"El Jubileo viene!" "The Jubilee comes!"*

Sign of Release

We arrived a week before the first of several mass gatherings, the one that would inaugurate the monthlong celebration. I spent that time ministering in the region of the Oriente, speaking at the churches of the Cuban believers and at outdoor gatherings. I was told that at every church in which I spoke, there would be informants planted among the people to report any word that could be taken as critical of or a threat to the government. As I spoke of the Jubilee, of freedom, and of God's revolution, my translator looked stunned and occasionally stumbled through his words, fearing we both would end up in one of Castro's prison camps.

Everywhere I went, I brought the shofar. Many of the Cuban believers saw it as a sign of release and freedom, which, of course, it was. There would be many stories told and retold by them of the signs that manifested on their island when the shofar was sounded. One of them happened in an unlikely place, just outside a convenience store.

And the Deaf Shall Hear

We had been warned that we were never to attract a crowd outside the walls of a church. But it happened anyway. Our hosts had taken us to a convenience store to pick up some needed items. I left the shofar inside the van. When we returned, we found the van surrounded by a large crowd. A man had peered into the van's windows and had spotted the shofar. He told the others. They gathered around the van and now pleaded with me to blow it. So I did.

The moment I sounded it, a loud shriek and then high-pitched shouting went forth from the crowd. A thin middle-aged man was jumping up and down. "What happened?" we asked. "The man is deaf!" they said. "But when you blew the shofar, he heard the sound!" The power, of course, came from God. But the shofar is given in Scripture as a sign and vessel of that power.

The Inauguration

The Jubilee was to be more than a celebration; it was to be a journey. It would move across the island from east to west. The first gathering, the celebration's inaugural event, was to take place in the city of Moa, near Cuba's easternmost end. From the time Communism first took hold of the island up until then, there had never been an event quite like it.

On the appointed day, Christians began converging on the chosen site to pray, worship, and proclaim the Word of God, outdoors, openly, and in mass numbers. Overseeing the event were soldiers, government security forces, and Communist officials nervously looking on. What took place in Moa would be reported to Castro and the central government in Havana. If the government felt that anything had gone wrong or anything posed a threat to its rule, the month of freedom would be in danger of being canceled at its inauguration.

Horn of the Israelites

It was the critical moment of the inaugural event. A Christian leader stepped up to the microphone to read a chosen passage of Scripture. It came from the prophets of Israel. It spoke of a land under a curse, a land that had turned away from God and was now filled with darkness, plagues, brokenness, loss, deprivation, want, poverty, barrenness, and hopelessness. The passage spoke of Israel, but now it was recited in view of Cuba. The government officials showed no reaction, perhaps unaware that the ancient words were being read and understood as applying to their nation.

The speaker then came to the verse, "Blow the trumpet..."[1] I set the shofar to my mouth and prepared to blow. One of the government officials turned to one of the organizers of the event and asked, "Isn't that the horn of the Israelites?" He had no idea what it signified.

The chosen Scripture called for a sacred gathering of prayer to be inaugurated by the sounding of the shofar. In biblical times the ones who would sound the shofar to usher in such gatherings would be the priests, the sons of Aaron. Those who invited me had no idea that I was descended from the priestly house, a son of Aaron. It was also the sons of Aaron who would sound the shofar in the year of Jubilee.

El Jubileo

I set the shofar to my mouth and blew. The Jubilee had begun. It would now move across the island from the eastern coast, through the region of the Oriente, through the major cities of Holguín and Camagüey, through a multitude of towns and villages, and finally to Havana. In every place it moved, there were open celebrations, worship, prayer, the Word of God, and the air of freedom.

In ancient Israel, the Jubilee was to last a year. The Jubilee of Cuba was set to last only a month—at least officially. The freedoms granted within that month would be removed at the month's end. But the Jubilee never stopped. It had given the believers of Cuba a new hope, a new confidence, and a new boldness. In the midst of repression, there would be revival. The four walls of the island's churches would not be able to contain the people who wanted to come inside. What had begun in that celebration would go on long after its official end.

———————————

So we journeyed with the Jubilee across the island, having no idea that a mystery was unfolding with every footstep. The mystery would center on one man, my translator, and would present a message to the island. And it would only be revealed in his last footsteps.

Chapter 5

THE RETURN OF THE EXILE

GOD SPOKE TO ancient Israel through prophetic acts.

Acts of the Prophets

The prophet Ahijah tore his cloak as a prophetic act to symbolize the nation's coming division. The prophet Jeremiah carried a wooden yoke of bondage before his nation's rulers as a prophetic act to symbolize his nation's coming bondage to Babylon. The prophet Ezekiel packed his belongings and departed in the sight of his fellow countrymen as a prophetic act foreshadowing their coming exile from the land. In each case, the prophet became a living sign and his act, a prophetic message to the nation.

Such acts could also be performed without any knowledge of their prophetic significance on the part of the ones performing them. The prophet Jeremiah was told to go down to the potter's house, and there God would speak to him. So he went and watched as the potter worked at his wheel to create a clay vessel. But the vessel was marred in the potter's hand. The potter then reworked the clay into a new vessel. It was a prophetic message to a marred and fallen nation on the verge of destruction. And yet it was brought forth by a man who had no idea he was bringing it forth.

A Man Called Felix

Before I embarked for Cuba, I had to find a translator. I asked the leader of the Spanish Ministry at Beth Israel, a man named Felix, who regularly translated my weekly messages, if he could do it. Felix was a man of godliness, humility, zeal, and passion for the ways of God. It had already been on his heart to go with me to Cuba. He immediately said yes.

As we made our way across the island, I shared of the Jubilee and Felix spoke of the Jubileo. I read the ancient ordinance of Leviticus 25: "Each of you shall return to his property..."[1] Felix then read the same from his Spanish Bible. Felix had planned on being on the island for only two weeks. But he was so moved by what he was seeing that he called his employer to ask for more time. His employer gave him one more week.

"We Knew You Were Coming"

A strange phenomenon accompanied us. Virtually everywhere we went, people would come up to us with a similar story. They said they knew we were coming. Some of them had had dreams about it. They saw our faces. Others told us that the Spirit had spoken to them about it. Others told us they had seen visions. Still others told us they just knew and were waiting for us to come.

As we moved with the celebration westward, we came to the province of Camagüey, a land of cows, citrus fruit, farms, and sugar cane. We arrived there at the end of the third week of the journey. It was Felix's last day on the island. It was there that a mystery, years in the making, would be revealed.

The Exile

When I asked Felix to come to Cuba, I had no idea of his past, beyond the fact that he was of Spanish descent. But as we journeyed through the island, he told me his story. He was of Cuban descent. In fact, he had been born on the island. With the coming of Castro and the revolution, Felix's family lost everything—their house, their land, their possessions. While he was still an infant, his family fled the island for America.

As an adult, Felix dedicated his life to Jesus. He was transformed. He began ministering God's love and salvation to the poor and to all who would receive it. But there was something missing. He had always dreamed and now prayed that one day he would return to Cuba, to the land that his family had lost. Though he never told me at the time, when I asked him to be my translator in Cuba, he knew his prayers had been answered.

It was on that day, the end of his journey, that Felix told me of the land of his birth—it was Camagüey. The journey's end had brought him back to his beginnings.

That day, Felix attempted to make contact with the pastor of a church not far from the region in which he was born. He was hoping they could quickly convene a meeting in which we could minister. When I asked the man in charge of our scheduling if we could fulfill Felix's request, he told me it would not be possible. The place where we were scheduled to minister that night had been planned for and set a good while back. I relayed the news to Felix. He was disappointed but accepted it.

The Farm

We set out for the appointed meeting in the late afternoon. The closer we came to our destination, the more rural it became. The buildings disappeared, then the houses, and then the road, which was now a dirt path that wound through something of a forest. And then we saw it.

It was a farm in the middle of nowhere. "Who are we going to minister to?" we asked our driver. "And how will they find us?" "They will come," he answered. And they would. They would be brought in on open-air grain trucks, at least fifty of them on each truck.

The owners of the farm welcomed us in and led us to an outdoor table on which they had prepared for us a meal. As we ate, their little children ran wild around the table, along with chickens and goats. As it neared time to minister, I looked for Felix, but he had disappeared.

Each Shall Return

Finally, I spotted him in the distance, walking toward me, along with some of the farm hands. Something was not quite right. He appeared shaken, dazed, stunned. "What happened?" I asked. "This place," he said, "this farm..." "What?" I asked again. "This is our land!" he said. "This is the land of my family! They showed me around. They told me the name of its owner. It was my grandfather! This is the land we lost! This is my land, my inheritance!"

In the ancient law of the Jubilee, God ordained that *each shall return to his own possession*. And now Felix had returned to his own possession. Three thousand years earlier, it was written, "each of you shall return to his family."[2] Felix had come home to the land of his family. As was ordained in the Jubilee, he had come back to that which he had lost. After years of dreaming and praying, Felix had returned.

A Panoply of Quirks

The mystery had unfolded with exact precision. It had brought us to the exact site on the exact day. And it had happened only because the national celebration happened to have arrived in Camagüey on Felix's last day on the island. And it was only his last day because his employer happened to allow him one more week and no more. And we were taken to that farm only because those in charge of our schedule happened to know the people who worked there.

Felix, in turn, had been on that journey only because I happened to ask him to go as my translator. I had asked him only because he happened to be the leader of the Spanish ministry. And he was the leader of the Spanish ministry only because he happened to be led to go to a congregation named Beth Israel. Such is the hand of God. The mystery and its journey were years in the making, decades in the making. Felix's life was itself a journey of restoration that could be revealed only on the day he returned to that farm in the middle of nowhere, his ancestral possession.

"I Am a Sign"

And then there was the journey itself. The journey was also a sign and a message. In Felix the people of Cuba were seeing one of their own, long separated and exiled, now come home to his inheritance.

Everywhere we went, I spoke of the ancient ordinance command that ordained that *each shall return to his own possession*. Everywhere we went Felix translated those words into Spanish. And every time he did, he moved one step closer to returning to his long-lost possession. In every place, I said the words "I am a sign to you." And in every place Felix repeated those words in Spanish. But he wasn't only repeating them. When God told the prophets to perform prophetic acts before the people, He told them that they would become *signs* to their nation. So Felix had become a sign to his nation. When the revolution came, he lost what had belonged to him. So too had the nation. The revolution had caused him to become an exile. So too it had caused Cuba to become a nation in exile. The revolution had cast a shadow over his life. So too it had cast a shadow over the island. But the message he gave was one of hope. There was an answer. There was a way, but it could be found only in God. In God was the power of restoration, freedom, and redemption. In God was the power of Jubilee.

The Dream

Long before I journeyed to Felix's homeland, he had journeyed to mine. There, in Israel, in Jerusalem, at the Western Wall, he bowed his head in prayer and asked God to bring him back to Cuba. He promised that if God would answer his prayer, he would build a church on his father's land and there preach the Word of God.

Now, as he stood on the land of his inheritance, he remembered his dream and his prayer. The people on the farm then led him across the property. They had something to show him. There, on the other side of the farm was the church. They had already built it. What he had dreamed of and prayed for throughout his life was already there, waiting for him.

To His Own Possession

They led him inside. It was now filled with the men, women, and children who had been brought in from the nearby villages. The church's pastor opened the service by reading a Scripture he had prepared for that night having no idea that the son of the land would return. The Scripture was this: "Each shall return to his possession."[3] He had just been led to recite it that night. And just happened to also be the message we had planned to give them.

That night, Felix ministered the Word of God in the church he had long dreamed about in the land of his inheritance. The prayer he had lifted to God at the Western Wall had been answered by the hand of God. His journey was complete and his Jubilee fulfilled.

What happened that night in that farm in the middle of nowhere was the manifestation of one side of the Jubilee—the side of blessing. But there was another. And it is this other side of the Jubilee that holds the secret to understanding the events that have come upon America. It is this that we will now open and, in so doing, find the next puzzle piece and key to the mystery.

This part of the mystery will also center on a specific place and a certain man but each of a very different nature from what we have just seen. The place is Havana, and the man—Fidel Castro.

Chapter 6

A SIGN FOR A DICTATOR

IT WAS NEW Year's Eve. The Cuban dictator Fulgencio Batista was hosting a holiday celebration at Campamento Columbia, a military base in Havana. Because of his anti-Communist stand, Batista had long enjoyed the support of the American government. But his seven-year reign over the island was marked by corruption, repression, and indifference. That New Year's Eve would ring in not only a new year but a new regime.

Batista's Farewell

In the midst of the celebration Batista informed his cabinet and his officials that he would be abdicating his office as president and would flee the island. In the early hours of the morning, Batista and his family, along with some of his closest supporters, boarded a plane headed for the Dominican Republic. On New Year's Day a new era began.

Batista had fled in the face of an uprising led by a tall, bearded, cigar-smoking revolutionary in army fatigues and an army of ragged guerrilla fighters. They had begun their revolt in the Sierra Maestra mountain range on the island's eastern end. After suffering a series of losses against Castro's forces and sensing the evaporation of his support among the Cuban military and the American government, Batista made the decision to abdicate. That day, the nation of Cuba came under the rule of Fidel Castro and his revolution. It was January 1, 1959.

The Revolutionary

Castro arrived in Havana seven days later. He had promised a democratic government, freedom of the press, free and fair elections, and the protection of individual rights. His entrance was greeted with cheers, jubilation, celebration, and great expectation. He had been hailed by many as something of a savior, the center of a quasi-religious euphoria. But the euphoria and hope of those first days would soon evaporate.

It wasn't long before Castro and his revolutionary government began dismantling the institutions and infrastructure of Cuban democracy. Those now deemed as enemies of the revolution were arrested, tried before revolutionary councils, and imprisoned. Many were executed. Others were assassinated without any trial. Others were tortured. The new government became famous for its many firing squads. The revolution had birthed a reign of terror.

The Prison Camp Island

Others were sent to labor camps, prison camps, and "reeducation" camps. The entire island had now become a reeducation camp. Cubans were indoctrinated from early childhood into Communist ideology. The indoctrination was everywhere, in newspapers, on radio and television, and on the posters and billboards that marked every Cuban city, town, and village.

Freedom of speech, assembly, and thought soon became a faded memory. Dissenting opinions could be punished by imprisonment and execution. Castro would eventually declare Cuba an atheist state. Those who followed the ways of God, those who even believed in God, were now enemies of the revolution. Ministers were imprisoned or killed.

The government was not content to implement its revolution inside the island's borders. Cuba soon became an exporter of Marxist ideology and revolutionary warfare. It supported Communist uprisings and militias across the world. It even sent its own soldiers into foreign lands with the aim of overturning governments.

The revolutionary nation was viewed by many as a danger to the global order. It was cut off from much of the world. It became a fortress island known for totalitarianism, deprivation, and repression. Many, indeed, saw themselves as prisoners in their own land. Others risked their lives trying to get out.

A Revolution in Reverse

We set out from Camagüey to Havana—the site of the final celebration and the center of Castro's government. In the midst of our journey, it dawned on me that we were walking in the footsteps of the Cuban revolution. The revolution had been launched at the island's eastern end. The celebration had been launched at the island's eastern end. The revolution had been centered in the region of the Oriente. Our time in Cuba had likewise centered in the region of the Oriente. The revolution had moved westward through the land of Holguín and then Camagüey. The celebration had likewise moved westward through Holguín and then Camagüey. The revolutionary march had culminated in Havana. The celebration and our journey across the island would likewise culminate in Havana.

The Jubilee sets in motion a reversal and an undoing. It sets free those who are bound, brings back those who are separated, and restores that which

23

was lost. So the Jubilean celebration was itself a reversal, an undoing. It followed in the path of the revolution but in reverse. The revolution had sought to drive God out of the public squares and ultimately out of the nation. The celebration was bringing Him back. The revolution had abolished freedom. The celebration was a manifestation of its restoration. The revolution had sought to stamp out all open manifestations of faith, worship, and Scripture. The celebration had opened the doors for the open manifestation of all three. And for those Cubans who couldn't witness it for themselves, it came to them as well through television broadcasts into their living rooms.

Havana

Havana was a city frozen in time, filled with dilapidated buildings of every color, billboards of Castro and Che Guevara, and American cars preserved from the 1950s. It was there, in the Cuban capital, that the monthlong Jubilean celebration would be sealed. In this was another parallel to the revolution. Castro's revolution was sealed in the mass rallies of victory held in the Plaza de la Revolución, Revolution Square. The Jubilee would conclude in the same city— in the same square.

And there would be yet another parallel—as we approached our final destination, we received word that Castro had decided that he would attend the event in Revolution Square. As he had once come to that square in the triumph of the revolution and many times after that to preach his revolutionary ideology, he would now go there not to speak but to silently watch. He would sit among thousands of Christians in Revolution Square in a gathering of faith, prayer, and worship, and in which the name of Jesus would be proclaimed.

Revolution Square

Castro had taken a strong interest in the celebration. He had taken a strong interest in us—even in me. On more than one occasion, it was relayed to me from sources in his government that the Comandante was watching me. Castro, of course, had many informants. But he had also been watching the events on Cuban television. At one point in our journey, it came back to us that he had inquired, "What is this Jewish man doing with the Christians?" And still, another time, we were informed that he had asked, "Who is this bearded man who is causing all this ruckus?"

On the day of the final event, Revolution Square was filled with thousands and thousands of believers. Then Castro arrived. He was, at that time, in his seventies and, except for his green army fatigues, looked more like an aged rabbi than a revolutionary commander. He made his way to the front row, where he was seated. The celebration began. The sound of worship filled Revolution Square, and the name of Jesus echoed through the city.

I had come there with a shofar, but was not led to sound it. I was led instead to hold it up for the entire event as the biblical symbol of freedom, restoration, hope, liberation, and the power of God. It was to be lifted up so that all of Revolution Square and all who watched by television throughout the island would see the sign of the Jubilee.

The Engraved Trumpet

I had another mission as well. Before I left for Cuba, I knew I was to bring a gift to give to Castro. The Cuban pastor who had come to our worship service the week before I left had alluded to it in his prophetic word. It was there at the final event in Revolution Square that arrangements were made with Castro's cabinet for that gift to be given.

I was to give Castro the sign of the Jubilee, the shofar. While in Havana, I was led to have it inscribed with Scripture. We found a shop that specialized in inscriptions. The man who actually did the inscribing wasn't at work that day. When we told the shopkeepers, "It's for the president," they rushed to the man's house. Shortly after that, he appeared out of breath at the shop. I showed him the Scripture, and he began carefully carving the letters into the shofar.

Word came from Castro that I and my translator would be granted access to the Presidential Palace. I had initially intended to give him one gift, but before the appointed day, I was led to add another. We entered the Presidential Palace and were greeted by a middle-aged woman, a member of Castro's cabinet, sent to receive the gifts. We presented them to her.

Three Gifts

The first was the shofar, the herald of the Jubilee, the sign of freedom throughout the land, restoration, return, reconciliation, liberty, and redemption, a message for the Cuban ruler.

The second was something Castro had outlawed—a Bible in Spanish. Years earlier he had outlawed its printing and distribution. But now he received one for himself.

The third was a message I had written to him in the form of a letter. I cannot give the details of what was in the message except to say it was a prophetic word—connected to the Jubilee and concerned freedom and the lifting of the curse.

The King's Palace

The cabinet member received the gifts. She also affirmed what we had been told by others—that the Comandante was very much aware of my journey across the island, very much interested, and very much watching.

Not long after that, Castro would send word thanking me for the gifts. We also received word that his cabinet had examined the shofar and were intrigued by it. They wanted to know how to use it.

As we left the Presidential Palace that day, I remembered the prophecy given to me by the Cuban pastor the week before I left for the island: "You will enter the king's palace." And so it had come true.

The shofar I gave in the Presidential Palace was not just a gift but a sign—a prophetic sign. Its meaning and mystery would be manifested in the years to come. It was a sign of the rise and fall of Fidel Castro.

Chapter 7

THE FALL OF KINGS

THE SHOFAR IS given in Scripture as an instrument to mark the changing of times, the beginning and end of epochs.

The Marker of Times

In ancient Israel the shofar had marked the holy days, the beginning of months, the reign of kings and their end. Could the shofar that was sounded throughout Cuba and given to Fidel Castro have served its ancient role as the marker of times, the beginning and end of epochs? And could the Jubilee be the key in determining the timing of those epochs?

The month of freedom had given Castro the chance to loosen the chains that had fettered the island, but he would not. He had allowed for a moment of freedom. He had opened up the island to a manifestation of the Jubilee. But in the end he would resist it and bring it to a close. And though for the Cuban believers the Jubilee would go on in the form of revival, Castro would not lessen the grip of his iron hand from the island.

The Fiftieth Year

But there are mysteries deeper than what is seen and recorded of human history, mysteries that lie behind it and direct its course. The Jubilee brings undoing, nullification, and reversal. Is it possible that such a mystery could manifest in modern history and lie behind the outworking and timing of events in the modern world?

According to the ancient ordinance, the Jubilee is the fiftieth year. It is important here to clarify. It is common to think of one's fiftieth year as beginning when one turns fifty. But one's fiftieth birthday marks the end of one's fiftieth year. One's fiftieth year begins on one's forty-ninth birthday, when one has completed one's forty-ninth year. It comes to its conclusion when one turns fifty. So the fiftieth and Jubilean year begins at the end of the forty-ninth year of the countdown and culminates one year later.

The Seventh Seven

The transformation of Cuba into a Communist regime, its repressions, its imprisonments and executions, the crushing hand of its government all centered on the rise and reign of Fidel Castro. His reign began in 1959. The Jubilean ordinance reads:

> And you shall count seven sabbaths of years for yourself,
> seven times seven years; and the time of the seven sabbaths
> of years...[1]

Seven sevens or seven Sabbaths of years set the timing for the Jubilee. So what then happens if we count seven sevens of years from the beginning of Castro's reign? The first seven is 1959 to 1966. The second: 1966 to 1973. The third: 1973 to 1980. The fourth: 1980 to 1987. The fifth: 1987 to 1994. The sixth: 1994 to 2001. And the seventh seven: 2001 to 2008. The seventh seven is the key.

> ...shall be to you forty-nine years...[2]

The seventh seven, the completion of the forty-nine years, and thus the beginning of the fiftieth, is 2008. The fiftieth year, the Jubilee of Castro's rise to power, is the year 2008. Could that year have been significant concerning his reign?

At eighty-one years old, beset by health problems, Castro sent a letter to Cuba and the world, posting it on the official website of the Communist Party newspaper *Granma*. It was his letter of resignation. He was resigning as president of Cuba, bringing his reign over the island to an end. It was truly the end of an era. When was that era brought to an end? In 2008, *the fiftieth year—the seventh seven of years, the year of Jubilee.*

The Prophecy on the Walls

What began when Castro heard the news of Batista's abdication at the start of 1959 came to its conclusion in 2008, the fiftieth year. The reign of Fidel Castro that had dominated the island and impacted modern history for over two generations came to an end with the Jubilee. Its ancient power to undo what had been done—had undone it.

The posters of my sounding the shofar along with the words *"El Jubileo viene!"* *"The Jubilee comes!"* remained on walls, fences, and vehicles long after I left the island. The words could be taken as prophetic—a message as to what would come in the year of Jubilee. When the Jubilee came, it would bring a release, a relinquishing, a nullification, and an undoing. It was a matter of counting. The seventh seven would usher it in.

Countdown for a Dictator

The mystery would go still deeper.

The day on which Batista set in motion his resignation as president of Cuba was December 31, 1958. It was then that he issued an invitation to his top officials to gather on New Year's Eve for a celebration at his Camp Columbia home. But the purpose of the gathering was to inform them of the end of his reign.

Starting the countdown from the exact day that Batista set in motion his resignation—seven sevens of years to the fiftieth year and seven sevens of days to the fiftieth day—the fiftieth day of the fiftieth year—what would it bring us to? The fiftieth day of the fiftieth year was February 18, 2008—the Jubilean day of the Jubilean year of Batista's resignation. Did anything of significance happen on that day?

On February 18, 2008, Fidel Castro set in motion the end of his reign as leader of Cuba.

Castro prepared his resignation in the Jubilean year and on the exact Jubilean day of the year and day that Batista prepared his resignation. December 31, 1958, constituted the last day of Batista's presidency. The Jubilean countdown from Batista's last full day as president brings us to the last day of Castro's presidency.

The Fiftieth Day of the Fiftieth Year

On the final day of 1958, Batista began planning for the end. His presidency was to be sealed with a letter of resignation. In the early evening of the fifitieth day of the fifiteth year from the last day of Batista's presidency, on his own last day as president of Cuba, Fidel Castro finished writing a letter that would bring his presidency to an end.

In the early evening of his last day as president, Batista ordered his military aide to come to his residence with two items—a passport and a list. The list had the names of those he had chosen to flee the island with him. By 10 p.m. of that New Year's Eve, Batista's top government officials became aware of his plan to abdicate. At midnight Batista wished his guests happy New Year and began the transfer of power.

Batista had prepared his resignation on December 31 and planned for it to go into effect after midnight on the first day of the new year. Fidel Castro had prepared his resignation on February 18 and planned likewise that it would only take effect after midnight. On February 19, 2008, Castro's resignation went into effect. It was the fiftieth day of the fiftieth year of the very day that Batista's resignation took effect.

The Last Letter

Not long after midnight, Batista read his resignation letter out loud to his top officials and gave it to them to sign. They passed it among themselves and affixed their signatures. The end of Batista's rule was now sealed.

On February 18, 2008, Castro gave his resignation letter to the government officials in charge of *Granma*, the official newspaper of the Central Committee of the Cuban Communist Party. After midnight it was in their hands to post it on their official site. The posting would officially mark the end of Castro's reign.

The signing of Batista's resignation letter by the top officials in his government marked the end of his reign and the beginning of Fidel Castro's. If one counts seven sevens of years and seven sevens of days from that year, that day—*and that time*—one is brought to February 19, 2008—in the early hours of the day. So it was then in those early hours that the Jubilean day began. In accordance with the ancient mystery, it was exactly then, *in the very first hours* of that day, that the announcement went forth to the world that Fidel Castro's reign had come to its end.

Hour of Abdication

After relinquishing his power, Batista headed for the plane that would take him along with his family and his top officials out of the country and into exile. All this took place around 3 a.m. After his plane took off, the news spread to the island and to the world that he had resigned and fled. On the fiftieth day of the fiftieth year from the moment of his departure, the official news site of the Central Committee of the Cuban Communist Party released Castro's announcement of resignation to the island and the world. It happened just around 3 *a.m.* That morning the world awoke to the news of Castro's resignation, on the Jubilean morning, the fiftieth day of the fiftieth year of the morning it had awoken to the news of Batista's resignation.

Modern Times and Ancient Mysteries

It is hard for the modern mind to fathom the possibility that behind the events, movements, and overall progression of world history lies a deeper story, an unseen hand, and a mystery. The story, the hand, and the mystery are ancient but as critical to the modern world as they had been to the ancient world. Castro's rule had been among the most consequential of modern history. It had constituted the first Communist regime in the Western Hemisphere. It had turned Cuba into a catalyst, a training ground, and an arsenal of armed revolutionary movements throughout the world. And at one point, with Castro's encouragement, it had brought the world to the brink of nuclear war. And yet greater, more critical, and more powerful was the ancient mystery that enfolded it.

The same mystery and the same invisible hand that caused an exiled Cuban son to unknowingly return to his ancestral possession had now caused a reigning Cuban dictator to relinquish his power in the set year, on the set day. Each was a manifestation of the Jubilee, one in space and the other in time. Remove any of the events leading up to them, the twists and quirks, or move any of them out of their place, and none of it would have come about exactly as it did.

The Parameters of the Mystery

Throughout his days of power, Castro had borne different titles and offices. But it was long after he came to power that he assumed the office and title of *president*. Had he not done so, he could not have paralleled Batista's resignation from the presidency in the fiftieth year. Had he not survived against many challenges or had he resigned at an earlier time, as most leaders do, it would not have taken place in the Jubilean year. Had he decided to resign even a week earlier or a week later, it would not have happened on the Jubilean day of the Jubilean year. And yet it is not so much that the mystery works inside the parameters of human history; it is that human history works inside the parameters of the mystery.

The Inscription

In the ancient world, kings were given signs foreshadowing the end of their reign. In the modern world, Castro was given such a sign. It came to him in the form of a shofar, the sign of the Jubilee, the release ushered in by the seventh seven of years. The sign spoke of an ancient countdown that would determine how much time he had left until the end of his reign.

It is written that God raises up kings to power and removes them from their thrones. Castro's reign had been among the longest of any leader in modern times. It had outlasted an American-sponsored invasion, multiple assassination plots, the Cold War, the fall of his principal benefactor, the Soviet Union, the extreme impoverishment of his nation, many American presidents, and a multitude of varied other crises. But it was brought to its end by the Jubilee. The ancient ordinance given in the book Castro had banned had determined how long it would last, even from his very first day in power.

Could the mystery of the Jubilee and its manifestation in Cuba provide the first puzzle piece in the calamitous events that overtook America?

Chapter 8

THE JUBILEAN DICHOTOMY

WE ARE ABOUT to see that the mystery that manifested on the island of Cuba would later manifest to America and the world. The manifestation would be of a very different nature, but the dynamics and parameters of time would be the same. In order to understand what would come upon America, we must understand the dynamics of the Jubilee as touching Cuba.

The Two Sides of the Mystery

The Jubilee has two sides. In the case of Cuba, the Jubilee was an unequivo-cally positive phenomenon. It brought freedom and blessing. For the first time since the revolution, they were free to gather, speak, and worship in mass and in the open. The Jubilee opened up the long-closed doors and broke down the formerly impenetrable walls.

In the case of the Cuban exile, Felix, the Jubilee was, likewise, a blessing. It brought the fulfillment of a lifelong dream and a fervent prayer. It gave back a measure of that which had been taken away and brought an exile home to his ancestral possession.

On the other hand, for Fidel Castro, the Jubilee was not positive or a blessing. Its promise of freedom was a danger to his hold on the island. He would seek to bring it to an end. But in the end the Jubilee would take away his power and remove him from office. It would reverse and undo his ascen-sion. It would bring his reign to an end.

The Repossessed and the Dispossessed

So on the one hand, the Jubilee brought blessing. On the other, it removed blessing. On the one hand, it empowered. On the other, it removed power. One the one hand, it restored what was lost. On the other, it took away what was held. It opened up one door and closed another. It is the dual nature of the Jubilee and its manifestations that will provide the key to the next mys-tery and to its significance for America.

The dichotomy goes back to ancient times and is intrinsic to the obser-vance itself. In the year of Jubilee, if one lost one's land, one would receive it back. The Jubilee brought restoration. On the other hand, for the one who had occupied one's land, the Jubilee bore a different dynamic. In order to be restored to one's land, the one occupying it had to relinquish it. The repossession of the one meant the dispossession of the other. The repossession and the dispossession were two sides of the same coin or of the same phenomenon.

To Give and Take Away

So the Jubilee was a double-edged sword. To those who had lost their possession, the Jubilee gave. But to those who had taken away the possession of others, the Jubilee took away. Fidel Castro had taken possession of Cuba. So when the Jubilee came, it took away his power and his position.

The Jubilee gives, and the Jubilee takes away. It is the bringer of restoration and restitution, a form of redemption on one hand and a form of judgment—even both at the same time.

———————————————

We are now about to see how this double-edged sword of the Jubilee actually determined a modern calamity of global and epic proportions.

Part III

THE WINDS OF HINNOM

Chapter 9

THE DEVER GADOL

THE PROPHET PONDERED the horrors of the valley. He knew that what took place there would spell the end of his nation. His name was Jeremiah. God had called him to warn His people of the end.

When Israel drove God out of its midst, its house did not stay empty. Other gods, dark spirits, came in to take possession of the space once filled by the presence of God. To each of the new gods was an altar. And the valley was filled with them.

The Fires of Baal and Molech

Among those gods was Molech, known as the "abomination of the Ammonites."[1] Molech was especially known for child sacrifice. But the practice extended to other gods. Foremost among them was Baal, chief of the Canaanite pantheon and the principal deity of Israel's apostasy. Both gods were represented in the valley.

What the Israelites had done in Hinnom had not gone unnoticed. The Word of God came to Jeremiah concerning it:

> And they built the high places of Baal which are in the
> Valley of the Son of Hinnom, to cause their sons and their
> daughters to pass through the fire to Molech.[2]

The sacrificing of children or of the weak and helpless was not an aberration of pagan culture—but common. The biblical view that all are made in the image of God and that human life is sacred and of immeasurable value was absent from paganism. So it was that when Israel turned away from God, it began partaking in this darkest of acts.

A Demonic Parenthood

How mothers or fathers could sacrifice their own children is virtually unfathomable. In ancient times they pierced them, left them to bleed, crushed them, or burned them in fire. At the same time in the world of paganism, children could be killed without rituals, as in the common practices of infanticide and abortion. It was largely the influence of the Gospel in the pagan world that ultimately brought child sacrifice to an end. Though many would object to the parallel between abortion and the child sacrifices of the pagan world, in their moral essence there is no meaningful distinction—they are the same.

The Return to Hinnom

The time of abortion's return to Western civilization is significant. It is no accident that the very first nation to legalize the practice was the Soviet Union—the world's first officially atheist state. It was only as Russia turned away from God and the Christian faith that it turned to the ancient pagan practice.

When a nation or civilization begins emptying itself of God, there is ultimately nothing left to protect its weakest and most helpless, its children, from being abused or murdered. It reverts to the ways of paganism or neo-paganism. By the same token, it is no accident that it was just when Western civilization, as led by America, was removing God from its culture in the late twentieth century, that it reopened the door to the ancient practice of child killing in the form of abortion.

An Invocation to Judgment

The prophet Jeremiah knew that the fires of Hinnom epitomized the fall of his nation. The sin was a massive one, a civilizational one. That made what God told him to do all the more ominous.

> Thus says the LORD: "Go and get a potter's earthen flask, and take some of the elders of the people and some of the elders of the priests. And go out to the Valley of the Son of Hinnom."[3]

The prophet was to take a clay vessel, bring it to the Valley of Hinnom, where the children had been sacrificed, and smash it in the sight of the nation's leaders. The smashed vessel would serve as a prophetic sign: a nation that kills its own children stands in the judgment of God. "*The blood of the innocent*"[4] invokes the judgment of God. The nation would be destroyed.

> ...it shall no more be called...the Valley of the Children of Hinnom but the Valley of Slaughter."[5]

As the people of Israel had brought death to their children, so death would return to them. It would come through what appeared to be natural events and yet which served as vessels of God's judgment.

A Great Plague

In view of the fact that the blood of the children invoked national judgment and calamity on ancient Israel, could the blood of children in the act of abortion invoke judgment and calamity on America and the modern world? In other words, as we have brought death to our children, could death also come to us? And if so, how would it come?

Jeremiah was given another prophetic word about the coming judgment. The people of the city that had shed the blood of its children would be struck down.

> *... they will die of a great plague.*[6]

They would die of what in Hebrew was called a *dever gadol*, a great pestilence, a plague of epic proportions, a dangerous and highly contagious disease, a mass contagion, a pandemic.

———————————

And so the question must now be asked: Is it possible that behind the coming of a great plague to the world and to America in the early twenty-first century, a *dever gadol*, a colossal pandemic, was an ancient and biblical mystery?

Chapter 10

SWORD OF THE CONTAGION

IN HIS SECOND inaugural address, Abraham Lincoln spoke some of his most profound words with regard to the calamitous war that had ravaged the nation.

The Bondman's Blood

They would be inscribed on the walls of his memorial in Washington, DC. He said this:

> Yet, if God wills that it continue until all the wealth piled by the bondsman's two hundred and fifty years of unrequited toil shall be sunk, and until every drop of blood drawn with the lash shall be paid by another drawn by the sword, as was said three thousand years ago, so still it must be said "the judgments of the Lord are true and righteous altogether."[1]

He was joining together the blood drawn by centuries of slavery and that drawn by four years of civil war, drop for drop, by the lash and the sword. Lincoln saw the war as a national judgment for the sin of slavery. The judgment was not focused on individuals. Among the stricken and the dead were the righteous and the unrighteous. The sin was national, civilizational. So too was the calamity.

Jeremiah, Lincoln, and COVID-19

So too it was in the case of ancient Israel. As Jeremiah had prophesied, the death of the nation's children in child sacrifice would bring death to the land. The second death would come through calamity, through the ravaging of war, of famine, and that of a "great plague." Behind such events lie a multitude of causes. Still, in the case of ancient Israel, the calamities were manifestations of judgment. So behind the coming of a "great plague" to the modern world would be a confluence of countless causes. And yet it may still represent the outworking of judgment.

So in view of the fact that the Scriptures identify the killing of children as among the most grievous of evils and one that especially invokes national judgment, and in view of the fact one of these judgments is that of a plague or disease—we must apply Lincoln's question to the plague that came on America and the world. Could it have come in the context of judgment? And as in the case of ancient Israel, could such a judgment be linked to the blood of its children?

Generation Hinnom

Could the generation upon which the plague came have been especially connected to the blood of its children? The answer is yes. The generation that saw the plague of COVID-19 was unique. It was that generation that was responsible for the killing of more children than any other in human history. It was that generation that, more than any other in modern history, had embraced and practiced abortion as a sacred right. Ancient Israel had shed the blood of over one billion of its children. The generation alive in 2020 had shed the blood of over one billion children.

Could the timing of the plague be connected to the killing of children? The plague came on the world in 2020. With regard to the West and, in particular, America, the generation that had pioneered the legislation that ushered in the age of abortion was then nearing its end. It was then, as well, that virtually every living adult had come to adulthood or spent most of it in an era in which babies were legally murdered. They had either partaken of it, championed it, allowed it, or done nothing to stand against or undo it. Of course, there were those who did stand against it, but they were the minority. It was this generation that had taken what didn't belong to them—life. It was Generation Hinnom.

Land of Missing Children

Could the plague's geographical origins and progression be linked to the blood of the children? The land in which more abortions were performed than any other was that of Communist China.[2] In sheer numbers it took the world's number one position in the killing of children. So the plague that struck the world in 2020 began in China.

At the same time, when it comes to abortion, America holds a unique and pivotal position. In sheer numbers it had been at the forefront of nations. At the time of the plague the number of children killed on American soil had exceeded sixty million.[3]

But beyond that, America was unique in that its example and influence had played a central role in leading other nations into the gruesome practice. And beyond that, its example was a particularly egregious one involving the killing of unborn children in the latter stages of pregnancy and development. And beyond all that, America not only had helped to spread abortion to the world by its example but had become an active agent in seeking to pressure, entice, or force other nations to join in the bloody practice.

So the plague began in China, the land in which more unborn children are killed than in any other, but would soon focus the center of its fury on America, the world's leading advocate in the killing of the unborn. The focus was so great that at one point, of all the world's recorded cases of the virus, one in three was manifesting on American soil.[4] And as we will see, as an angel of death passing through the land, the plague, in its striking of the land, would become even more precise.

The Dark Jubilee

As we saw in the case of Cuba and Fidel Castro, the Jubilee can function as a sign revealing an ancient biblical dynamic at work in the course of human events beyond that of the natural realm. Is it possible that, as in the case of Cuba, the dynamic of the Jubilee was at work in the case of the plague that came upon America and the world?

It came in the year 2020. What happens if one counts back from the year of its coming to the span of the Jubilee? The Jubilean countdown brings us to the year 1970. Did anything happen in that year that bears significance with regard to our question? The answer is a very definite yes.

Abortion on demand began on American soil not in 1973 but three years earlier. 1970 was the year that America began killing its unborn children on demand. Thus 2020 was the Jubilee of abortion in America. And so the ancient principle—death would be answered by death. The first year ushered in one form of death; the Jubilee of that year would usher in another.

The Taking Away

Jeremiah had warned his nation that the slaughter of its children would be answered years later by the slaughter of its citizens. The death they had set in motion would ultimately come back on them. So the death that America had set in motion in 1970 would come back on it in 2020.

We must now consider the other side of the Jubilee. The Jubilee gives and takes away. It brings restoration but also restitution—and the repossession of the owner means the dispossession of the occupier. If you had taken that which didn't ultimately belong to you, then in the year of Jubilee, that which you had taken would be taken away from you. The Jubilee takes away that which the taker has taken. In 1970, America took life. So in the year of Jubilee, 2020, life was taken from it—and from the generation that had taken it.

Breath

As in the case of Lincoln's words concerning the Civil War, the calamity was not a matter of individual judgment. It struck the righteous and the unrighteous alike. The sin belonged to a civilization. So too would the judgment.

Abortion is specifically the sin of the older against the younger, the older lives and the younger dies. In 2020, the Jubilee of abortion, the dynamic was reversed. The plague overwhelmingly spared the young and overwhelmingly focused its fury on the old. The young overwhelmingly survived, and the old perished.

The act of abortion robs the baby of breath. Its lungs never empty of fluid and never fill with air. The baby is not allowed to breathe. In 2020, the year of Jubilee, a plague came on the land and struck its victims' ability to breathe. Their lungs could not fill with air. The plague had robbed them of their ability to breathe. A generation had taken away the breath of others. Now it was their breath that was taken.

America, by its example and influence, had spread death in the form of abortion to the nations. Fifty years after setting that death in motion, death returned to it.

———————————

This is only the beginning of the mystery. I first introduced it in *The Harbinger II*. But we are now going to go deeper, to reveal what could not then be revealed, as we look at the *entrance of a specter*.

Chapter 11

ENTRANCE OF A SPECTER

IN *THE HARBINGER II*, in a chapter called "The Plague," the man known as the Prophet opens the mystery behind the calamity that came upon America and the world in 2020. But there is much more than I could have revealed then—mysteries of stunning precision. We now open them.

The Footsteps of Molech

America began practicing abortion on demand in 1970. In a biblical context, the beginning, the first act or event, the first day, or "first fruit" is of particular significance. So if we had to identify the entrance of abortion on demand onto American soil, the first step of that entrance, what would it be?

The year 1970 would see abortion legalized in four states. Of those four, two were first in time and most primary. One constituted the first American state to legalize the practice. But the other was the first to legalize the practice on the continent. It would also be the most central and pivotal, by far, in introducing and spreading it across the nation. The reasons for this were several.

First, the law by which it legalized it was the most expansive. At the time, it was called "the most liberal abortion law in the world."[1] Second, the law had no limitation with regard to one's residence. Thus anyone could come to the state and have an abortion performed. So thousands and thousands of babies were aborted in the state from mothers who resided elsewhere. Third, the state would soon become America's abortion capital. Fourth, by virtue of the last two reasons, the state would become central in spreading the practice and its acceptance throughout American society. And finally, its legalization of abortion on demand would strongly influence the United States Supreme Court in legalizing the practice across the nation.

The Dark Entrance

The state was New York. It was, by far, the most critical American state in abortion's entrance into the nation. It was New York that introduced abortion to continental America. It was New York that enacted the most extreme of abortion laws up to that point. It was on New York soil that more babies were killed than in any other American state. It was New York that was foremost in the spreading of the practice across the nation. And it was New York that laid the groundwork for the ruling of *Roe v. Wade*, the Supreme Court decision that made abortion the law of the land three years later. In fact, the Supreme Court ruling would refer to New York's abortion law.

Is it possible then to find and identify the first act, the first event in the coming of abortion to New York?

Constance Cook was a Republican member of the New York State Assembly. She was first elected to the Assembly in 1963 and served until 1974. It was Cook, along with Democratic Assemblyman Franz Leichter, who was responsible for writing the bill that would, upon its passage, ultimately transform New York, abortion, and America. The bill would legalize abortion on demand in New York and lead to its dissemination throughout the nation.

So when was it set in motion? It was set in motion on the day it was introduced into the New York State Legislature. It was introduced into the Legislature on *January 20, 1970. January 20, 1970,* was the seminal day, the first fruit of abortion on demand's entrance into the nation.

Patient Zero and the Western Entrance

As the year 2020 began, the world watched with increasing alarm the reports of a new virus originating in the Wuhan province of China. The contagion was soon identified as a new strain of the coronavirus with pneumonia-like symptoms. In the second week of the new year, China reported the first death to be associated with the virus. Up until then every confirmed case of infection had been confined to China. But that would soon change.

A few days after the report of that first fatality, a thirty-five-year-old American man returned home to Seattle after a visit with his family in the Wuhan province of China. He began feeling sick. At first, it was just a cough. But it was soon followed by increasingly severe symptoms. He decided to get tested.

The test samples were rushed on an overnight flight to a lab in Atlanta. The next day, the results came back. The man was infected with COVID-19. It was the first official confirmation that the contagion had entered American soil.

He was placed in a plastic-covered isolation gurney and transported to a containment ward designed for highly contagious diseases. Those assigned to his care wore helmets and face masks, while a robot took his vitals. But it was too late. He had already come into contact with others. He would become one of the central conduits for the spreading of the plague into America. The specific strain of the contagion that he had brought to Seattle would later be found throughout the nation. He would become known as *patient zero*, America's official herald of the plague.[2]

The Day of Two Specters

Abraham Lincoln drew the connection between the blood drawn by the lash of slavery and that drawn by war. Jeremiah spoke of the connection between the blood of the children sacrificed on the nation's altars and the judgment that would come by sword and plague. What about the two deaths that entered American soil, one in 1970 and the other fifty years later, in 2020?

What happens if we take the beginning of abortion, its first fruit, its first act, the seminal day of its entrance, January 20, 1970, and count forward the full span of the Jubilee, fifty years? Where does it take us?

It takes us to *January 20, 2020.*

January 20, 2020, was the day the plague officially struck America. It was the day of patient zero, that day it was confirmed that the contagion had entered the nation.

Date of Entry—January 20, 1970 / January 20, 2020

Thus the plague began ts entrance into America on *the same exact date* that abortion on demand began its entrance into America. Beyond that the two dates were joined together by the exact fifty-year duration of the Jubilee. Or in other words, the death brought by abortion and the death brought by the plague each entered the land on the same exact day.

The Jubilee brings reversal and restitution. So on the Jubilee of the day that began America's taking of life, the plague would come to take the lives of the generation that had taken the lives of the children. The one was the inversion of the other—and the two days would be joined together by the Jubilee, fifty years to the year, to the month, to the week, and to *the exact day.*

No human hand could have joined those two events. The plague came, as plagues come, through the smallest and most microscopic of causes and effects. But the timing of those microscopic actions and interactions was exact.

The Seeding

Each of the two events represented the first fruit—the first fruit of abortion and the first fruit of the plague. And each was a *seeding*. The seeding on January 20, 1970, would bring death to countless children. The seeding on January 20, 2020, would bring death to countless adults. Each represented the beginning of the beginning, a single act of introducing a single law and a single case of contagion. Neither would remain single. Each seed of death would become fruitful and multiply. Each of the two days would constitute the beginning of something ominous. Death would beget death. And the second death would come on the exact Jubilean day of the first. In the year of return would come the return of death.

At the moment America was about to embark on a course that would lead to the killing of millions of unborn children, a word was given. The origins of that word were ancient, going back three thousand years to the miraculous birth of an ancient nation.

Chapter 12

THEY WHO OPEN THE WOMB

AMERICA WAS FOUNDED after the pattern of ancient Israel. Those who laid the first of its foundation stones in Massachusetts Bay spoke of its calling in terms of a holy commonwealth, an Israel of the New World. And in the days of the American Revolution, the nation's departure from English rule was likened to the exodus of Israel from the rule of Pharaoh.

The Law of Birth

One of the distinctions that separated Israel from the nations that surrounded it was the prohibition against the killing of children. The neighboring Canaanites were especially known for offering their children as sacrifices to their gods. Israel was warned by their prophets never to take part in such horrors.

Just after Israel's exodus from Egypt, it was given a unique law concerning birth, the womb, and one's children. It would become known as the Law of the Firstborn. Implicit in the ordinance was another scriptural principle— one's child was a gift from God. Thus one could not do to one's child as one pleased or as the pagans did to their children.

You shall set apart to the LORD all that open the womb.[3]

The child of one's womb was holy. They were to be treated as such. Birth was sacred. Life was a miracle. And one's children, as represented by the firstborn, belonged to God.

A Word From God

Every Sabbath day in synagogues across the world, the Jewish people recite an appointed passage of Scripture. The passage is called the *parasha*. Each passage is appointed from ages past to be read on a specific Sabbath day. So every week on the Sabbath the scrolls are opened in virtually every synagogue and the appointed passage is read, chanted, and proclaimed—the same passage throughout the world.

Just before America set in motion the laws that would legalize abortion in New York on January 20, there was an appointed Scripture to be chanted in the synagogues of America and the world. It was the last Scripture to be chanted before those critical days of America's descent into child killing. Of what did it speak?

It spoke of the nation's children. It spoke of the moment of birth, the moment the unborn child opens the womb. And it declared that the child who opens the womb is sacred, set apart, and belongs to God and is to be consecrated to Him.

They Who Would Never Open the Womb

So just at the moment that America was to embark on legalizing the killing of its unborn children, to stop them from opening the womb, to take the miracle of life, the gift of God, and dispose of it—it was then that this Scripture was proclaimed throughout its cities and towns.

It would be proclaimed especially in New York, the center of America's Jewish population. New York was the very place where abortion would be first set in motion.

The children who would be killed because of that week would eventually number into the tens of millions. They would never *open the womb*. They would be terminated before they could. And yet the Word of God and the appointed word for that moment declared them holy, sacred, and precious. And so it was proclaimed in the land just before America embarked on its dark journey and before any of those lives, precious to God and belonging to Him, were killed in the womb.

We are now going to open the mystery of two days—the days when everything changed. We will find that lying behind them was an ancient mystery.

"THE DAY EVERYTHING CHANGED"

Is IT POSSIBLE for us to identify the exact moment abortion on demand actually began in America? And if so, would it bring forth a revelation?

The Hawaiian Death

On February 20, 1970, the Hawaiian House of Representatives passed its abortion bill. Four days later, the Hawaiian Senate passed the same bill. It was then sent to the governor. The governor was a Catholic and believed that abortion was wrong. It wouldn't be until the middle of March that the next step would be taken.

Up to the middle of March, abortion's entrance into America was spotty and in steps. It had gained momentum and, in the case of Hawaii, had gained the needed votes. But it hadn't actually been enacted.

Fifty years later Americans would watch nervously as signs of the plague appeared in their land. Its advance was likewise spotty and scattered. With regard to the total population, its effect was minuscule. Up to early March, the numbers of those Americans infected with the disease was reckoned to be, at most, a few hundred out of a population of over three hundred million. The plague was approaching, but had not broken out. It had not yet fallen on the nation.

Month of Impact—March 1970 / March 2020

With the entrance of abortion to America, the moment when everything changed came in March 1970. It was then that the Hawaiian governor, though without putting his name on the bill, decided he would let it pass. And so the legalized killing of children in America began in March 1970.

We have seen the ancient biblical connection between the killing of children and the entrance of death, in this case through a plague. We have seen the mystery Jubilee in the plague that came on the land fifty years after the killing of children began. So as abortion on demand came to America in 1970, the plague came to America in 2020. But it could be even more exact.

If the *actual killing of children* on American soil began in the month of March 1970, then the mystery would ordain that death would come to America fifty years later—*in March of 2020*. Did it?

It did. The plague fell upon the nation *in March of 2020*, the Jubilean month of the children's blood.

As March began, the number of Americans infected with the virus stood at around 300. As March ended, the number had skyrocketed to around 175,000. It had taken over a month to get from one case to 300 cases but less than a month to go from 300 to over 175,000.[1] As March of 1970 had marked the coming of the children's blood on American soil, March of 2020 marked the coming of the plague to American soil. And yet the correlation would be even more exact.

In the *Middle* of March

The legalization of abortion came more specifically in *the middle of March* 1970. Therefore, if the mystery is to hold, we would expect death and calamity to come to America exactly fifty years later—*in the middle of March* of 2020.

And so it did. The plague fell not only in the month of March but *in the middle* of that month.

In fact, the events of that time were so dramatic that for most Americans *the middle of March* 2020 would be indelibly burned in their memories of the coming of the virus and the changing of their lives.

It was in *the middle of March* that America became a nation under quarantine.

It was in *the middle of March* that the nation's president ordered a ban on non-US citizens entering the land from twenty-six European nations.

It was in *the middle of March* 2020 that the World Health Organization declared the plague a *pandemic*, noting that cases of disease beyond China had increased *thirteen-fold*.[2]

It was in *the middle of March* that the American president issued a proclamation that declared that America was now in a *State of Emergency*.

It was *the middle of March* when, in the view of the lightning speed of the pronouncements made by its government and the events that surrounded them, much of the nation went into a state of panic.

And it was in *the middle of March* that Americans witnessed the beginning of something unprecedented—for the first time in its history, America was being shut down. Stores were shut down; schools were shut down; businesses were closed; movie theaters, Broadway theaters, sports stadiums, even churches were shut down. The nation went into a state of paralysis. Life was frozen. Cities turned into ghost towns. People stayed hidden behind the walls of their homes, afraid to venture out in fear of the deadly plague that was now passing through the land.

Date of Impact—March 11, 1970 / March 11, 2020

And yet could the mystery be even more exact?

In mid-March 1970, Hawaiian governor John Burns informed his state that it would now be legal to kill one's unborn child:

> House Bill 61, relating to Hawaii's century-old abortion law, is now Act 1 of 1970. The measure became law without my signature.[3]

With that announcement, abortion on demand came upon American soil. What day was it? *March 11, 1970.* This is the exact date when abortion on demand became legal on American soil. What then happens if one takes the years of the Jubilee and begins a countdown starting from that day?

It leads to the date of March 11 of 2020. So the exact Jubilean day of abortion on demand in America is March 11, 2020.

Did anything significant happen on that day? The following is the title given to an article on National Public Radio:

March 11, 2020: The Day Everything Changed.

"While some changes happened gradually, there was one day that marked the beginning of the new normal. March 11, 2020. On that day in the United States, the pandemic future arrived all at once."[4]

The pinpointing of *March 11, 2020,* as the date the plague fell, the day that *everything changed,* is virtually universal. From other articles:

> "March 11, 2020, began in one reality and virtually ended in a new one."[5]

> "The Day Everything Changed: A Timeline of March 11, 2020"

> "On March 11, 2020, the American public finally began to come to grips with a stark reality..."[6]

> "...on March 11, 2020, the day COVID swallowed everything.... So many forces of history years in the making converged on March 11 and were all subsumed by something few thought possible just weeks earlier."[7]

> "March 11, 2020, was the day everything changed."[8]

> March 11, 2020, was the day that Dr. Anthony Fauci, director of the National Institute of Allergy and Infectious Diseases was

summoned to Capitol Hill to testify before the House Committee on Oversight and Reform. When he was asked by Members of Congress what he believed would happen, he said, "Things will get worse."[9]

March 11, 2020, was the day that the World Health Organization announced the what had come upon the world and was now gripping America was nothing short of pandemic.

March 11, 2020, was the day the Dow Jones Industrial Average plunged more than 1,400 points.

March 11, 2020, was the day that the stock market closed 20 percent lower than its February peak to enter bear market territory.

March 11, 2020, was the day that the eleven-year American bull market came to an end.[10]

March 11, 2020, was the day multiple US cities started banning large public gatherings.

March 11, 2020, was the day that high-profile universities such as Princeton and Notre Dame suspended their classes.

March 11, 2020, was the night, as one article put it, that "sports, as we knew them, ended."[11]

March 11, 2020, was the day that would be marked as the official beginning of the lockdown in America.

March 11, 2020, was the day that the American president came on the air in prime time to address the nation concerning the plague. It was in that address that he made the stunning announcement that America would be, in effect, quarantined from Europe.

March 11, 2020, was the day everything changed, the day the full force and reality of the plague began to fall on America.

"The Day Everything Changed"

Thus the day the plague fell upon the nation was one Jubilee, fifty years, to the *exact day* that abortion officially came to American soil. Most Americans knew that what they were witnessing that day was historic and unprecedented. But they had no idea it was part of an ancient mystery as old as the prophet Jeremiah and the Valley of Hinnom. Nor did they have any idea of its connection to the ancient evil that America had embraced on the same date, exactly fifty years before. But it was fitting that March 11, 2020, should be called "the day that everything changed"—as it was the Jubilean day of the other day, fifty years earlier, the other day *that everything changed*.

With regard to its timing, the plague was uncannily precise. But now we will see that its precision manifested not only in the realm of time—*but space*—as we uncover the *American Gehenna*.

Chapter 14

THE AMERICAN GEHENNA

ONE CANNOT SPEAK of the coming of abortion to America and the coming of the plague without speaking of the *place* to which they came. I began pointing to that place in *The Harbinger II*. Now we go deeper.

Valley of Slaughter

When Jeremiah prophesied to his people of the children they had sacrificed, he spoke not only of the coming judgment but of *the place* to which that judgement would come:

> Because they have forsaken Me and made this an alien place...and have filled this place with the blood of the innocents (they have also built the high places of Baal, to burn their sons with fire for burnt offerings to Baal...), therefore...this place shall no more be called Tophet or the Valley of the Son of Hinnom, but the Valley of Slaughter.[1]

In other words, the judgment would return to the place where the evil had been committed. As they had slaughtered their children in the Valley of Hinnom, so the valley would become the site of their own slaughter. The site would later be called Gehenna, a name that would become synonymous with hell. If the Valley of Hinnom was the ground on which Israel had slaughtered its children, what then would America's Valley of Hinnom—the American Gehenna—be?

Finding Hinnom

It would have to be the central ground on which the blood of its children was shed. There is only one possible place—New York. New York was the nation's abortion capital, the ground on which more of its children were killed than any other. It was and is America's Valley of Hinnom. The mystery would thus ordain that the plague would turn its focus and fury to the ground of New York. And that is exactly what happened.

The most critical span of time in New York's legalization of abortion was March 1970 into the first ten days of April. From the first days of March up to its final days, New York's abortion bill came up in no fewer than *eight* of its legislative sessions. And then, in early April, it all came to a head.

Adding fifty years to that pivotal time period brings us to March 2020. March of 2020 would, in turn, be critical with regard to the plague's entrance into New York. The plague officially came to New York on the first day of March. In March of 1970, the movement to legalize abortion in New York gained strength and momentum, so the plague gained momentum and strength in New York fifty years later, in March of 2020.

Capital of the Plague

March of 1970 was also critical in the legalization of abortion in America. So it was in March of 2020 that the plague's focus turned to America. By March 24, *one of every three* new cases was appearing in America. And on March 26, the nation crossed a critical threshold—it overtook China to become the plague's global epicenter.

And as New York was central in the coming of abortion to the land, so it would be central in the coming of the plague. When America became the global epicenter, *almost one out of every two cases* was focused on just a small sliver of America—New York. And a massive part of those cases was, in turn, focused on the even tinier sliver of New York City.[2] As precise as the plague had been with regard to its days and timing, so too it was with regard to its place and grounds. Death had returned to the time from which it came but also to the place.

As with the Valley of Hinnom, the place where the children's blood was shed became the center of another death. New York had become the plague's new global epicenter and capital. The ancient mystery had ordained it.

Dark Milestone—April 10, 1970 / April 10, 2020

Abortion was first legalized in Hawaii. Less than one month later it came to the American mainland through New York. It was finalized by vote in the New York State Senate on April 10. Adding the fifty years of the Jubilee brings us to April 10, 2020.

It was fifty years later, in the second week of April 2020, the plague's fury as touching New York reached its peak. It was the Jubilean week of New York's legalization of abortion. At that same time, another dark milestone was passed—New York now had more cases of the plague *than any other nation* on earth. In fact, compared with China, it had almost *twice as many*. When was that dark milestone reached? It happened on *April 10*, the very same day that the state had cast its final and deciding vote to legalize abortion[3]—it happened fifty years later on *the exact same day*. The two ancient elements, the children's blood and the deadly plague, were again joined together in exact precision.

———————————

During the days of the plague's fury, the epicenter of the epicenter of the epicenter, New York City, was eerily quiet. Its streets were empty of cars, its stores and squares empty of people. But its mortuaries were filled and over-flowing. As the death prophesied by Jeremiah had returned to the ancient Valley of Hinnom, death had now returned to the American Gehenna.

The Scripture assigns much significance and even mystery to the gates of a city or kingdom. What about the gates of America? We are now going to reveal how America's gates were central in a modern mystery, one that even involved the plague's genetic markers.

Chapter 15

THE EASTERN AND WESTERN GATES

JEREMIAH WAS TOLD to go to the Valley of Hinnom by the Potsherd Gate in order to give his prophecy concerning what the nation had done to its children. The valley was by the *gate*. The nation had committed its darkest and most gruesome of evils there *by the gate*.

The Eastern Gate

America is not a walled city, but it does have gates, entranceways to and from the rest of the world. Could the gates of America, like the gates of ancient Israel, be linked to the darkest of the nation's sins?

America's greatest and most famous gate is and has always been that of New York City, the gate through which millions have come in and gone out. In the case of Israel, its children were murdered by the gate. So too in the case of America, it was by the gate that the nation had murdered its children.

In the Scriptures, the gate was also connected to calamity and judgment. Judgment would come as the nation's enemies broke through the gates to bring destruction. Judgment began at the gate. And so too a biblical form of judgment, the plague, came especially to the gate of America, New York.

Death Through the Gate

But a gate is not only that which one comes to—but that which one comes *through*. So New York was not only the gate *to which* abortion came but the gate *through which* it spread to the rest of the nation.

When New York legalized abortion in 1970, it was only the beginning. Because of its expansive abortion law, because of the multitudes who came to the state to have abortions, New York became the primary gateway through which abortion came to America.

The state's role as the nation's abortion portal was colossal. In 1970, the first year of its legalization, of all the abortions performed in America, *over 45 percent* of them were performed in New York! In its second year, 1971, *over half* of all abortions in America, *55 percent*, were performed in New York. And in the last year before *Roe v. Wade*, *over 51 percent* of all abortions in America were performed in New York.[1] So of all abortions performed in

America from 1970s until *Roe v. Wade, most of them were performed in New York*. New York was the nation's gate of death.

Gate of the Plague

This leads us to the next question—If New York served as the central gate and portal through which abortion spread to America, is it possible that it also served as the central gate and portal *through which the plague spread* to America?

To discover the answer, we must add to the ancient mysteries of the gate, of judgment, and of the Jubilee—the discoveries of modern virology and genomic sequencing.

The mystery of the Jubilee would point to the fiftieth year, or 2020, as the year of inversion and return. The principle of return and inversion would indicate that the gate and portal through which the one form of death spread to the nation in the 1970s would be the same gate and portal through which another death, a plague, would spread through the nation fifty years later. Did it?

"The Primary Gateway" and Seeder of Outbreaks

The answer comes from the discoveries of modern virology and genomic sequencing as concerning the plague's spread across America. An article in the *New York Times* reveals it:

> The research indicates that a wave of infections swept from
> New York City through much of the country before the city
> began setting social distancing limits to stop the growth.
> That helped to fuel outbreaks in Louisiana, Texas, Arizona
> and as far away as the West Coast.[2]

So not only was New York, and specifically New York City, the center of the plague; it was the *central gate through which it came*. The article continues the conclusions of a Yale epidemiologist:

> We now have enough data to feel pretty confident that New
> York was the primary gateway for the rest of the country.[3]

Thus the same *primary gateway* of death through which abortion came to America would now become the *primary gateway* of death through which the plague would come to America.

We have seen the critical role that March of 1970 played in abortion's entrance into both New York and America. That makes the next discovery concerning New York City and the first days of March 2020 even more pro-found:

> By early March...the city became the primary source of new infections in the United States, new research reveals, as thousands of infected people traveled from the city and seeded outbreaks around the country.[4]

The Eastern Portal—1970 / 2020

When we looked at New York's role as the nation's gateway of abortion, the results were stunning. The state or city accounted for more than half of all the cases of abortions performed in America. What about its role as the gateway for the plague?

The answer is no less stunning. *Of all America's cases of the pandemic, more than half of them* came through the gate and portal of New York. The city, one of the scientists commented,

> acted as the Grand Central Station for this virus, with the opportunity to move from there in so many directions, to so many places.[5]

According to the research, the percentage of American cases that origi-nated in New York was a *colossal 60 to 65 percent*.[6] It had a precedent. Fifty years earlier, out of all children legally killed in America, the percentage of those killed in New York was likewise colossal. Or to put it another way, for *most Americans* who were struck by the plague, it came to them through the gate of New York City.

The Other

Though abortion on demand came to the American continent through New York, there was one other state on the American mainland, and only one, that followed New York's lead in legalizing abortion that year. Its legaliza-tion would come by referendum and much later in the year. It was the state of Washington.

So in 1970 abortion came to the American mainland through two portals. Though, as with every other state, the impact of the state of Washington with regard to abortion could not compare with that of New York, it still played a pivotal role as the only other state in mainland America to legalize the act. So the legalized killing of children came to the American mainland through two gateways, one on its East Coast and the other on its West—through an eastern gate and a western gate.

The Western Gate

What then happens if we approach the western gate in view of the ancient mystery? In accordance with the Jubilee there would be a return—the gate through which death entered the nation from the west in the form of abortion would, in the Jubilean year, be the gate through which death in the form of a plague would enter from the west in the form of a plague. And this is exactly what would happen.

In the Jubilean year of abortion's entrance into America through the western gate, death would return and again enter through the same gate. In other words, the plague would enter America through Washington State.

Two Gates and Two Years

So as abortion came to the American mainland through two gateways, in the Jubilean year, a plague would come to the American mainland through two gateways. The two states through which the plague entered the land in 2020, New York and Washington, just happened to be *the same exact two states* through which abortion entered the land fifty years earlier, one through the nation's eastern gate of death, the other, through its western gate of death.

The Western Portal—1970 / 2020

The genetic markings left in the wake of the plague bore witness to the ancient mystery, as they pointed to the nation's gates. In the case of the eastern gate, as we have seen, the findings were overwhelming, accounting for more than half of the nation's COVID cases, just as it had accounted for more than half of the nation's abortions. But what about the western gate?

The findings as concerning the western gate were also striking. The genetic markers revealed that in states such as a California, Oregon, and Wyoming, *one-third of all cases* bore the genetic markers of having entered the country through Washington State. Even in states such as Illinois in the Midwest, it was found that 27 percent of cases had come through the western gate. And even in states as far away as Georgia on the East Coast, 30 percent of cases were found to have come through the western gate.[7]

Patient Zero at the Gate

There was one more connection.

The plague made its official entrance into America on January 20, 2020, when it was confirmed that it had entered America through *patient zero*.

But *where* in America did that take place? Patient zero landed in

Seattle—the state of Washington. In other words, he entered the continent through the *same western gate* through which abortion had spread to the nation. Through patient zero the plague struck the nation at its western gate and there ignited its first official outbreak before spreading through the nation.

It was the convergence of space and time at the two same gateways. For the day that marked the plague's entrance into America from the western gate was January 20, the same day that abortion began its entrance into America through the *eastern gate.* So on that day of the plague's arrival, both the eastern and western gates, through which the nation's sin had entered, were joined together. The plague came to the nation's western gate one Jubilee, fifty years, to the exact day that abortion had come to its eastern gate. It was the year and day of return—so it was there and then that it returned.

The Genetic Witnesses

The two gates would now usher in an era in which millions of Americans would be struck or struck down. The overwhelming majority of these would bear the plague's viral markers. The plague's viral markers would point to either one or the other of the two gates—the eastern or the western.

In other words, those struck by the plague would bear in their bodies the markers that joined them to the same two gates through which the nation's darkest of sins had, fifty years earlier, entered the land. The genetic sequences would bear witness to the two gates of darkness.

The ancient mystery had been fulfilled. The calamity had returned to the gate, and death, to the place of the children's blood.

We must now ask the unasked question—that which is framed by the words of the ancient prophets and at least one American president. None of them had the ability to quantify the calamities of their day and to arrive at the answer—but we do.

Chapter 16

THE WINDS OF HINNOM

IT WAS THERE from the beginning, implicit in Jeremiah's prophecy over the Valley of Hinnom and Lincoln's second inaugural address. It is a question that must have seemed in past times as it does now—almost unaskable. We must now ask it.

The Unasked Question

Jeremiah had foretold the correlation between the blood of the children shed in the Valley of Hinnom and the blood to be shed in Jerusalem through war. Lincoln had posed the possibility that the war could go on until every drop of blood drawn by the lash of slavery was matched by another drawn by the sword of war.

In each case, the judgment was connected to the evil that invoked it. The children's blood in the Valley of Hinnom would be answered and matched with blood of the nation that shed it. The blood of American slaves would be answered and matched by the blood of American soldiers. Death will be answered and matched by death.

So now the question that must be asked: Is it possible that the ancient correlation between sin and judgment—the killing of children and a deadly plague—could involve not only their times, days, dates, events, locations, durations, and origins, but their scope, their magnitude, their breadth, and their immensity?

In other words, could there be any connection or correspondence, between the numbers of children killed by abortion and the numbers of Americans killed by the plague?

The Three-Year Window

If so, in what periods of time could the two be measured and compared? It is already clear. There is one clear window of time concerning the entrance and establishment of abortion in America—that which begins with abortion's entrance into the nation and ends with its establishment in the Supreme Court decision that made it the law of the land. Its entrance into America began on January 20, 1970, and its establishment was sealed on January 22,

1973—or, for the purpose of available statistics, the three-year period of 1970, 1971, and 1972, ending on December 31.

With regard to the plague, it would have to begin with the same parameters, with its official entrance into America. So the window begins on January 20, 2020. The second window of time would have to parallel the first period. So the parameters of the second period with regard to the plague would start in late January 2020 and go to late January 2023—or, if we were to compare it with the statistics available for abortion—the three-year period of 2020, 2021, and 2022 and ending on December 31.

Of course, with all such figures, there will always be the factor of under-reporting on one hand or overreporting on the other. We are also dependent on the availability of the statistics. National statistics on abortion for the period of our inquiry were typically recorded by year as opposed to by month. On the other hand, we certainly have an idea and can arrive at a general number in each case.

So could there be any connection or correspondence between the number of children killed in abortion between 1970 and the start of 1973 and the number of Americans killed by the plague fifty years later in between 2020 and the start of 2023?

The Children's Number

As to the number of children killed in the first three years of abortion's entrance into America and up to *Roe v. Wade*—we have the yearly abortion statistics from the Johnston Archive. These are also the same statistics listed by the CDC, the Centers for Disease Control and Prevention, on abortion as reported from 1969 to 1972.

According to these statistics, the number of abortions in America for the first year of our period, 1970, was 193,491.

The number for the second year, 1971, was 485,816.

And the number for the third year, 1972, was 586,760.[1]

Adding up the totals of each year brings the total number of abortions for the three-year period to *1,266,067*.

The Plague's Number

What about the number of Americans killed by the plague in the three corresponding annual periods of 2020, 2021, and 2022?

For this we have the CDC mortality statistics. They include not only the statistics of deaths attributed solely to the virus, but the other deaths caused by COVID-19, such as pneumonia and influenza. It thus represents the total number of deaths caused by the virus.

We have the total excess deaths in America as recorded in the CDC mortality statistics as attributable to the virus in the period beginning in late January to January 21, 2023. The number is 1,286,050.[2]

Statistical Convergence

Thus the number of Americans dying from the plague in that period is 1,286,050. And the number of children killed by abortion in the corresponding period is 1,266,067.

In view of the data and its margins of error, the two figures are statistically identical.

1,266,067 / 1,267,965

But it goes further. The numbers of excess deaths by COVID contain an extra twenty-one days in January that the abortion statistics are without for the lack of monthly recordings. The number of excess deaths for those twenty-one days is 18,085.[3] If we adjust accordingly, subtracting the number from the total excess deaths of the three-year period, it comes out to 1,267,965.

So the number of American children killed in the first three-year period of legalized abortion is *1,266,067.*

The number of Americans killed by COVID in the first three-year period of the plague is 1,267,965.

1,266,067 and 1,267,965—again, the figures are statistically identical—and even more so.

1.3 Million / 1.3 Million

Another major study on the mortality rates caused by COVID-19 was undertaken by the British newspaper *The Economist*. It is considered one of the most comprehensive and rigorous studies made of the excess death rates caused by the virus. The results involve estimates but provide a ballpark figure.

For the three-year period beginning January 1, 2020, and ending January 23, 2023, *The Economist*'s estimate of those Americans killed by the plague directly or through complications comes out to approximately *1.3 million.*[4]

The comparable number of children killed by abortion in the parallel three-year period falls at 1.26 million. But again, the abortion statistics do not include the twenty-three days of January covered in the *Economist's* study. If one adds in an average daily rate of abortions in accordance with that period and multiplies it by twenty-three for the days accounted for in

The Economist's study, it brings the number of abortions for the three-year period of January 1970 to January 22, 1973, to *1.3 million.*

Percentages of Correlations

How close is the correlation of the CDC's number of total deaths caused by the plague—1,267,965—and its number of children killed by abortion in the corresponding period—1,266,067?

The percentage correlation is 99.85 percent!

As for *The Economist*'s approximate figures on COVID deaths compared with the number of children killed by abortion?

The correlation of 100 percent!

Conclusions

When Lincoln pondered the correspondence of blood drawn by the lash of slavery with the blood drawn by the Civil War, there were no statistics on the lashings of slavery.

When Jeremiah prophesied of the correspondence of the children sacrificed on the altars and the slaughter of his countryman by the sword, there were no statistics on either. We don't know how close the correspondence was.

But in this case we do. The correspondence is stunningly precise. And all the other correspondences we have seen between the two—their inceptions, their inversions, the years, the months, the dates, the locations—they were all warning of this one.

What would we have expected of a nation that had shed so much innocent blood? We would have expected the winds of Hinnom. And so they came. But America has not killed 1.3 million children. At the time of this writing, it has killed over 60 million children. The winds of their killings have not yet fully blown. And can we rest in the assurance that they never will?

We will now open up a very different stream of mystery, one of kings, priests, temples, and gods—and one particularly infamous queen. The replaying of this mystery is specific, precise, and exact. And it holds the secret of one of the most memorable leaders in recent times.

Part IV

JEHU AND THE TEMPLE OF BAAL

Chapter 17

THE PROTOTYPE

THE TEMPLATE WE are about to uncover is over two and a half thousand years old. It contains ancient events, ancient movements, and ancient people. And yet it will provide us with precise revelation concerning events, movements, and even people of the modern world, even of our own day.

The Tupos

In 1 Corinthians 10, the apostle Paul writes of the fall and judgment of the ancient Israelites. Then he adds,

> Now all these things happened to them as examples, and they were written for our admonition...[1]

Behind the English word *examples* is the Greek word *tupos*. *Tupos* can also be translated as a pattern, a model, a template, a prototype. In other words, what happened to ancient Israel as recorded in the Scriptures happened and was recorded as examples, as patterns for future generations. Thus they serve as templates to give instruction, warning, insight, and revelation. Such templates, though they may be prophetic, are not the same as prophecies. They are not so much foretelling a specific future event as revealing principles and patterns that future events may follow or be conformed to. The underpinnings of such things derive from God's sovereignty and omniscience. He who knows every event and every moment of human history, past, present, and future, is able to weave into those events, moments, and history, patterns, templates, and paradigms.

The correspondence between the ancient template we are about to open and modern American history is detailed and precise. Whether or not it has replayed itself or found parallel in past times or will do so again in the future, it has done so in our time and with intricate specificity.

Man of Controversy

I first opened the template in the book *The Paradigm*. We will now center a single piece of that template, a man of controversy, an enigma, and his relationship to a certain pagan temple. Since the book was released, the mystery and the template have not stopped unfolding and progressing. We will first set up the template with regard to the man of controversy—and then of his connection to a pagan temple. Then I will open up what I never revealed in *The Paradigm* or any book—namely that which has come true *after* the book was released.

It will involve one of the most controversial events of modern times—and the ancient mystery that lies behind it.

Chapter 18

A MAN NAMED JEHU

COULD AN ANCIENT figure and mystery lie behind one of the most controversial leaders of our time?

Beyond Politics

The mystery contained in the ancient template is not a political one. It touches every realm, including that of politics, but it is not *of* the political realm. It is beyond it. The pieces of the template will fall where they will fall regardless of politics. And though the template involves people, leaders, and prominent figures on the American national stage—it is not ultimately about them. They are only pieces of a larger picture. None of them move and act with any awareness of their place in the template or of the ancient mystery they follow.

This especially applies to the piece of the template paradigm on which we will center our focus—the man of controversy. It is not about him. It doesn't matter what one thinks of him or where one stands regarding him. The template, in that sense, is neutral. Its purpose is to reveal.

The Unlikely Vessel

The northern kingdom of ancient Israel was racing away from God. Not only was it a departure; it was now a war. Those who sat on the nation's thrones and those who stood at the pinnacle of its culture actively campaigned against the ways of God. And those who held true to God's ways now found themselves marginalized and vilified. If the nation's course continued unaltered, the end would be judgment and destruction.

It was then that a man named Jehu began a campaign to take the nation's throne. He was an unlikely figure. He was not a member of the ruling house, nor a politician, and many would see him as unqualified to sit on the king's throne.

A Man Named Trump

In the first two decades of the twenty-first century, America's fall from God was accelerating and solidifying its hold on the ruling institutions of government and culture. Those who sought to uphold the ways of God, those who held to the values and faith on which the nation had been founded, now found themselves marginalized, vilified, and increasingly treated as enemies of the mainstream culture.

It was then that a man named Trump began a campaign to take the White House. He had no idea, but he was following after the pattern of an ancient king—Jehu. He would walk in his footsteps and repeat his acts. Jehu was the prototype, and Trump, the antitype.

Like Jehu, Trump was an unlikely contender. He was not a member of America's political establishment. He was not a politician. And many saw him as unfit to govern. Jehu was a controversial and polarizing figure. He was loved by some, hated and feared by others. So too was Trump.

The Enigma

Though Jehu would invoke the name of God, the Bible never speaks of him as a man of God. As to where his heart was, it was a mystery—and it remains a mystery to this day. By his ways, acts, and nature, he could be judged as an ungodly man. Even Scripture calls his relationship with God into question:

> But Jehu took no heed to walk in the law of the LORD God of Israel with all his heart; for he did not depart from the sins of Jeroboam.[1]

And yet the Scriptures are also clear that Jehu was used of God. Regardless of his ways and intentions, he was an instrument. Even those ways and acts that could be seen as reckless and ungodly were used to bring about judgment and reformation. Jehu was a vessel of God's purposes, even if a most unlikely one, even if in spite of himself.

As did Jehu, Trump would invoke the name of God, but few would speak of him as a man of God. As with Jehu, Trump was an enigma. And as for where his heart was at with regard to God, that remained a mystery. Many judged him as an ungodly man. And yet Trump was used of God. He had been, as was Jehu, an unwitting vessel. As with Jehu, his faults and ways did not nullify the fact that he was used as an instrument for God's purposes. Nor, as with Jehu, did the fact that he was used as an instrument for God's purposes nullify his faults and ways. God will use whom He will.

Madman Driver

Jehu was a warrior, a fighter. Trump was a fighter, a man who fought with almost everyone and thrived on it. The biblical account of Jehu's rise to power presents a picture of wildness, impulsiveness, and unpredictability. Trump was seen by supporters and opponents alike as wild, impulsive, and unpredictable.

Jehu's ascent to the throne began as he mounted a chariot and embarked on a race to the capital city and the seat of governmental power. Jehu was said to have driven his chariot as one who was "crazy," a "madman."[2] Trump's race to the White House was described in similar terms.

The Alliance

In the midst of his race to the throne, Jehu made an alliance with the religious conservatives of the land. So in the midst of his race to the White House, Trump made an alliance with the religious conservatives of the nation.

More specifically, Jehu formed an alliance with one particular man who represented the religious conservatives of the land, Jehonadab. Jehonadab was known for his piety and his lifestyle of abstinence from alcohol. Jehonadab accepted Jehu's invitation to join him in his chariot. The two then rode together in Jehu's race to the throne.

Trump, likewise, made an alliance with one man, Mike Pence. Pence would, likewise, represent the religious conservatives of the land. As was Jehonadab, so Pence was known for his piety and his lifestyle of abstinence from alcohol. Pence accepted Trump's invitation to join him in the race to the White House. The two would finish the race together.

In the Twelfth Year

Jehu would succeed King Joram. Joram had been in power on the national stage for twelve years when Jehu came to power. Trump would succeed Barack Obama. Obama had come to the national stage in the Democratic Convention of 2004. Trump came to power in the presidential election of 2016. As Jehu came to power at the end of Joram's twelve years, Trump would come to power at the end of Obama's twelve years on the national stage.

The Former First Lady

The last major figure to stand in the way of Jehu's ascent was the nation's former first lady. And so in order to become king, Jehu would have to come head to head with the nation's former first lady.

The biggest obstacle to Trump's ascent to the presidency was the nation's former first lady, Hillary Clinton. In order to become president, Trump would have to come to a showdown with the former first lady.

When Jehu came face to face with the nation's former first lady, it would mean the downfall of the latter. Jehu prevailed and proceeded to take the crown of kingship.

Though virtually every poll showed Clinton winning decisively against

Trump, the biblical paradigm said the opposite—that when the two came head to head, the former first lady would fall and Jehu would prevail. So against almost all odds and all polls and in one of the greatest upsets in American presidential history, the first lady was defeated and Trump won the presidency.

Twenty-Two and Fourteen Years

How long was Hillary Clinton on the national stage? She came to it with her husband and remained on it with him for twenty-two years. After her husband's presidency she served as senator and Secretary of State for twelve years. She retired from public life for two years. She returned to run for president for two more years.

So her time on the national stage was twenty-two years with her husband and on her own, fourteen years. Her ancient prototype, the former first lady of Israel whom Jehu defeated, was on the national stage for twenty-two years with her husband and on her own, fourteen years.

What could a modern president have to do with the ancient god, Baal, and his temple? Everything...

Chapter 19

THE HOUSE OF FALLEN CHILDREN

AFTER DEFEATING THE former first lady, Jehu then directed his attention to the capital city of Samaria. The city was filled with corruption, immorality, and apostasy. Jehu had come to the capital with one agenda—*to drain the swamp*. After defeating the former first lady, Trump turned his attention to the capital city, Washington, DC. He had one agenda—*to drain the swamp*.

Children of Baal

For Jehu, there was one swamp and obstacle that stood out above all others. Jehu would confront it. It had to do with Baal. Baal was the chief of the foreign gods that Israel had turned to when it departed from God. And the worship of Baal was especially associated with the nation's former first lady.

In her office as queen, she had introduced an especially virulent form of Baal worship into the land. She used the powers of state to force the people to worship Baal, the chief god of her Phoenician homeland. Those who refused to do so could be put to death. Under her rule, Baal worship became the official religion of Israel.

The elements of Baal worship were typical of pagan religion—rites of nature, sensuality, sacrifices, and sexual immorality. It was the sacrifices, though, that made Israel's worship of Baal especially dark. As Baal demanded the sacrificing of their children, the land would be filled with their blood.

Gods and Kings

Paralleling ancient Israel's embrace of child sacrifice is America's modern embrace of abortion. In the case of Israel, the practice of child sacrifice was embarked on only as the nation turned away from God. So too in the modern case, abortion came to America only after the nation began its departure from God.

When the Israelite King Ahab and his wife, Jezebel, forcibly promulgated the worship of Baal across Israel, Jehu was one of their commanders. Therefore, he served, defended, and supported the worship of Baal, along with its sacrifice of children. But Jehu turned against the house of Ahab and against the cult of Baal, and thus against child sacrifice.

In the same way, Trump was originally a supporter of abortion. He had been friends with the former first lady and her husband, Bill Clinton. But as did Jehu, Trump would turn against abortion. When he began his race to the White House, he did so as a staunch opponent of the practice.

Showdown

During Jehu's ascent to power, the most prominent advocate of Baal worship was the nation's former first lady. During Trump's ascent to power, the nation's most prominent advocate of abortion was the nation's former first lady, Hillary Clinton. As the two ancient figures came head to head in what would be their final showdown, so the two modern figures came head to head in their final showdown, in their last debate, in the autumn of 2016. It was in that debate that Trump directly challenged Clinton in front of the nation concerning the blood of America's children. She supported the practice. But as did Jehu, Trump opposed it and pledged to war against it.

Temple of Baal

When Jehu arrived in the nation's capital, Samaria, he was confronted by a massive national temple dedicated to Baal. If he was to rid the land of Baal worship, he would have to bring down the great temple. It was that temple in the capital city that stood as the center of Baal worship and thus the axis of the system that caused children to be sacrificed. Jehu gave the orders, and the Temple of Baal was destroyed:

> Then they broke down the sacred pillar of Baal, and tore down the temple of Baal and made it a refuse dump to this day. Thus Jehu destroyed Baal from Israel.[1]

The fall of the Temple of Baal both epitomized and inaugurated Jehu's reign. It is one of the central dynamics of the paradigm: *when Jehu rises, the Temple of Baal must fall.*

Palmyra

When Trump began his rise to power in the launching of his presidential campaign, there stood, across the world in Palmyra, Syria, a Temple of Baal. It was ancient. It had stood there from the days of the Roman Empire, for almost two millennia. But according to the paradigm, when Jehu rises, the Temple of Baal must fall.

Trump announced his candidacy in June of 2015. Two months later the ancient Temple of Baal that had withstood the world for nearly two thousand years *fell to the ground*. The ancient paradigm had manifested: when Jehu rises, the Temple of Baal must fall.

The Foreshadowing

And yet the fall of Baal's temple would be the prophetic foreshadowing of a coming change. The change would alter American politics and culture. But before that change would come, there would be another manifestation of the ancient template, of Jehu and the Temple of Baal. It would replay before the nation, before the world.

Those who witnessed its replaying would have no inkling. Those members of Congress who spent countless hours in committee investigating it would likewise have no idea. But behind the event that stunned America and the world was an ancient mystery.

I wrote *The Paradigm* in 2017. The event we are about to open happened over three years after its release—yet it was foreshadowed in the paradigm revealed in the book.

What we are about to see is the mystery that the world could not, at the time, see and that the United States Congress could not, in the subsequent years, find. It is a mystery that I have never, until this moment, revealed in any book.

Chapter 20

JEHU AND THE TEMPLE OF BAAL

Is it possible that behind one of the most jarring political events of modern times lies a biblical mystery? Is it possible that the answer to an event that the American government spent incalculable effort, energy, and time investigating lies not in the political or ideological realm but in an ancient template and an event that took place over two and a half thousand years earlier?

The Rematch

In the biblical template, the rise of Jehu is linked to the fall of Baal's temple. The template, as we have seen, manifested in the rise of the modern-day Jehu and the fall of the ancient Temple of Baal in Palmyra, Syria. But could there be another manifestation? And if the war of Jehu and the Temple of Baal framed the beginning of Jehu's reign and the beginning of Trump's rise to the presidency, could it also have framed its end? Or could his presidency end with a replay, a rematch, of the battle revealed in the template?

January 6

It was the first week of January 2021, the week that would determine the future of the United States Senate and the American presidency. It would all pivot on the middle of that week, Wednesday, when the results of the Senate race in Georgia would be known and thus which party would control the Senate. It was also the day that the votes of the 2020 presidential election would be officially sealed. Wednesday was critical, as it would give the Democrats control of Congress and the presidency. It would seal the end of Trump's days in power. It would all converge on January 6. What happened on that day is not condoned by the template, but it is revealed and foreshadowed.

The National Temple

The Temple of Baal that stood in the nation's capital city, Samaria, was, in effect, the national temple of Israel's northern kingdom. So the first question we must ask is this: Is there a building in Washington, DC, that could be deemed its national temple? It is commonly assumed that America has no national temple. But there is one.

It has been called the *Temple of the American Republic*, the *People's House*, America's *Secular Temple*, and the nation's *Temple of Democracy*. It is the United States Capitol Building. The Capitol Building's place as America's national temple appears on its very walls where it is written: "We have built no temple but the Capitol..."[1] Even the building refers to itself as a temple. It was modeled after the pagan temples of the ancient world, particularly those of Greece and Rome and more specifically the Roman Pantheon, the temple of all gods.

The Pagan Prayer

But it is not such architecture that makes a building pagan but what happens on the inside. In the ancient Temple of Baal, prayers and worship were lifted up to a pagan god. The Capitol Building has traditionally seen prayers and invocations lifted up to the God of the Bible. But as the week of January 6, 2021, began, something changed.

It happened on January 3, the first working session of the new Congress. The new Congress was inaugurated with a prayer offered by the Democratic congressman Emanuel Cleaver. I had written of him years before in *The Paradigm*. He was the man who had given an unknowingly prophetic address at the Democratic Convention that nominated Hillary Clinton. He would now offer up an unknowingly prophetic prayer.

The problem with the prayer was the god to whom Cleaver prayed. He sealed it with the name Brahma.[2] Brahma is an eternity away from the God of the Bible. Brahma is a Hindu god, one of three gods ruling deities, the others being Vishnu and Shiva. Brahma has four heads. He originally had five, but the god Shiva cut one of them off when he was caught lying. Brahma is a pagan god. And so on January 3, 2021, the 117th Congress was consecrated to a pagan god and America's national temple became a house of prayer—to a pagan god—as in a pagan temple.

The Agenda

Beyond prayer, the Temple of Baal housed practices and agendas that stood in opposition to the ways of God. It promoted sexual immorality and the sacrifice of children. On that first week of 2021, it was not just a pagan prayer that inaugurated the new Congress—it was an anti-biblical or pagan agenda that did. The new Democratic-controlled Congress would bring to Capitol Hill an agenda that stood in stark opposition to biblical morality and values as touching sexuality, religious freedom, gender, and the lives of unborn children. The new Congress came to the Capitol Building prepared to enact the most proabortion agenda in American history.

So it was not only the prayer that turned America's "temple" into a pagan one—it was the agenda. That first week of 2021 was when that agenda took full control of Capitol Hill and of the Temple of the American Republic. And it all happened when *a Jehu was still in power and in the capital city*. These were the ingredients of the ancient template. It was a battle waiting to happen.

Jehu's Assembly

The tenth chapter of the Book of 2 Kings records that Jehu called for an assembly in the capital city. So President Trump called for an assembly in the capital city, Washington, DC, on January 6. Jehu's gathering would ultimately be directed at the national temple in the capital city. Trump's gathering of January 6 would likewise be directed on America's national temple—the Capitol Building.

The ancient template would center on two gatherings or two groups of people gathered in that city: the priests and worshippers of Baal, who would convene inside the temple, and the supporters of Jehu, who would stand outside the temple. So on January 6, the gathering that convened inside the Capitol Building represented the victory of an anti-biblical agenda. The gathering that took place outside the Capitol Building represented the supporters of the modern-day Jehu, Trump.

Jehonadab in the House

It is of note that the ancient template tells of both Jehu and his partner, Jehonadab, playing a prominent role in what would happen in the Temple of Baal. So both Trump and Pence would play a prominent role in what happened on January 6 in the Capitol Building, America's national temple.

In the ancient template, both Jehu and Jehonadab go to Baal's temple. Trump had planned to go down to the Capitol Building that day, but his security team prevented him. But Pence, the modern-day Jehonadab, did indeed enter the national temple that day in accordance with the paradigm. It is worthy of note that though we can assume that Jehonadab left the building after entering it, the account gives no record or indication that he did. On January 6, Pence entered the Capitol Building. He never left but would remain there through the night.

Those Outside the Temple

In the ancient template, Jehu directed the multitude of his supporters to go to the Temple of Baal and stand outside it. On January 6, Trump, in effect, directed the multitude of his supporters to go to the Capitol Building and stand outside in protest.

Jehu's supporters stood outside the national temple while proceedings took place inside. Trump's supporters stood outside the national temple while proceedings took place inside. The supporters of Jehu would not stay outside the Temple of Baal. And the supporters of Trump would not stay outside the Capitol Building.

The Siege

In the biblical account of Jehu's war against the Temple of Baal, his supporters were given the word, "Go inside."[3] Upon that, the people of Jehu laid siege to the temple. So on January 6 the supporters of Trump would do likewise. They believed they had the authority to *go inside*. So they went inside. They laid siege to it.

In the ancient template, the followers of Jehu entered the Temple of Baal and dramatically and violently interrupted its proceedings. On January 6, the followers of Trump entered the Capitol Building and dramatically, if less violently than the ancient case, interrupted its proceedings. In the ancient template, Jehu's followers go inside the temple to shed blood—and they do. On January 6, though it was not the majority, among those who had entered the Capitol Building were those calling for blood and those who had prepared for violence.

Desecration

In order to prevent the Temple of Baal or the ground on which it stood from ever being used again as the site of pagan practices, Jehu's people defiled and desecrated it. So on January 6, among those who entered the Capitol Building were those who sought to defile and desecrate it.

In view of Jehu and the Temple of Baal, the reactions of members of Congress in the wake of January 6 are especially significant and consistent. The incoming Senate majority leader said,

> "This *temple* to democracy was *desecrated*."[4]

A senator speaking that night from Capitol Hill said,

> "This sacred place was desecrated....This temple to democracy was defiled."[5]

The Speaker of the House spoke of those who engaged in the

...desecration of this, our temple..."[6]

Shmonim Ish—The Eighty Men

In the wake of January 6, the government began its crackdown against those involved with breaching the Capitol Building. At the end of the week, the Washington, DC, Police Department announced the number of those they arrested in connection with the Capitol Hill riot. The number made headlines:

80 Arrested for Civil Unrest at US Capitol and Around DC

> Metropolitan Police Department arrested 80 individuals in connection with the civil unrest at the U.S. Capitol and around D.C.[7]

So the number of those connected to the siege of the Capitol Building was 80. The ancient template gives the number of Jehu's men who laid siege to the Temple of Baal with two Hebrew words:

Shmonim Ish

The translation of "Shmonim Ish"? *Eighty men!*
So it is written in the ancient template:

> Jehu had appointed for himself men on the outside, *80 men*...[8]

The same exact number. No one could have orchestrated the connection. But the template had been there for over two and a half thousand years.

The Secret of America's Temple

There appears to be a secret hidden in the walls of America's temple, its Capitol Building. In the years before it was planned and built, an English scholar traveled the Middle East. There he surveyed ancient ruins, ancient structures, ancient temples. He wrote a book detailing his findings, with descriptions and drawings. The book was hugely influential among scholars and architects of the day.

One of the ancient buildings he surveyed and wrote about was the *Temple of Baal.* It is believed that his book influenced those designing the United States Capitol and that part of the Temple of Baal is actually embedded into the Capitol Building.

Further, the particular Temple of Baal that he surveyed happened to be the Temple of Palmyra, Syria. In other words, *it was the same ancient temple* that would fall to the earth two months after Trump began his rise to power.

Templates and Prototypes

As the ancient Jehu contended against the great national temple, the modern-day Jehu contended against America's great national temple. The modern Jehu had no idea of the ancient template, or of his ancient prototype, or of the role he was to play. But nor did the eighty participants in the January 6 siege of the Capitol Building have any idea of the eighty who laid siege to the Temple of Baal on Jehu's behalf. It didn't matter. The parallels were not natural. The template manifested regardless.

The Reign of Baal

The siege against Baal's temple and its subsequent fall framed the beginning of Jehu's reign. The fall of Baal's temple likewise framed the beginning of Trump's ascent to power. But in the case of Trump, just as it had framed the beginning of his reign, it would also frame the end. It is no accident that the ancient template replayed itself on the very day that sealed the end of his presidency.

It was, in a sense, a rematch. Only this time, the modern Jehu and his forces would not prevail. It was a sign that the agenda of Baal would be prevailing in America and his influence would rest on the thrones of both political and cultural power.

But what happened on January 6, 2021, was not the end of the story, not of the template, and not of the battle of Jehu and the Temple of Baal. There would be another manifestation. In many ways this one would be the most significant. It would become the key to joining together the mysteries of Jehu and those that preceded them—as well as those that would follow. We now open this last manifestation of Jehu and the Temple of Baal.

Chapter 21

BREAKING THE GODS

BAAL'S CONNECTION TO child sacrifice was as infamous as that of the god Molech. When judgment finally fell on Israel's northern kingdom, the nation's obituary appeared in 2 Kings 17. Prominent among the causes of its destruction was that the people

> ...served Baal. And they caused their sons and daughters to pass through the fire.[1]

Destroying Baal From Israel

It was the cult of Baal and the act of child sacrifice that caused the nation's destruction. That cult and that act centered and was embodied in the Temple of Baal in the nation's capital city. So when Jehu came against that temple, he was coming against an institution, a religion, a priesthood, a system, and a practice. He was waging war against the systematic murder of the nation's children. And thus, as the account reads, not only did he destroy a temple, but he drove out a god and his cult: he *"destroyed Baal from Israel."*[2]

In this, Jehu was unique. He was the only ruler in the history of Israel's northern kingdom who actively sought to drive Baal out of the land and to end the practice of child sacrifice. Even in the less apostate kingdom of Judah, the number of kings who sought to do likewise was minuscule.

Destroying Baal From America

As he walked in the template of the ancient king, Donald Trump would likewise wage war against the systematic killing of children. And as Jehu was unique among the kings of the northern kingdom in his war against Baal, Trump was unique among American presidents in the post-*Roe v. Wade* era in the effectiveness of his war against the killing of children. Jehu had *destroyed Baal from Israel*; Trump would seek to do similarly with regard to abortion in America.

His administration would be overwhelmingly consistent in its attempts to protect the unborn. Trump would become the first sitting American president to address the annual March for Life in Washington, DC. His administration would act to protect the freedom of those whose conscience prohibited them from funding or assisting in the killing of the unborn. And as Jehu cut off all state support for the cult of Baal and child sacrifice, Trump cut off all state funding for abortions around the world and sought the defunding of abortion organizations from the federal budget.

Bringing Down the Temple

In his campaign of 2016, Trump promised that as president, he would appoint judges who would stand for life, and that would lead to the overturning of abortion as the nation had known it. And so the paradigm of Jehu and the Temple of Baal was about much more than a building. In the case of Trump, it was about bringing down an institution, a ruling, and a practice. And the unique role that he would play in bringing it down was no accident but a prerequisite of the ancient paradigm.

Baal Comes to New York

One month before his final debate with Hillary Clinton and less than two months before the election, something strange happened. An object appeared on the streets of New York City, a foreign object. It was a representation of a Middle Eastern object, from Palmyra, Syria, the city of the Temple of Baal that had been destroyed just after Trump began his rise to power.

It was an arch. Some called it the Arch of Baal. It was the arch that, in ancient times, led the worshippers of Baal into his temple. It was erected on the grounds of City Hall. It was unveiled at the order of city officials to the playing of music meant to evoke the worship of Baal—and to the cheers of those gathered to witness it.

Baal's temple had fallen when the American Jehu had begun his rise. But now an object linked to that temple was erected in the land of the modern-day Jehu. In fact, it was standing in the land of both presidential contenders—New York. And it was standing in New York City, where the blood of more children had been spilled than anywhere else in the nation. There was even a written sign placed by the arch identifying it with the Temple of Baal.

So now, just as the American Jehu was on the verge of coming to power—a reign that would threaten the bloody practice linked to the worship of Baal—an object bearing the name of the god and connected to his temple appeared in the land.

First Act

In order for Trump to make good on his promise to appoint Supreme Court justices who would stand for life, several factors had to fall into place, each of which was beyond his control. First, he had to win the election. Against all odds and the conclusions of virtually every poll, he did. Second, the doors would have to open to the Supreme Court—meaning Supreme Court justices would have to resign or die during the window of his presidency. They did.

Trump made his first Supreme Court nomination less than two weeks after becoming president. To replace the deceased justice Antonin Scalia, he nominated Neil Gorsuch. Gorsuch was confirmed on April 7, 2017. Since Gorsuch was a conservative justice replacing another conservative justice, the appointment did not alter the balance of the court but preserved it.

Second Act

The following year in June, another Supreme Court vacancy opened up as Justice Anthony Kennedy announced he would be resigning. Though Kennedy was considered a moderate, when it came to issues such as gay marriage and abortion, he voted with the court's liberal wing. Trump chose Brett Kavanaugh to replace him. Unlike Kennedy, Kavanaugh was a conservative and decidedly pro-life. If he was to be confirmed, it would alter the court, giving it a pro-life majority.

Thus the confirmation hearings became a battleground, a focal point of the culture wars. A flurry of accusations, defenses, and counteraccusations swirled around the nomination. Behind the controversy was the issue of life and abortion.

And then something strange happened.

Baal Comes to Washington

The media was blind to it. And most people never realized it happened. But in the days of the Kavanaugh hearings and the fury that surrounded them, an object appeared in Washington, DC. It appeared on the National Lawn, facing the Capitol Building, the place in which the hearings were taking place. It was a foreign object—from Palmyra. The Arch of Baal was now standing in the nation's capital and representing the Temple of Baal.

So while the battle over abortion and life raged on Capitol Hill, the object representing the Temple of Baal, the ancient god of child sacrifice, appeared in front of it. The elements of the ancient paradigm again manifested—Jehu, as embodied by Trump; Jehu's war against the cult of Baal and the systematic killing of children, as embodied by his Supreme Court nomination; and the Temple of Baal and child sacrifice as embodied by abortion and that arch.

The arch was a gateway through which worshippers entered into Baal's temple. So it was first erected in New York City, the gateway through which child sacrifice had spread to America. So too it was erected in Washington,

DC, the nation's capital and the gateway through which child sacrifice spread to the nation through *Roe v. Wade.*

Third Act

After a storm of controversy, contention, and accusations, Kavanaugh was confirmed by the United States Senate on October 6, 2018, by a margin of two votes, and only because the Senate happened to be in control of the Republicans. The court was now solidly pro-life. And the implications were enormous.

Still, one more Supreme Court justice and one more vote would be needed for the paradigm to be fulfilled. This would also come to pass apart from anyone's intent or control. It would happen at the very end of the Trump presidency, so close to the end that it was doubtful that it would happen at all.

It would come to a head only eight days before the presidential election that would mark the end of Trump's presidency. But it would go through. And it would give the court an even stronger and more decisive pro-life majority. It was this third Supreme Court justice that would provide the critical vote in a ruling that would alter the nation's course.

Breaking the Pillar

Trump's appointing of the three Supreme Court justices would prove to be among the most consequential acts of his presidency. The first appointment was set in motion less than two weeks after the start of his presidency, and the last would be completed near the end.

When Jehu brought down the Temple of Baal, he was doing more than destroying a building; he was bringing down an institution. Abortion was America's form of Baal worship. It rested on one critical Supreme Court ruling—that of *Roe v. Wade. Roe v. Wade* was a modern-day version of the Temple of Baal. It was the vessel, the structure, that allowed for the sacrifice of children. So the modern-day Jehu would seek to bring down the modern-day Temple of Baal.

The Nullifiers

Had Trump not risen to power just when he did, all this would have never happened. He had to be lifted to the presidency and exactly when he was. Trump's four years in power were just enough to set in motion the three Supreme Court justices and secure the three votes needed to bring down the modern Temple of Baal.

He would put forth his last and most critical nomination at the end of his presidency in *2020*. And so Jehu's bringing down of Baal's Temple, the breaking of abortion, would be set in motion in *the fiftieth year of abortion's entrance into the land—the year of Jubilee.*

The Jubilee nullifies, undoes what was done. Jehu nullified the Temple of Baal. Now the two nullifiers would come together—the modern-day Jehu and the ancient Jubilee. No one could have planned it. And no one could have orchestrated it. But it would all converge at the exact and appointed time.

———————————

And yet with all that, it still would not have happened had there not been another stream of events and mysteries, and another convergence in the pieces of the puzzle. This one would as well be connected to the Jubilee, but of a different nature. It would come from the Jubilee's other realm. And although its movement went almost unnoticed, when it fulfilled its mission, it would change the course of American history.

Part V

THE JUBILEAN REDEMPTION

Chapter 22

A DARK CONCEPTION

WHEN ABORTION BEGAN its entrance into American society and law, it did not come at once but step by step, law by law, and state by state. But there would be another entrance, different from the others. It would not be initiated by a state legislature or a government official. It would begin when a troubled young woman visited the office of a Texas attorney, Henry McCluskey.

What was conceived in that office would take years to come to fruition. But when it came, its impact on American culture would be seismic. It would change the lives of millions, born and unborn.

The Making of Jane Roe

Norma Leah McCorvey was twenty-one years old when she discovered she was pregnant. It was her third child. She had a drinking problem and partook of illegal drugs. She wanted to abort the baby. McCluskey referred her to two attorneys who were looking for a white pregnant woman to use as the plaintiff in a lawsuit that they wanted to mount over abortion. Upon meeting with them, McCorvey was told that her unborn child was "just a piece of tissue."[1] She agreed to become their plaintiff, believing it would allow her to continue to drink and partake of drugs without having to worry about her unborn child.

The Jubilee of *Roe v. Wade*

The lawsuit was filed against Dallas County District Attorney Henry Wade, representing the state of Texas. McCorvey was given a new name for the purpose of the suit, *Jane Roe*. So the suit would become known as *Roe v. Wade*. Though the case would become famous because of the 1973 Supreme Court ruling bearing the same name, it did not begin in 1973. It began in the same critical year in which abortion began its entrance into America. *Roe v. Wade* was filed in 1970.

Thus the year 2020 was not only the Jubilee of the year in which abortion on demand was set in motion in America—it was also the Jubilee of the year that *Roe v. Wade* was set in motion. In other words, *fifty years after* Roe v. Wade *began, in the Jubilee of its conception, the plague came to America.*

Month of Conception—January 1970 / January 2020

Roe v. Wade began with that meeting in McCluskey's office. When did it take place? It happened in January 1970. Fifty years forward from that meeting takes us to *January 2020*, the Jubilee of *Roe v. Wade*. *January 2020* was the month that the plague began in America. It was the Jubilee of the month that *Roe v. Wade* also began in America.

The most accurate reports put that initial meeting between McCorvey and McCluskey in *late January* of 1970. That would put its Jubilee in *late January of 2020*. And so the plague entered America in *late January of 2020*.

Month of Fruition—March 1970 / March 2020

The meeting of McCorvey and McCluskey was the critical moment in the conception of the lawsuit that would alter American history. Two months later, it would come to fruition when the case known as *Roe v. Wade* was filed against the state of Texas.

It was filed in *March 1970*. Fifty years from that filing takes us to *March 2020*. So too the plague came to fruition in America, falling at full force and impact, in *March 2020* when America went into a state of emergency, lockdown, and paralysis. It all happened in the Jubilee of the conception and fruition of the lawsuit that would become famous as *Roe v. Wade*.

We have again seen the principle of restitution, life for life. But what about the Jubilee's other work, that of restoration and redemption? That too would manifest. It would come as had the plague, with precision and at the appointed times.

Chapter 23

A CASE OF NULLIFICATION

WE HAVE SEEN that the Jubilee is a two-sided phenomenon. To the one who has taken or occupied the ancestral land of another, the Jubilee takes away. But to the one who has lost it, the Jubilee restores. Each of the two sides involves a return and an undoing of what was done. But one manifests in the form of restitution, justice, or judgment, and the other, in the form of restoration and redemption.

The Other Side

We have seen the first side in the form of a plague and in the taking away of life from the generation that had taken away life. But what about the other, the side of restoration and redemption? What about an undoing that brings not death but life? The Jubilee of 2020 saw death moving across the land. Could there have been another moving—not of death but life?

Dobbs v. Jackson

Roe v. Wade had begun as a suit filed against the state of Texas. If the Jubilee is a return and reversal of that which was done, we would expect to see a return to a suit filed against a state. And that is exactly what took place.

In March 2018 the Mississippi legislature passed a law that prohibited abortion after the fifteenth week of pregnancy. A Mississippi abortion clinic immediately filed a lawsuit against the law. The suit, which would be known as *Dobbs v. Jackson*, would end up in the US District Court for the Southern District of Mississippi. The court ruled against the state and for the abortion clinic.

The Filings

Roe v. Wade had also ended up in a US District Court. Likewise, the court ruled against the state and for abortion. The state of Texas would appeal the decision, sending *Roe v. Wade* to the Supreme Court. When the District Court ruled against Mississippi and for the abortion clinic, the state likewise filed an appeal. And just as with *Roe v. Wade*, it would cause the case to go to the Supreme Court. And as with *Roe v. Wade*, the ruling would be pivotal and historic.

Days of Appeal—June 1970 / June 2020

Everything was now returning to where it had been fifty years earlier. *Roe v. Wade* was sent on appeal to the Supreme Court in 1970. The case that would bring about its reversal, *Dobbs v. Jackson*, was sent to the Supreme Court on appeal in 2020, fifty years later.

The event that caused *Roe v. Wade* to be appealed was the ruling of the US Court of Appeals for the Fifth Circuit. With the release of its verdict, both sides began working on the appeal to be sent to the Supreme Court. That verdict and the beginning of the Supreme Court appeal took place in *June of 1970*. The sending of *Dobbs v. Jackson* on appeal to the Supreme Court took place in *June of 2020*—fifty years, one Jubilee, to the month that the appeal of *Roe v. Wade* began.

Could an ancient queen, an ancient villain, an ancient decree of evil, and another decree of good lie behind two of the most pivotal Supreme Court cases in history? The answer lies in the mystery of Sivan 23.

Chapter 24

THE MYSTERY OF SIVAN 23

THE BOOK OF Esther recounts how the Jews of Persia were saved from annihilation. It began with the rise of the brutal Persian official Haman.

The Ordinance of Evil

Haman devised a plan to exterminate the Jews of the Persian Empire on the thirteenth day of the month of Adar. Upon securing the king's approval, the plan was sealed.

But before the set day, Esther, the Jewish queen of Persia, along with Mordecai, her cousin, exposed Haman's plans before the king and brought about his downfall. But the evil decree, his plan of annihilation, was still in effect to be carried out on the appointed day.

Esther appealed to the king, saying,

> If it pleases the king, and if I have found favor in his sight and the thing seems right to the king and I am pleasing in his eyes, let it be written to revoke the letters devised by Haman, the son of Hammedatha the Agagite, which he wrote to annihilate the Jews who are in all the king's provinces.[1]

The Ordinance of Nullification

The king's answer was to allow for a second decree to be written:

> You yourselves write a decree concerning the Jews, as you please, in the king's name, and seal it with the king's signet ring.[2]

So a new decree was penned. Its purpose was to nullify the power of the first decree. It authorized the Jews of Persia to assemble on the appointed day and protect themselves with whatever force was needed. It was a decree of life in answer to a decree of death. It was committed to writing by the king's scribes and then sent forth to every province of the empire. The account specifies the day on which the decree was committed to writing to be sent forth:

So the king's scribes were called at that time, in the third month,
which is the month of Sivan, on the twenty-third day; and it
was written, according to all that Mordecai commanded...[3]

Sivan 23

So it was sealed to be sent throughout the empire on the twenty-third day of
the Hebrew month of Sivan, Sivan 23. Sivan 23 was thus commemorated in
the Jewish calendar as the day to pray for the annulling of evil decrees. One
Jewish writer notes:

The holy books teach us that this day is a very powerful day
for prayers to nullify decrees and anything bad, evil and
horrible against us.[4]

A prayer is given in Hebrew to be recited by the Jewish people on the Sivan
23 for the nullification of all evil decrees:

O Lord, my Rock and my Redeemer. From you I am asking
mercy!...Bestow your mercy on all of us, to transform all
evil to good, annul all harsh decrees concerning us, tear up
the evil of our sentence...[5]

Against the Evil Decree

The Supreme Court ruling in *Roe v. Wade* was, in its effect, *a decree of death
and destruction*. As in Haman's decree against the Jews of Persia, it opened
the door "to destroy, kill, and annihilate"[6] the innocent of an entire nation.
So the effect of *Roe v. Wade* was to destroy millions of innocent lives, the
number of Jews living in Persia multiplied many, many times over. It was a
most evil decree.

The decree of Haman would be nullified by the decree of Mordecai. It
would be undone by the same means and in kind, by a decree sent forth to
undo a previous decree, a royal ordinance to nullify a royal ordinance.

In the case of *Roe v. Wade*, the same pattern was replayed. The evil decree,
in this case, was a Supreme Court ruling. So it had to be nullified and undone
by the same means and in kind—by a Supreme Court ruling, that of *Dobbs
v. Jackson*.

When did the case that would nullify *Roe v. Wade* go forth? When was it
sent to the Supreme Court? It went forth on June 15, 2020. But that was the
date on the Western Gregorian calendar.

On the biblical calendar, it was sent to the Supreme Court on a different
date—*the twenty-third day of Sivan—Sivan 23!*

The Day of Revoking

In other words, the case that would revoke the evil decree of *Roe v. Wade* was sent to the Supreme Court on the ancient day when the decree of life was sent forth to nullify the decree of death. The document that would nullify *Roe v. Wade* went forth on the same day that the document nullifying Haman's decree of death went forth.

It was sent to the Supreme Court on the same day that prayers were lifted up across the Jewish world to nullify, revoke, and tear up the decrees of evil. Of course those who prayed those prayers had no idea the document was being sent, and those who sent the document had no idea that those prayers were being uttered.

The Decree of Haman and Mordecai

The decree of Mordecai was joined to the decree of Haman not only in its purpose and impact but in the pattern of its going forth. Below is the record of how each of the two decrees were issued—first, the decree of death as issued by Haman, and second, the decree of life as issued by Mordecai:

> Then the king's scribes were called on the thirteenth day of the first month.[7]

> So the king's scribes were called at that time, in the third month, which is the month of Sivan, on the twenty-third day.[8]

> ...and...written according to all that Haman commanded...[9]

> ...and...written, according to all that Mordecai commanded...[10]

> ...to the king's satraps, to the governors who were over each province...and to every people in their language.[11]

> ...to the...satraps, the governors...to every province...to every people in their own language...[12]

> In the name of King Ahasuerus it was written, and sealed with the king's signet ring.[13]

> ...And he wrote in the name of King Ahasuerus, sealed it with the king's signet ring...[14]

> ...The couriers went out, hastened by the king's command.[15]

...by couriers on horseback...bred from swift steeds.[16]

The Decree of Roe and Dobbs

So Mordecai's decree would follow the same pattern, steps, and path, of the decree it was meant to nullify. In other words, the redemption would go forth just as had the evil; the ordinance of life would take on the form as the ordinance of death.

So too the case that was sent to the Supreme Court on Sivan 23 of 2020 would follow the same pattern, steps, and path of *Roe v. Wade*, the case it was to nullify. In its initial hearing, in its judgment by a federal court, in its appeal to the Supreme Court, and in its timing, *Dobbs v. Jackson* would parallel the steps, the path, and the timing of *Roe v. Wade*. And by so doing, it was also paralleling the Sivan 23 decree of Mordecai, which was, in turn, paralleling the decree of Haman. It was a mystery within a mystery within a mystery.

Dobbs v. Jackson was sent to the Supreme Court on the Sivan 23, the day of the decree that nullifies the decree of death and destruction.

It was sent in the year 2020, abortion's Jubilean year.

And it was sent to the Supreme Court in the year that president who walked in the footsteps of Jehu would complete his third nomination to the court to nullify the evil decree.

So it was sent. What happened when it arrived?

Chapter 25

RECEPTION

BOTH CASES ARRIVED in the Supreme Court. But their arrival did not, of course, guarantee a hearing. Of the seven thousand or so cases sent to the court each year, only about 2 percent are accepted and heard.

Year of Reception—1971 / 2021

In 1970 there was no guarantee that the court would hear *Roe v. Wade* or that, fifty years later, it would hear *Dobbs v. Jackson*. But in 1971 the Supreme Court announced it would take up and hear the case of *Roe v. Wade*. Fifty years later brings us to the year 2021. In 2021 the court announced it would take up and hear the case of *Dobbs v. Jackson*. Thus in the Jubilee year of the court's taking up of *Roe v. Wade*, the court took up *Dobbs v. Jackson*.

Month of Reception—May 1971 / May 2021

The court announced it would take up *Roe v. Wade* in the month of *May*. The court announced it would take up *Dobbs v. Jackson* fifty years later in the month of *May*—the same court, the same act, the same matter—*and fifty years later—one Jubilee—to the same month*.

Of Life and Death

On the day of *Roe*'s hearing, the attorney for the plaintiff argued that to abort one's pregnancy was a personal right. When questioned if that meant a child could be aborted up to the moment of birth, the attorney answered that it did. The state of Texas argued that once a child is conceived, one does not have the right to end its life.[1] On the day of *Dobbs*' hearing, the arguments centered on using the issue of "viability" to determine whether a child could be aborted. In other words, the child could be aborted if he or she could not at that point survive outside the womb. The abortion clinic argued for that measure of viability to be used in determining whether an abortion could be performed. Mississippi argued that the measure was wrong.[2]

Mississippi was not seeking the overturning of *Roe v. Wade* but for the right of states to uphold restrictions on abortion beyond that of viability. But the outcome of *Dobbs v. Jackson* would turn out to be far more consequential and significant than what the state had imagined. So *Dobbs v. Jackson* would serve as an instrument, a Jubilean instrument, through which a reception would come.

Year of the Hearing—1971 / 2021

Roe v. Wade was heard before the Supreme Court in 1971. Fifty years later takes us to its Jubilean year—2021. The hearing of *Dobbs v. Jackson* that would bring the reversal of *Roe v. Wade* took place in 2021, *the Jubilean year* of Roe's first hearing.

Month of the Hearing— December 1971 / December 2021

When in 1971 did *Roe v. Wade* receive its first Supreme Court hearing? It happened in *December*. One Jubilee forward brings us to *December 2021*. When did *Dobbs v. Jackson* receive its hearing? It happened in *December 2021*. The Jubilean case was heard in the fiftieth year of the case it was to annul, in its Jubilean month and within twelve days of its fifty-year culmination point.

The Thirteenth Day of the Twelfth Month

We must take note of one more convergence. We have seen how the case of *Dobbs v. Jackson* was sent forth to the Supreme Court on Sivan 23, the same day that Mordecai's decree was sent forth to the Persian Empire to nullify the decree of Haman.

The purpose of each was to undo a decree of death. Mordecai's decree went forth to nullify Haman's decree. And Haman's decree was linked to the *thirteenth day of the twelfth month*.

Dobbs v. Jackson went forth to nullify *Roe v. Wade. Roe v. Wade* would receive its hearing before the Supreme Court on *December 13—the thirteenth day of the twelfth month*.

Thus both the ancient and modern issuance that went forth on Sivan 23 did so to nullify a decree of death linked to the *thirteenth day of the twelfth month*.

Could an error, a glitch, a breaching of protocol, a breaking of order have happened according to an appointed order? Could a wrong have taken place at the right time?

Chapter 26

THE LEAK

THE NEXT MAJOR event in the case of *Dobbs v. Jackson* did not happen according to any procedure, plan, or protocol.

The Leaked Draft

It went against all protocols concerning Supreme Court deliberations. It was the court's practice to tightly guard the confidentiality of all internal communications and opinions concerning any case under consideration. But what happened in the case of *Dobbs v. Jackson* broke those conventions.

In the spring of 2022 the news organization Politico published a document that had been obtained through a Supreme Court leak. Apparently one of the court's employees decided to release an internal communication to the press. It was a draft written by Justice Samuel Alito in the case of *Dobbs v. Jackson*. The draft did not necessarily represent a final decision, but it stunned much of the nation and the world—as it indicated that *Roe v. Wade* could or would be overturned.

Shock Waves and Violence

The leaked document sent shock waves through the media and culture. Within hours of its release, protests and demonstrations broke out in Washington and across the nation. Proabortion protesters demonstrated outside the Supreme Court building, along with pro-life protesters. An unprecedented weight of pressure fell on the court. Proabortion spokespeople threatened a "summer of rage" if *Roe* was overturned.[1]

The Department of Homeland Security began preparing for violent attacks against government officials, ministers, and organizations involved with abortion. Soon after the leak, a wave of attacks was launched against crisis pregnancy centers and pro-life churches. Crowds gathered outside the homes of the Supreme Court justices presumed to be in favor of *Roe*'s overturning. A man was arrested near the home of Justice Kavanaugh for attempted murder. In response to the protests Congress passed a law to increase protections for the justices and their families.

The Other Leak

Many described the leak as unprecedented. But there was a dramatic precedent. And it concerned a case just as monumental as that of *Dobbs v. Jackson*. The case was *Roe v. Wade*.

The leak in the *Dobbs* case came from a document penned by Justice Alito and circulated among his colleagues. The leak in *Roe* came from a document penned by Justice Douglas and circulated among his colleagues.

The leak in *Dobbs* appeared in an article by Politico. The leak in *Roe* appeared in an article by the *Washington Post*. The Politico article focused on the court's internal deliberations. The *Washington Post* article focused on the court's internal deliberations.

The one occurrence was again the parallel of the other. We must now turn to the question of timing.

Year of the Leak—1972 / 2022

When did each of the two leaks occur?

The leak in *Roe v. Wade* took place in *1972*. Adding the fifty years of the Jubilee takes us to the year *2022*.

The leak in *Dobbs v. Jackson* took place in *2022*.

Thus even the leak in each case followed the timing and dynamic of the Jubilee.

Could the parameters given in the Book of Leviticus have determined a modern event that altered American history?

Chapter 27

THE JUBILEAN REDEMPTION

THE SUPREME COURT ruling in *Roe v. Wade* was handed down on January 22, 1973. With that one decision, abortion on demand became the law of the land. By the time of its Jubilee, over sixty million children had been killed.

The Leviticus Parameters

So when exactly was the Jubilee of *Roe v. Wade*? The answer is found in the Jubilean ordinance of Leviticus 25:

> And you shall count seven sabbaths of years for yourself, seven times seven years; and the time of the seven sabbaths of years shall be to you forty-nine years....And you shall consecrate the fiftieth year.[1]

Seven times seven of years from January 22, 1973, *takes us to January 22, 2022.* The Jubilean year of *Roe v. Wade* thus *begins on January 22, 2022, and concludes one year later.* All but twenty-two of its days take place in 2022.

The *Roe v. Wade* Jubilee

We have seen the continual unfolding of convergences between the case that legalized abortion and the case that would undo it. Now we come to the final event, upon which all the rest hangs.

The Jubilean year of *Roe v. Wade began on January 22, 2022, and ended on January 22, 2023.* For the mystery to be complete, the final event of the Jubilee, the return and the undoing, would have to take place within the parameters of those days. So when was *Roe v. Wade* overturned?

The Supreme Court would hand down its ruling in the case of *Dobbs v. Jackson* in June of 2022.

That places it in between the two parameters of January 22, 2022, and January 22, 2023.

Thus the overturning and nullifying of *Roe v. Wade* took place in the Jubilean year of *Roe v. Wade.* It had all happened in accordance with the ancient mystery and within its parameters of time as ordained in the Book of Leviticus. The year of Jubilee is appointed to bring undoing and reversal. So in the

Jubilean year of *Roe v. Wade*, the ordinance of death had been reversed. And the reversal of death meant life.

After over sixty million deaths, the lives of the innocent would now be saved and the nation would be given a new chance to save them. The Jubilee had thus brought a form of redemption.

The Single Vote

And it all happened through a single vote. While the Mississippi ban on abortion was upheld by a slightly more decisive vote, the reversal of *Roe v. Wade* came by the vote of a single Supreme Court justice. Every change that would stem from that ruling, even the changing of a nation's course, hung on that one solitary vote. And yet when *Dobbs v. Jackson* was sent to the Supreme Court, that single vote did not even exist. It would only come into existence by a series of twists and quirks, events that were, once again, beyond anyone's control.

———————————

The vote that overturned *Roe v. Wade* would fall into place only through another stream of mysteries—through an ancient calendar and a mystery of appointed days.

Part VI

THE APPOINTED DAYS

Chapter 28

A MYSTERY OF DAYS

I s IT POSSIBLE that the most critical of years, 2020, the year of the plague and lockdown, of disorder and chaos, and so many other dramatic events, was actually determined by a three-thousand-year-old calendar—even the holy days of ancient Israel?

The Appointed Times

If so, it would not be the first time that significant historical events were marked by them. The Bible itself gives us the first precedents. The crucifixion of the Messiah, as in the sacrifice of a lamb, took place on the Passover, the day of the sacrificed lamb. So too the coming of the Spirit upon the first believers in Jerusalem, the day known as Pentecost, took place on the appointed Hebrew holy day of Shavuot. Even such post-biblical events of significance in Jewish history as General Allenby's liberation of Jerusalem from Turkish rule in December 1917 fell on the eve of Hanukkah, the ancient Jewish festival that celebrates the liberation of Jerusalem.

Holy Days and Judgment

So could one of the most dramatic, consequential, and ominous years of modern history, 2020, have been marked by the ancient holy days of the Bible? And as the year bore the signs of biblical judgment, could those holy days have also manifested with the trappings of judgment?

We now open up the mystery of the holy days, a revelation that will provide the next puzzle piece and key in the larger mystery. We must begin with the first of all celebrations given to Israel and the one that opens the sacred calendar—Passover.

Chapter 29

DAY OF THE LAMB

BEFORE ANY OF the other festivals and appointed times of ancient Israel, there was Passover. Passover was the first of all appointed festivals, historically and on the sacred yearly calendar.

Passover 2020

The first and second days of Passover are the most central to the feast. They are the two days on which the seder, the commemoration and celebration of the exodus, is traditionally held. In 2020 the first two days of Passover fell on April 9 and 10. It fell just as the full weight of the plague had fallen on the world. It fell as billions throughout the world saw their lives altered in a way they could never before have imagined. In an instant, everything was changed. The world had drawn to a near standstill as an invisible and strange specter of death moved across the world.

Festival of the Plague

One of the unique aspects of Passover is that it focuses on *the coming of a plague.* So in April of 2020, the ancient holiday that tells of the coming of a plague *fell in the midst of the coming of a plague.* Passover recounts the story of a plague that passed through the land of Egypt, leaving a trail of death in its wake. So in the days of Passover 2020, people all over the world watched in fear and anxiety as a plague passed through their lands, leaving a trail of death in its wake.

The bond between the Passover and the plague is so strong that the holiday's name is derived from that very connection:

> And when I see the blood, I will *pass over* you; and *the plague* shall not be on you to destroy *you.*[1]

No other biblical holiday or major holiday of any kind bears such a connection. In 2020 it all came together.

The Passover People

The plague that fell on Passover was unique in that it was not indiscriminate in its striking. So too the plague that had brought the world to a standstill during the days of Passover was not indiscriminate. It had focused its weight of its fury on America.

Outside of Israel, the land in which Passover was most widely celebrated in 2020 was America. Except for Israel, America had more Jewish people than any other nation on earth. And within America the Jewish population was especially centered in one small area—New York, and, specifically, its metropolitan area. And that was the same area on which the plague had focused its fury. And it was during Passover, the feast of the plague, that the plague's impact on New York would reach its peak. So as Jewish people throughout the New York metropolitan area commemorated the festival of the plague, an actual plague was raging around them.

Feast of Lockdowns

But Passover not only involved a plague but a measure of prevention taken in light of it. On the first Passover, the people of Israel were told to go inside their homes and stay there until the plague passed through the land. In other words, Passover also involved a *lockdown*, a lockdown imposed upon the nation because of a plague. Passover was *the first recorded national lockdown in world history*.

In 2020 Passover came to a world in which the people had been ordered to go into their homes and stay there until it was safe to come out. When the Passover came to America, the lockdowns were at their peak. During the feast of the plague, approximately 95 percent of Americans were in lockdown, most of these confined to their homes.

After 3,000 Years

So as the Jewish people observed the ancient feast and recited the ancient account of how the people of the land were directed by their leaders to stay inside their homes until the plague had passed them by—they did so at the same time that their leaders had told them to stay inside their homes until a plague had passed them by.

And in the land of Israel, that same Passover, in view of the plague that was passing through the land, the government had ordered the people to stay inside their homes from Passover eve to Passover morning. It was the first time such a thing had happened in over three thousand years, since the day of the first Passover when Moses gave his nation the same command.

Passover World

And though America had become the center of the plague, it had, of course, come upon the entire world. During the days of Passover, the world's lockdown was at its peak, with an unprecedented half of the entire human population sheltered behind the walls of their homes.

The Scriptures speak of the Gospel, the message of Messiah, in terms of Passover. The New Testament faith began on Passover with the crucifixion. The one revealed as Messiah, Yeshua, Jesus, is spoken of as the Passover Lamb, the only hope and answer to judgment. It was always a Passover faith.

In the latter part of the twentieth century, much of the *Christian West*, including America and Europe, began noticeably departing from the Christian faith. By the early part of the twenty-first century there was more and more talk of the end of a *Christian America* and the decoupling of Western civilization from Christianity.

Thus it is worthy of note that as America and other nations had fallen away from their *Passover faith* and from the *Passover Lamb*, in 2020 the Passover came back and was manifested itself in force. The same civilization that had departed from Passover was brought back into it, a plague, a judgment, and the command to stay inside one's home until the plague had passed. The only thing missing was the Lamb. A civilization that had turned away from the Lamb now found itself in need of Him.

Passover is the first of the appointed times and holy days. It leads to another. And it would be this other ancient holy day that would hold the key to the next dramatic event of that most dramatic year. And this one too would carry the dynamics of judgment.

Chapter 30

DAYS OF FIRE AND BREATH

PASSOVER, THE FIRST great festival of Israel, ushers in the second. In the midst of the first festival, the countdown begins for the second.

The Festival of Sevens—Shavuot

The countdown is similar to that of the Jubilee except that instead of years it consists of days.

> Seven Sabbaths shall be completed. Count fifty days to the day after the seventh Sabbath; then you shall offer a new grain offering to the LORD.[1]

The second of the great festivals and appointed gatherings of Israel receives its name from this countdown: *The Festival of Weeks* or *Sevens*, or, in Hebrew, *Shavuot.*

Shavuot was linked to the great summer harvest, a period of several months in which the Israelites went out into the land and reaped their fields and vineyards. The summer harvest would approach its end only with the coming of the autumn holy days.

By calculating the days of the countdown from the first Passover, the rabbis concluded that Moses went up Mount Sinai to receive the Law on the day of Shavuot. So the holiday became, as well, a commemoration of the giving of the Law at Sinai.

Pentecost

When the Bible was translated from Hebrew into Greek, the festival of early summer was given a new name, *the Feast of the Fiftieth Day*, or, in Greek, *Pentecost.* It is by this name that most people know it.

The Book of Acts records that the Spirit of God fell upon the first believers on the Day of Pentecost. Thus the Hebrew feast of early summer took on new meaning. It became known as the day when the Spirit of God came upon the disciples to empower them to go forth to the nations, to proclaim the Gospel to the ends of the earth.

Festival of the Law

If the first appointed feast manifested in the form of judgment, could the second do so as well? Passover leads into Shavuot. So the first shaking of America led into a second. In the spring of 2020, as the nation was still reeling from the coming of a plague, a second shaking was unleashed. Many believed that the plague's disruptive impact on America's social order paved the way for what was to come.

Whereas Shavuot, or Pentecost, marked the giving of the Law, now it would mark the removal of law. It all began when those entrusted with upholding and enforcing the law were judged as having broken it. As a result of his brutal treatment at the hands of law enforcement officers, an African American man, George Floyd, died on the streets of Minneapolis.

His death set off a wave of anger and protests, lawlessness, violence, and destruction. It began in Minneapolis but then spread to other American cities. There were multitudes of calls to defund or eliminate law enforcement officers altogether. And in some places, their presence was, in effect, eliminated, as sections of cities became as war zones.

Lawless

The protests, violence, demonstrations, riots, and destruction broke out in over 140 American cities. Before the summer was over, the number of demonstrations or riots would exceed ten thousand. The amount of damage caused by the riots skyrocketed into the billions. At least nineteen people would lose their lives. Over fourteen thousand people would be arrested. The number of those who had taken part was estimated at between fifteen million and twenty-six million. More than half of all American states had to call in the National Guard. Even the nation's capital appeared to be under siege. It was believed to be the largest or most widespread movement of protests, disorder, and riots in American history.

And all this came upon a nation already badly traumatized by a deadly plague still moving through its borders. And it was more than the riots. The same season that gave birth to the riots gave birth to an explosion of violent crime throughout the nation. So at the time of the second festival, the celebration of the Law—there came lawlessness.

Festival of Breath

But there was more to the appointed day. Under its Greek name, Pentecost, the second festival became most widely associated with the Spirit. It would become known as the Day of the Spirit. The Gospel of John records Yeshua, Jesus, foretelling the event:

> And when He had said this, He breathed on them, and said to them, "Receive the Holy Spirit."[2]

The Spirit was linked to breath. The connection was intentional. The word for *spirit* in the Old Testament is the Hebrew *ruach*. *Ruach* also means *breath*. The word for *spirit* in the New Testament is the Greek *pneuma*. *Pneuma*, likewise, also means *breath*. The Day of the Spirit is the Day of the Breath. The gift of the Spirit is the gift of the breath. And the breath of God brings life.

The Removal of Breath

So if the season of Shavuot, Pentecost, was connected to the giving of breath, what would happen if it came in the form of judgment? It would mean the taking away of breath. What ignited the explosion of those days was the death of George Floyd in the streets of Minneapolis. The last words he uttered before he died were "I can't breathe." So in the season of the *ruach*, the *pneuma*, and the breath, breath was removed.

And all that which then came upon the nation, the explosion of violence, protests, chaos, and destruction, began with the taking away of breath. The season that once gave birth to a movement of life and to a people filled with the breath of God now gave birth to a movement of death and to multitudes chanting the words "I can't breathe" in cities across the nation. And it was all happening in a land already under the shadow of a plague that robbed people of their breath.

As the Passover of that year spoke to a civilization that had turned away from the Lamb, so the Pentecost that followed spoke to one that had become empty of the Spirit, the breath of God.

Festival of Fire

But there was more to the ancient holy day, an element that would become its sign:

> When the Day of Pentecost had fully come, they were all with one accord in one place....Then there appeared to them divided tongues, *as of fire*, and one sat upon each of them. And they were all filled with the Holy Spirit...[3]

That same element appears in the words of John the Baptist when he spoke of the baptism of the Holy Spirit:

He will baptize you with the *Holy Spirit and fire*.[4]

The element even appears in the giving of the Law on Mount Sinai, as celebrated on Shavuot, Pentecost:

> Now Mount Sinai was completely in smoke, because the LORD descended upon it *in fire*.[5]

Fire is the primary symbol used to represent the Pentecost recorded in the Book of Acts. It is known as the day of holy fire, the fire of God's Spirit, and the fire that literally appeared over the disciples when the Spirit came.

A Different Flame

The fire of Pentecost was a blessing. But to a nation under judgment, Pentecost now came with a different fire, a fire not of blessing but judgment. Fires now blazed in the streets of America, in its stores, its businesses, its homes, and even its police stations. Fires now lit up its cities and night skies. The fire had fallen at the appointed time of fire but not for good, but destruction.

May 28, 2020

In the year 2020, when did the feast known as Pentecost and Shavuot fall? On both the Jewish and Christian calendars, it fell in the last days of May. When did the shakings that would set cities on fire come upon America? They came upon America in *the last days of May*.

In the days leading up to Pentecost, the fire was kindled. George Floyd was killed, and the first protests began in Minneapolis.

But on May 28 it reached its critical mass. It was that day that major protests erupted not only in Minnesota but in the major cities of other states. And that night, it all exploded. It was then that rioters overtook the Minneapolis police station of the third precinct and set it on fire. And it was then that the nation and much of the world took notice and realized something major was beginning.

And it was that same evening of fire, Thursday night, May 28, that an ancient feast began—the Feast of Shavuot, Pentecost. It started just before sunset as Jewish people began lighting the candles of the holiday—shadows of the fires that would be lit that same night.

Shavuot would be observed in the Jewish world into the weekend, when it would usher in Pentecost Sunday. That Pentecost Sunday, as Christians celebrated the day of holy fire, a very different fire spread across the nation.

Summer Harvest

Shavuot is also the holiday that consecrated the summer harvest. In the year 2022 it would launch a summer harvest of fury and violence. Among the signs given in the Bible of a nation under judgment are those of lawlessness, violence, division, and destruction, not to mention pestilence and plague. All these were now manifesting across America and at the same time.

———————————

In the season of Passover, the feast of the plague and lockdown, came a plague and the lockdown. Then, at the time of Shavuot, Pentecost, the feast of law, breath, and fire, came the removal of law, the removal of breath, and the sending of a different fire.

But the ancient calendar was not finished. It would now move into an entirely different realm. The next ancient holy day was very different from those that preceded it. And its manifestation would focus on one specific city and one particular building. What would it bring?

Chapter 31

THE HEAVENLY COURT

WE NOW COME to the most sacred and awesome time of the ancient biblical calendar, known as the Days of Awe.

Yom Teruah

In biblical times, as the end of the summer harvest drew near, the focus returned to the Holy City of Jerusalem. These were the days of *teshuvah*, a Hebrew word that means both return and repentance. It was the season ordained from ancient times to return to God, to get right, to repent, to forgive, and to be forgiven.

The days of national repentance and return were heralded on the first of the High Holy Days. The day had been ordained by an ancient decree as mysterious as it was brief:

> Speak to the children of Israel, saying: "In the seventh month,
> on the first day of the month, you shall have a sabbath-rest,
> a memorial of blowing of trumpets, a holy convocation."[1]

It would be called Yom Teruah, or the Day of the Trumpet Blast. It would become known as the Feast of Trumpets. Later on it would also be called Rosh Ha Shannah, the Jewish New Year. But it was not the New Year—it was the opening of the seventh month, the final month of the sacred calendar. The sounding of the trumpet or shofar was in this case a spiritual alarm, a reminder that judgment was coming and that each must be prepared to stand before God. It was a wake-up call to get right, to repent, to return.

Day of the Judge

The Feast of Trumpets was also known as Yom Ha Din, the Day of Judgment. The judgment alluded to was not so much that of calamity or disaster but rather that handed down by a judge or magistrate before whom one has been summoned to stand. The Hebrew prayer known as the U'Netanneh Tokef and recited on the Feast of Trumpets describes the judgment:

> You alone are the One Who judges, proves, knows, and
> bears witness; Who writes and seals, who counts and
> calculates; Who remembers all that was forgotten. You will

open the Book of Chronicles....The great shofar will be sounded and a still, thin sound will be heard. Angels will hasten, a trembling and terror will seize them—and they will say, "Behold, it is the Day of Judgment."[2]

The image given is that of God as the judge of all. According to the prayer, God is not only the judge but the witness who bears testimony, the attorney who proves the case, and the recorder who writes down all that is of note. He is all in all.

Thus the judgment given on the Feast of Trumpets and the Days of Awe is that of a verdict issued by a presiding judge after the defendant has been given a hearing. The context is judicial. The imagery is that of a courtroom. And this is precisely the context and imagery through which the Jewish world views the High Holy Days—that of a judge, a court, and a judgment. So as the summer draws to a close, the Jewish are fixed on a court.

The Heavenly Court

The observances, teachings, and prayers of the High Holy Days do not, of course, refer to just any court but to the court that stands high above all other courts. It is known as the *heavenly court*. Such verses as found in Psalm 82 and describing God presiding in a heavenly court and rendering judgment on the earth are cited as its scriptural foundation:

> God takes his stand in the divine assembly; among the divine beings he renders judgment.[3]

The central text of rabbinical Judaism, the Talmud, describes the deliberations of the heavenly court. On the Feast of Trumpets, it says, the books of the heavenly court are opened. And for those who have forgiven those who have sinned against them...

> ...the heavenly court in turn forgoes punishment.[4]

So the Days of Awe are focused on the heavenly court and the verdicts to be rendered from its deliberations.

The Most Supreme of All Courts

The year was now approaching late September. It was the time of the Feast of Trumpets and the Days of Awe, when a nation is to turn to the judicial realm, the matter of judgment, and to a court. Would the mystery continue to manifest?

As the sacred calendar turned to the realm of the judicial, so at that very moment, the eyes of America turned to the realm of the judicial.

The sacred calendar turns to the *most high* of courts. There is only one institution that could constitute the most high, of course, with regard to America—the Supreme Court. Indeed, the court spoken of on the Feast of Trumpets' liturgy is known as *the supreme* of all courts.

And so as the sacred calendar turned to the most high court, at that same moment, the eyes of America turned to the nation's most high court.

And as the Feast of Trumpets calls all to look to Him *who judges, proves, knows, and bears witness*, the Most High Judge, the eyes of America were turned to a judge, the highest of judges in the nation's judiciary, one of the nine to sit on the Supreme Court.

Who Pass From the Earth

It was believed that the judgments handed down by the heavenly court during the Days of Awe included those that determined who would live or die. The prayer spoken on Rosh Ha Shannah speaks of the court's verdict on

> …how many will pass from the earth and how many will be created; who will live and who will die; who will die at his predestined time and who before his time…[5]

And so as the sacred calendar turned to the days on which it was believed that the heavenly court passed its verdict as to who would *pass from the earth*, a verdict was passed. And one then passed from the earth. One who had sat on the nation's highest of courts, Judge Ruth Bader Ginsburg, passed from the earth.

Sunset

In the year when the themes of each of the ancient holy days manifested in concrete physical realities and events, so too did it manifest on the Feast of Trumpets—the turning to the court, the highest of courts, the judge, the passing of the verdict, and the passing from earth. It all happened at the time appointed by the sacred calendar.

In 2020 the Feast of Trumpets started at sunset on Friday, September 18. When did Judge Ginsburg pass from the earth? On Friday, September 18, the Feast of Trumpets.

That Friday night, as the liturgy of the Jewish world spoke of the judgment of the most high court concerning who would pass from the earth, the nation's most high court released the news to the world that one of its justices had passed from the earth.

As with all Hebrew holy days, the Feast of Trumpets began at sunset, Friday evening. On September 18, 2020, in Washington, DC, the sun set at 7:11 p.m. The Supreme Court announcement of Justice Ginsburg's passing went forth just after the sunset.

Judges and Judgment

That Judge Ginsburg passed from the earth on the day that speaks of being summoned to appear before the heavenly court could be seen as a sign that all must stand before God and that even the highest of judges will be judged in the court of the Most High. And all the judgments and verdicts of man will be judged by the judgment and verdict of God.

This brings us to the other side of the mystery. All the correlations and manifestations of the ancient holy days led up to this one. And they all took place in the Jubilean year of abortion. The Jubilee brings inversion. The generation that brought death now saw death come upon it. And now on Yom Ha Din, the Day of Judgment, death came to one of them who sat as judge in the Supreme Court.

It was the Supreme Court that played the most central and critical role in the sanctioning and establishing of abortion throughout the nation. In this, it was usurping the role of the heavenly court, passing verdict as to who will live and who will die. Its ruling passed judgment on millions of the most innocent, causing them to die before their time.

The Overturning

The Jubilee is the time of the return. So now it would all return to the Supreme Court. Here on Yom Ha Din, the Supreme Court was the defendant, America was the defendant, and both were guilty. Here on the Day of Judgment, the heavenly court would begin passing judgment on the judgment of man, the judgment of the Supreme Court—and would overturn it. And it would all begin at nightfall of Yom Ha Din, the time that sets in motion the return and repentance. The very death of Judge Ginsburg at that time would set in motion a return and a repentance—and would begin the overturning.

"Remove the Evil of the Decree"

That same night, Jewish people gathered together in synagogues throughout the nation to pray and seek mercy from judgment. They recited in unison the last line of the appointed U'Netanneh Tokef prayer. It was this:

But repentance, prayer and righteousness *remove the evil of the decree!*[6]

The evil of the decree can be taken as an ordained calamity or misfortune. But in the case of America, the words could be taken another way. An evil decree had gone forth from the Supreme Court, *Roe v. Wade*, and it had led to the death of multiplied millions of children. But that night, as they chanted the words "Remove the evil of the decree," a Supreme Court justice was removed, the very event that would make possible the removal of the evil decree.

The case of *Dobbs v. Jackson* had been submitted to the Supreme Court just three months before Judge Ginsburg's passing. And it was submitted on Sivan 23, the Day of the Revoking of the Evil Decree. Now in the court to which it was submitted, and on the day when the words "Remove the evil of the decree" are pronounced, the judge's passing made possible that the evil decree could actually be removed.

The Autumn Window

Had the Supreme Court justice not passed from the earth at that exact time, every other return and reversal of the Jubilee would have come to nothing. The passing had to have taken place at the time of the ancient holy day.

From the day of that passing, the American president who walked in the template of Jehu would have just four months left in power—and a window of just over *one month* before the election that would, in effect, nullify his ability to act in the matter. And just as small was the window left for the Republican-led Senate to do likewise.

And it was the very summer that marked the fiftieth anniversary of the summer that *Roe v. Wade* was sent to the Supreme Court. And it was that very same summer, the Jubilean summer of that sending, that *Roe*'s Jubilean parallel, *Dobbs v. Jackson*, had likewise been sent to the Supreme Court. As in the Jubilean ordinance, everything was coming home, returning to the place of its ancestral origin, which in the case of *Roe v. Wade* was the Supreme Court.

Had Judge Ginsburg still been on the bench when *Dobbs v. Jackson* was taken up by the court, the evil decree would never have been revoked. The single vote on which the revoking would rest still did not exist and could not exist before the sunset of that holy day that spoke of the heavenly court and its judgment. It was only the passing of the judge that would bring the required vote into existence to *overturn the evil decree.*

What took place in those days was yet again beyond the realm of any human agency or plan. The hand that moved all things into their places was not of flesh and blood. Every stream of every mystery, that of the Jubilee, of Jehu and the Temple, of the ancient appointed times and holy days, of Yom Ha Din and the heavenly court, each one had to converge with one another at the exact time and place to pass through the window that opened up on the night of the ancient holy day.

The day that had been ordained from ages past to set in motion the turning of a nation at sunset would do so again and at sunset. The heavenly court had made its decree.

And yet for all this, there was still another mystery that would have to converge with all the others and apart from which the others would never have come to their fulfillment. What began at the sunset would open the door for the next mystery. And this one would begin in Egypt, in the River Nile.

Part VII

CHILD
OF THE NILE

Chapter 32

THE BOY AMONG THE REEDS

THEY WERE CASTING babies into the river. It was a campaign of mass infanticide—a civilization warring against a generation of infants.

Children in the Nile

The civilization was Egypt. It had enslaved the people of Israel who had settled within its borders. But Israel was multiplying. The Pharaoh saw it as a threat and launched a war of extermination against the Hebrew babies. So he commanded his people,

> Every son who is born you shall cast into the river...[1]

So the Egyptians began hunting down newborn Hebrew children. When they found a boy, they took him down to the Nile River and cast him into the waters to certain death.

The Ark Baby

The biblical account then tells of a baby boy born of the Hebrews. Fearing for his life, his mother kept him hidden three months after his birth. But when she could no longer hide him,

> ...she took an ark of bulrushes for him, daubed it with
> asphalt and pitch, put the child in it, and laid it in the reeds
> by the river's bank.[2]

To save her baby from death, she placed him in the ark and set him in the Nile River. The child was now floating in the same waters into which the other Hebrew babies had been cast. After he was found by the Pharaoh's daughter, his life was saved and he was brought up as her own son.

The baby was, of course, Moses. In his adulthood, he would flee the land of Egypt and then, years later, return there, sent by God on a mission to set His people free. When Pharaoh refused his demand for freedom, Moses became the vessel of Egypt's judgment, the instrument through which the Ten Plagues would fall on the kingdom.

Breaker of Death

It is of significance that the first of the nation's plagues began in the same waters into which the Hebrew babies had been cast, the Nile. In other words, the nation's judgment had returned to the place of the nation's sin. The nature of that first plague would highlight the connection—the waters of the Nile would turn to blood just as the blood of the Hebrew children had once reddened its waters. And the man through whom the judgment came had once floated down the same river while other Hebrew babies were being killed in its waters. It was Moses, as well, who oversaw the coming of the tenth and final plague, that of the judgment that would slay the sons of Egypt. As Egypt had sought the death of Israel's sons, now it would witness the death of its own. It was no accident that the plagues began in the place where the male babies of Israel had been killed and would culminate with the slaying of the nation's sons.

And it was no accident that it was one of the Hebrew babies that Egypt had sought to kill and who had floated down the waters of death who was now being the instrument by which the kingdom would be broken.

So it was a child born in the midst of the Egyptian slaughter who, years later, would be used to break the ancient powers that carried it out.

Is it possible then that a child born of the American slaughter would be used to break the modern powers that carried it out?

Chapter 33

CHILDREN OF THE SHADOW

T HE CRITICAL WINDOW in America's embrace of abortion on demand began in January 1970 with its entrance into the States and ended in January 1973 with the Supreme Court ruling that made it the law of the land.

The Firstfruits of Slaughter

The unborn children of that window were the first over whose lives hung the specter of legalized murder. They were the firstfruits of the generations that followed them and over whom that shadow would also loom. Over one million of that generation who were alive in their mothers' wombs during that window of time would not be alive at its end.

In the case of ancient Egypt, it was one of the Hebrew babies that had survived the days of slaughter who, years later, would break the power that had spilled the children's blood.

What about the American slaughter of its children? Could there have been a child born in that critical three-year window of abortion's entrance into America up until the ruling in *Roe v. Wade*, a child born in the days of that first slaughter, whose life would be spared and who, years later, would be central in the breaking of the power behind that slaughter? There was.

The Girl Among the Reeds

The child was a baby girl, conceived in the midst of the three-year window. She was born in New Orleans on January 28, 1972. Her parents gave her the name Amy. Years later she would become famous as Supreme Court Justice Amy Coney Barrett. *Roe v. Wade* would be overturned by a single vote. She would be the one to cast it. Without her coming onto the court at that exact time and without the casting of her vote as she did in the case of *Dobbs v. Jackson*, *Roe v. Wade* would never have been overturned. Her life was the missing piece of the puzzle.

In the Shadow of Roe

So the person who would break *Roe v. Wade* and begin the turning back of abortion was the child born in its shadow. She would, in fact, be the first justice to sit on the Supreme Court born in the days when it was legal to prevent her from being born. It was the outworking of the mystery that went back over three thousand years to the baby in the Nile.

It was not only that she came into the world in that critical window of the emerging slaughter but that it was at the equally pivotal time when *Roe v. Wade* was moving through the American judicial system on its way to become the law of the land.

In fact, she was likely conceived in the same month the case that would overturn *Roe v. Wade* would also arrive at the same court. The case would be given two Supreme Court hearings. Barrett was born in between those two hearings. And so, in accordance with the mystery, the one whose birth was framed by *Roe v. Wade* would arrive at the Supreme Court just when the case that would overturn *Roe v. Wade* would also arrive at the court.

Princess of Egypt

Everything had to be in its exact place. Had Judge Ginsburg not died on that Feast of Trumpets, Amy Coney Barrett might never have come to sit as justice on the Supreme Court and certainly not at the time when the pivotal case concerning abortion had come before it. But so too it was in the case of Moses. The princess of Egypt just happened to have come to the Nile as a baby floated down its waters. Without that the Exodus would never have happened as it did. So with Amy Barrett, everything had to happen just as it did for *Roe v. Wade* to be overturned.

Judge Ginsburg was of the generation that had legalized the killing of the unborn. Judge Barrett was of the generation whose killing in the womb had been legalized by Judge Ginsburg's generation. Now the one would be taken away and the other would come into her place. And for the first time, a child born in the days of abortion on demand would sit on the Supreme Court and rule for the children who had not yet been killed. And it all came to pass in the year of the abortion Jubilee, when all is reversed, inverted, and undone.

The overturning of *Roe v. Wade* would involve the Jubilee not only of America's sin but of the one who would overturn it.

Chapter 34

CHILD OF THE NILE

MOSES CAME INTO his calling as the deliverer of his people in the days of plague. Judgment had come upon the land. Amy Barrett came into her calling, likewise, during the days of plague. Her nomination, her confirmation, and her swearing in all took place in the days of masks, social distancing, and death, the plague's first year on the land.

Year of Arrival

The child who was born when abortion was advancing through the legal and judicial halls of America would be raised to the Supreme Court just as the case of *Dobbs v. Jackson* was sent to the court in June. She was nominated in late September. *Dobbs v. Jackson* had just been sent to the court that summer.

As she had been born when *Roe v. Wade* was pending before the court, so she would come to the court just when *Dobbs v. Jackson* was pending before it.

The Jubilee of Amy Coney Barrett

But the mystery would involve more than the Jubilee of abortion. What happens if one takes the Jubilean countdown of Leviticus 25 and applies it to the life of Amy Barrett? Seven times seven years from the day of her birth brings us to January 28, 2021. That day marks the completion of her forty-ninth year and the beginning of her fiftieth and Jubilean year.

Amy Barrett was sworn into office as a Supreme Court justice at the end of October 2020. Three months after being sworn in to the court, her Jubilean year began. And so the great majority of her first year on the court was her year of Jubilee.

And it was then, in her Jubilean year, that the Supreme Court took up the case of *Dobbs v. Jackson*, in May 2021. When the case received its hearing in December 2021, it was heard before Barrett in her Jubilean year.

And when Amy Barrett first cast the deciding vote that would overturn *Roe v. Wade*, it was the year of her Jubilee in which she cast it.

Moses in the Courts of Pharaoh

The Jubilee of Amy Barrett and that of *Roe v. Wade* would converge for six days. The Jubilee of *Roe v. Wade* would then continue. And in the midst of it

Roe v. Wade would be overturned. And when *Roe v. Wade* was overturned, Barrett, who had cast the deciding vote, was *fifty years old.*

As the Hebrew boy taken from the Nile into Pharaoh's palace was appointed to one day return there and fulfill his appointed part at the appointed time to set his people free, so the girl born in the days when *Roe v. Wade* made its way through the halls of the Supreme Court was appointed to one day enter those same halls to fulfill her appointed part at her appointed moment.

For Amy Coney Barrett was America's child of the Nile.

In the next section, the mysteries we have seen thus far will now converge into the span of a single day.

Part VIII

DAY OF THE TURNING

Chapter 35

THE RETURN

IS IT POSSIBLE to change the course of history? Can the prayers of a remnant alter the path of nations?

Turn to Me With All Your Heart

In the Book of Joel, God speaks of a nation turned from His ways and battered by calamity, a devouring plague, and devastation. Then comes a call and an answer:

> "Now, therefore," says the LORD, "Turn to Me with all your heart, with fasting, with weeping, and with mourning." So rend your heart, and not your garments; return to the LORD your God, for He is gracious and merciful.[1]

The call is to return. The Scripture is directed at a nation—for a national return, or the return of those representing and interceding for the nation. If that were to happen, God would bring healing and restoration. He would turn the nation's curse into a blessing and would restore the years *the locusts have eaten.*[2]

If My People

I have long held the conviction that without revival America will be lost, and without repentance, there can be no revival. As God called Israel to return in its last days before judgment, He was now calling America. I have long spoken of this call to America. In *The Harbinger,* I wrote of it. I quoted the promise given to King Solomon of national restoration in 2 Chronicles 7:14.

> If My people who are called by My name will humble themselves, and pray and seek My face, and turn from their wicked ways, then I will hear from heaven, and will forgive their sin and heal their land.

The Sacred Assembly

But the call to return in the Book of Joel contains an even more specific manifestation:

> Blow the trumpet in Zion, consecrate a fast, call a sacred assembly; gather the people.[3]

The return manifests as a day of prayer and repentance and, more specifically, in the form of a sacred assembly, a solemn convocation, of intercession before God on behalf of the nation.

Lincoln's Call

Throughout American history, there have been several such days. Among the most dramatic came in the midst of the Civil War, a day of prayer and repentance called for by Abraham Lincoln and the United States Congress. It was not long after that day that Union forces prevailed at Gettysburg and Vicksburg. Those two victories, a day apart, are cited as the two decisive turning points of the Civil War. They would lead to the Union's victory and the nation's preservation.

The Hand and the Scripture

A more recent such gathering took place in 1980, at a time when America had been so badly traumatized by a barrage of national crises, including the taking of fifty-two American hostages in Iran, a deteriorating economy, and an energy crisis, that many believed it was the end of the American age. It was then that Christians from around the nation gathered in Washington, DC, on the National Mall to pray and intercede for God's mercy. The theme of that day was 2 Chronicles 7:14: "If My people…" The consequences of that gathering were dramatic and included the election of a new president, the release of the American hostages from Iran in the same hour that the new president was inaugurated, and a national turning that some would call Morning in America. It all began when the new president laid his hand on the Bible and took the oath of the presidency. His hand rested on a Scripture. The Scripture was 2 Chronicles 7:14: "If My people…"

The Gathering

In the wake of 9/11, I had a vision of a national day of prayer and repentance for America. I saw it centering on a sacred assembly in Washington, DC, on the National Mall. In the ensuing years, I was brought into contact with a great and humble man of God, Kevin Jessip, who had been faithfully holding a similar vision for such a day and such a gathering. Through the years, we would touch base, pray, and seek God's will concerning it.

Then, in 2018, we both felt a sense of greater urgency, that the time of the vision was drawing near. It had to take place in 2020. Kevin was able to reserve the National Mall for late September of that year. In the autumn of 2019, I was praying about what the next book I was to write would be. I felt a strong sense that 2020 would be a year of dark events and great shakings and that these would be part of the continuation of the mystery I had written of in *The Harbinger*. Therefore, I was led to write the book I had for years held off on writing, the sequel to *The Harbinger*, to be known as *The Harbinger II*.

In January of 2020 I began writing. Soon after came the shakings and dark events I had sensed would be coming. It began with a plague—COVID-19. By March, with the national lockdown and bans on public gatherings, it became doubtful whether such an event could even take place. Nevertheless, we continued planning it.

The Return

Though the event had been planned to include a program that would go into the night, I felt strongly that the core event, the central time of prayer and intercession, had to conclude at five in the afternoon. So the event was planned to culminate at that hour, after which those gathered could leave or stay for a night of afterglow that would begin an hour later.

Up to then, it was called the National Day of Prayer and Repentance. The title was accurate but generic. I felt another strong leading that it needed another name, simpler, easier, and summing up its purpose. I realized it was all there in *The Harbinger*. It was the calling that ran through the book:

> ...the nation was being called to *return* to God in prayer.[4]

> ...behind the Harbingers—behind everything is the word *return*![5]

> It's the word of the prophets....A voice was calling, calling the nation back to God, and crying out, '*Return*.'"[6]

I told Kevin. He was in total agreement. From then on, the event would be called *The Return*.

The Storm Gathering

As the time of The Return approached, the shakings that had come upon the nation showed little signs of abating. The plague was still raging; the summer of fires, riots, demonstrations, and violence had further traumatized the nation; much of life was still shut down, and many still kept hidden behind the walls of their homes.

That September, *The Harbinger II* was released. It spoke not only of the progression of the mystery and the continuing signs of national judgment but also of the past days of prayer and sacred assembly that had altered the nation's course. Now we were planning another. Would it affect the future? I had cautioned others that with such things, the impact is not often seen at the time but in later days and that regardless of the result, we were called to take God at His word and do what He called us to do.

When I Send a Plague

There were signs of something unique concerning The Return. The sacred assembly called for in Joel takes place against the backdrop of a plague that had come upon the land. So The Return would take place against the backdrop of a plague on the land.

The context of the most famous of verses on national repentance, 2 Chronicles 7:14, is this:

> When I...*send a plague* among my people, if my people, who are called by my name, will humble themselves and pray...[7]

Again, the context specifically mentioned a *plague*. We were now in that context. The plague had come. Now it was time to humble ourselves and pray.

Days of Awe

The Return was scheduled for September 26, 2020. The date had been set two years earlier, when it was reserved for the National Mall. But just eight days before it was to happen, Judge Ginsburg was taken from the court on the same day that ushered in the Feast of Trumpets. But the Feast of Trumpets was never a conclusion—it was a beginning. It ushered in the Days of Awe.

The Days of Awe were given for a nation to humble itself before God and come before Him in the confession of sin, repentance, and prayers for His mercy. And this, of course, was the exact purpose of The Return. So The Return would fall on one of the Ten Days of Awe and would be one of them.

As the Feast of Trumpets ushers in the Days of Awe and Repentance, so that which happened on the Feast of Trumpets, the death of Justice Ginsburg, would usher in a corresponding event that would take place on the day of one of the days of repentance.

THE POTTER'S JAR

IT WAS THE morning of The Return. Storm clouds hovered over the capital. They had showered the capital city the night before and were threatening to do so again. Beyond the weather, with lockdowns, quarantines, bans, and social distancing, we had no idea who would show up.

The Day

But they did show up. They came by the thousands and thousands, from all walks of life, black, white, Asian, Hispanic, every ethnic group, Jew and Gentile, old and young, from all over America and beyond. They came with one purpose: to humble themselves and pray, to seek God's face, to repent, to intercede, and to plead for mercy on the land. As I stood on the stage with the Capitol Building in back of me, I looked out to the multitude. It was a sea of color filling the National Mall all the way up to the Washington Monument.

There would be many who would approach the stage that day to pray and intercede, to share, and to lead in worship—in all, over one hundred fifty people. They included spiritual leaders, cultural figures, governmental leaders, Hollywood celebrities, recording artists, worship leaders, men and women of prayer, leaders from around the world, and everyone from the daughter of Billy Graham to the niece of Martin Luther King Jr. They came with the same purpose, to humble themselves and pray.

Beyond those on the Mall, many more were watching by television, online, in churches and homes, in America and around the world. We were told that those taking part in The Return throughout America and the world numbered in the millions.

A Most Critical Hour

At 9 a.m. I opened The Return with an ancient Hebrew prayer and then the promise of 2 Chronicles 7:14. Then I said this:

> We are standing at a most critical hour. The time is late. A great nation is hanging in the balance....We've witnessed the darkest year in living memory, a year in which the world and specifically America has been shaken to its core as it has never been in modern times, by plague, by

economic collapse, by paralysis, civil disorder, fires, riots, and a division that threatens to tear apart the national fabric....This is a Sacred Assembly. We've come here with a holy purpose....We will pray and worship and intercede... until we've accomplished what God has called us to do.[1]

Many others then took the stage and led in sharing, prayer, the confession of sin, and intercession for God's mercy on America and the nations.

A Thousand Angels Swearing

At 11 a.m. I gave what was to be the word of The Return. I began:

Two and a half thousand years ago, the prophet Jeremiah stood outside the walls of Jerusalem, by the Valley of Hinnom. In his hand was a potter's jar.[2]

I had been led to frame the message by speaking of the prophet Jeremiah as he overlooked the Valley of Hinnom where the nation's children had been sacrificed. I spoke of America's departure from God and the many sins of that departure, but I was especially led to address the millions of children the nation had murdered:

What we once revered we now revile, and what we once knew to be wrong we now celebrate. We too have profaned the sacred and have sanctified the profane. And as for our children, our most innocent possession, we have sacrificed them on the altars of self-indulgence. It was here in this city... that their collective murder was blessed and given sanction. But a thousand laws, and a thousand Supreme Court rulings, and a thousand angels swearing on a thousand Bibles cannot alter one iota of this basic measure of morality—to shed the blood of an unborn baby is to murder a human life, and the most innocent of human lives. The people of ancient Israel lifted up thousands of their children on the altars of Baal and Molech. And by doing so, they invoked their own destruction. But we have lifted up millions. And our collective hands are covered with blood...[3]

The Broken Vessel

I was then led to direct my words to the nation's leadership, starting with the Supreme Court:

> Supreme Court justices, you open up your sessions with the
> words "God save this Supreme Court." But if you overrule
> the rulings of God, if you judge the judgments of God, if you
> strike down the eternal precepts of God, then how can God
> save your court? Know then, there stands a court much higher
> and there sits a judge who is much more supreme. And before
> His judgment all judges will stand and give account.[4]

At one point I had to stop because of the peals and rumbles of thunder over the nation's capital. And yet it went with the message. I thought of the Scripture "The LORD thundered from heaven, and the Most High uttered his voice."[5]

Jeremiah's prophecy over Hinnom focused on a single object, a clay vessel, a potter's jar. I was led to bring to Washington a clay vessel I had gotten from a pottery house near my home. Jeremiah was told to smash the jar as a sign of the destruction that would befall the nation if it continued on its present course. I was led to do the same. As I spoke of America and warned of national judgment, I smashed the vessel onto the stage into countless pieces.

While It Is Still Day

Then I shared of the hope, God's will to save and restore, His call to mercy and redemption:

> And the voice of God is calling out:
> "Return! Return! Return! Return, America, for you have
> fallen in your iniquity. Return, America, while it is still
> yet day. And there is set before you life and death. Choose
> life and not destruction. Return, America, and I will have
> mercy on you."[6]

And finally, I spoke of the Spirit and the promise of revival. I went down on my knees to the wooden floor of the stage, and the thousands on the National Mall did likewise on the grass and soil. The Mall was now filled with men, women, and children, kneeling, bowed down, sitting, stretched out, with faces to the ground, and some turned to the heavens, in deep intercession for America, pleading for God's mercy and the moving of His hand.

The Day of Shuvah

Of the Ten Days of Awe, one that was given special prominence was called Shabbat Shuvah. It was the Sabbath that bridged the Feast of Trumpets to Yom Kippur. In 2020, Shabbat Shuvah fell on September 26. The Return fell on

Shabbat Shuvah. No one had planned it that way. It just happened. And it was only in the weeks leading up to the event that I realized it.

The word *Shabbat* simply means Sabbath. So The Return took place on Saturday, the biblical Sabbath. But the word that describes the day's unique nature is *Shuvah*. What does *Shuvah* mean?

It means *the return*! Shabbat Shuvah literally means the Sabbath *Day of the Return*! Without our planning it, the *day of The Return* was appointed for the ancient *Day of the Return*!

The Appointed Scripture

Since Shabbat Shuvah is a Sabbath, there was a Scripture appointed from ages past to be read on it. It begins with these words:

> O Israel, *return to the LORD your God,* for you have fallen
> because of your iniquity.[7]

The passage calls a nation that had once known God but has fallen away, to return to the Lord. That was the message of The Return.

But there was another Scripture also appointed for Shabbat Shuvah. It was the blueprint for The Return—the Book of Joel:

> Blow the trumpet in Zion, consecrate a fast, call a sacred
> assembly; gather the people.[8]

The Next Holy Day

And so in synagogues throughout America and across the world, Jewish people were observing Shabbat Shuvah, the Day of the Return, while believers throughout America and the world were taking part in the Day of the Return. And as Jewish people were chanting the ancient words calling for a sacred assembly and a national gathering of repentance to seek God's mercy—it was actually taking place on the National Mall.

It was the next manifestation in the mystery of the holy days. The year had begun with the plague and lockdown on Passover, then moved to the breath and fire on Pentecost, and then to the halls and judgments of the most high court on the Feast of Trumpets. Now it moved to the next holy day, that of Shabbat Shuvah, the sacred assembly of return, as ordained in Joel 2. And now this too had come to fulfillment.

The Day of Turning

The word *Shuvah* can also be translated as "the turning." So the Day of Shuvah can be translated as "the Day of the Turning." Is it possible that the holy day known from ages past as the Day of the Turning and that now manifested in The Return, or the turning, could set in motion the actual turning of a nation?

———————————————

It is in the answer to that question that all the mysteries and puzzle pieces we have seen thus far would now come together.

Chapter 37

THE TURNING

THE TURNING OF a nation—how does it happen? In this case the odds were against it.

The First Window

Up to September 18 and the passing of the Supreme Court justice, it was an impossibility. After that, it had only the smallest of windows to squeeze through. Though President Trump had appointed two Supreme Court justices, it would not be enough. A third vote was needed.

The window was even smaller than it appeared. The upcoming elections would be held on November 3. After that the president would be leading a lame duck administration. His power to push through a highly contested Supreme Court nomination would evaporate. So too the power of a Republican-led Senate would, on the same day, begin to dissipate.

Since the election would be held on Tuesday, it meant that, for all intents and purposes, the process of nominating and confirming a new Supreme Court justice had to be completed within the week that ended on Friday, October 30, just forty-two days after Judge Ginsburg's death. And yet heading into late September, the president did not even have a nominee.

The Second Window

But that wasn't the only window. The other had to do with the case of *Dobbs v. Jackson*, which had just come to the court in the summer before Judge Ginsburg's death. The court had not yet accepted it, and there was no guarantee it would. And even if it did, it was all hanging on what would happen with the seat vacated by Judge Ginsburg.

So what was now at stake was not only the deciding vote in a future Supreme Court case but the case itself. Both had come into play at the same time. And each was hanging by a thread. And a case carrying the chance of reversing *Roe v. Wade* might never again be sent to or received by the court.

The Third Window

And there was yet another window, an ancient and spiritual one—the Ten Days of Awe—the time span given to turn from one's sins, to repent, to undo, to make good, and to return to God. In the Jewish world, after the ten days are over, it was believed that the window would close and one's destiny would be sealed.

America had the smallest of windows in which to turn from its sin and undo its evil. It had the chance to repent for the blood of the over sixty million children it had shed and to undo its fifty-year-old transgression. But the windows would soon close. And judging from the ensuing events, the president's effective window to nominate a new Supreme Court justice was not much more than that of the Ten Days of Awe.

The window had opened on September 18 with the passing of Justice Ginsburg. It was the same day or night given to a nation to turn, repent, and *revoke the evil decree*. They both began on the exact same day, the exact same hour, and with the exact same sunset.

The President's Day of Awe

In 2020 the ancient time given for repentance came to its close at the end of September, after which, according to Jewish belief, every action was sealed before the high court of heaven. At the same time, the president had a political and logistical window in which to act. Without intending it or realizing its significance, the day on which he chose to act was one of the ten sacred Days of Awe.

The timing appeared strange. The president would set in motion his third Supreme Court nomination not on a weekday but on the weekend. There, on the White House lawn, he would nominate to the Supreme Court the American child of the Nile, the first to be born among the slaughter of children, Amy Coney Barrett. He would thus be setting in motion the single vote that would overturn the ruling that had shed the blood of millions—*the revoking of the evil decree*.

It was among the most critical acts of his presidency. When would it be set in motion? It was set in motion on Shabbat Shuvah, *the Day of the Return*.

As *shuvah* can be translated as "return" and "turning," so it was appointed that on the Day of Turning the turning would actually begin. Shabbat Shuvah was appointed for repentance to undo what had been done. So it was on that day that a nation set in motion its repentance and the undoing of what it had done.

The Physical and Spiritual Realms

What was taking place in the spiritual realm at The Return on the National Mall was taking place in the physical realm on the White House lawn. While we prayed on the National Mall for repentance and turning, the president was at the White House taking an action that would turn America from the evil of its past.

That the two events were happening simultaneously on the same day was not the result of any human intent or design. The president just happened to choose that Saturday, September 26, because of political and logistical reasons. One week earlier, none of those reasons and factors existed. They only came into being because of the removal of a Supreme Court justice on the Feast of Trumpets. And according to the ancient calendar, what begins on Trumpets is linked to what happens on Shabbat Shuvah, the Day of the Return.

In the Footsteps of the Mystery

What would happen on the White House lawn was the playing out of what appeared to be random events. And yet they would all converge with The Return. But The Return was planned to take place on that specific day *two years before it happened*. So The Return was not following the events that overtook the Supreme Court and then the White House. But what happened at the Supreme Court and then on the White House lawn was following after the mystery that lay behind The Return.

The converging of mysteries would go even deeper and manifest even more dramatically. It would all happen in the twinkling of an eye and to the ancient vessel of God's power.

Chapter 38

5:04:33

THE SET TIME of prayer and intercession at The Return approached its climax of *5 p.m.* It was the one time parameter I felt strongly about. When the president made his decision to begin his Supreme Court nomination on Saturday, September 26, he had to decide when in the day to do it. He chose *5 p.m.*

The Hour of Convergence

Thus the president would set in motion his most consequential Supreme Court nomination just as the prayers and intercession of The Return were coming to their climax. So it was not only that the Supreme Court nomination and The Return would take place on the same day—but that the two were now converging at the same time of that day, in the very same hour.

But it was not just the hour but what would happen within that hour. When The Return was in its planning stages, I was strongly led that it had to culminate with trumpets, with the sound of the shofar.

The Sound of God

So in late afternoon, I stood overlooking the National Mall with a tallit, the Jewish prayer shawl, draped over my head and a shofar in my hand. I would sound it seven times as the people interceded for seven purposes of God. Before I set it to my mouth, I said this:

> In the Scriptures, God ordained the trumpet as a vessel of His power. At the sound of the trumpet, the armies of God triumphed. At the sound of the trumpet, the walls of Jericho fell down. The enemy would flee. The power of the Jubilee was unleashed. The blessings of God would break forth....
> This is a sign of His power....We're going to believe for the breakthrough of God.[1]

The Release of His Power

It was to be a releasing of God's purposes and power. As I began sounding the seven blasts, I had no idea at the time that another event was crystalizing nearby at that very moment—the gathering on the White House lawn that would set in motion the overturning of *Roe v. Wade*. It was all happening at the same time, the sounding of the trumpets and the setting in motion.

In ancient times and beyond, the sounding of the shofar ushered in the time of teshuvah, the Hebrew word for turning and repentance. So now, as the shofar sounded in Washington, DC, it ushered in the event that would begin a turning back with regard to the children's blood.

The shofar was, of course, also the sound of the Jubilee. So now, in the Jubilean year of 2020, the Jubilee's reversal and undoing would be set in motion by the sound of the Jubilee.

The Secret Story

Behind world history is a secret story, guided by the hand of God. In this case it took place in public as millions watched. The overturning of *Roe v. Wade* was marked by the hand of the Almighty.

The sound that once broke the walls of Jericho now filled the National Mall. And the walls that enshrined abortion in America would begin to crumble. Though most would have no idea, the overturning of abortion began with the sound of repentance, the sound of the Jubilee, the sound of God's power, and the sound of Jericho.

And there was more.

The Final Act

The White House event ran slightly behind schedule, a few minutes past 5 p.m. The president walked through the columns of the White House into the Rose Garden where the assembled guests were waiting. To his left was Amy Coney Barrett.

I had planned for one last prophetic act to be performed at The Return to seal—one final blast of the trumpets—the blast of several trumpets at once.

In the Bible the sound of the trumpet marked not only the appointed times of God but the appointed *moments*. The shofars of Jericho are an example of it. It was at the exact *moment* of the blast that the walls fell down. So too in the Book of Revelation, seven angels are shown sounding seven trumpets. The blasts are matched by an immediate corresponding event in the heavens or on the earth.

The Sealing

I announced the final act:

We are now going to seal this sacred time.[2]

I called to the stage those who would sound the trumpets. Six men with prayer shawls and shofars ascended the platform and spread out across the stage behind me as Kevin Jessip stood to my right. I instructed those gathered on the Mall that at the sound of the trumpets they were to shout just as the people of Israel had shouted at the sound of the trumpets at Jericho when the walls came down.

That one final blasting of the trumpets was to be the sealing of everything that had been done at The Return, every prayer, every intercession, every word, every declaration, every plea, every act—it would now all converge into that one moment and that one final blast and shout.

It was not about the shofars, the shofar blowers, or me. It was about God's power. The shofar was only a symbol of that. The final sounding would take place in the wake of a half century of prayers lifted up by God's people and coalescing into that moment.

I looked back at the men behind me and asked if they were prepared. They set the shofars to their mouths and lifted them up in readiness. I turned back to those on the Mall, equally ready and awaiting the moment.

It was now a few minutes past 5 p.m. When I called for the men with the shofars to come to the stage, the president had just reached the podium on the White House lawn from which he would speak. As those gathered on the National Mall were anxiously waiting for the trumpets to sound, those gathered at the White House were anxiously waiting for the president to speak.

"Go!"

I then proclaimed the final declaration and prayer to seal The Return and pray for the releasing of God's power:

> From here, Lord, as we seal The Return and the power of God, now, Lord, let the sound of Your power go forth to the world...in Jesus, Yeshua's name...[3]

And then I gave the word:

> Go![4]

It was that moment that the blast went forth from the trumpets on the stage and the shout went up from the multitudes gathered on the National Mall. So it is written in Psalm 47,

> God has gone up with a shout, the LORD with the sound of the shofar.[5]

And that was the moment.

The Moment

On the White House lawn, the president was standing at the podium before the gathered guests. He opened his mouth to speak:

> I stand before you today to fulfill one of my highest and most important duties.[6]

That was the moment that began the nomination of the one who would cast the critical vote to overturn *Roe v. Wade*. It began in the instant when the president began to speak. It would alter American history.

So when was it?

5:04:33

I said, "Go!" and the trumpets blasted:

It was *5:04 p.m.—4 minutes—and 33 seconds*.

When the president opened his mouth to set in motion the overturning of *Roe v. Wade*, it was *5:04 p.m.—4 minutes—and 33 seconds*!

The turning, the undoing of abortion, the altering of history began at the exact moment the trumpets began their blasting and the shout of the multitude went up—*the exact same moment*.

The overturning of the ruling that made abortion the law of the land was set in motion on September 26, 2020, at five o'clock, four minutes, and thirty-three seconds to the ancient sound of God—at the very same moment.

The Exact and Countless Moments

The president was delayed in starting the White House gathering. And because of the applause that greeted him, the nomination was further delayed by another minute. The Return was also running late. There were well over a hundred fifty people who took the stage to speak, worship, or pray that day. Had any of them gone on a moment too long or stopped a moment too short, or had those who had gone over their time *not* gone over their time, or not gone over their time for the exact number of seconds that they did, if there had not been the exact number of extra words, extra notes, words not spoken, notes not played, pauses, changes, twists and turns as there were—and each lasting the exact number of seconds they lasted or saving the exact number of seconds they saved—the convergence would never have happened.

It was the confluence of countless factors at the White House that altered the timing of the president's announcement coalescing with another confluence of countless factors at The Return that caused the blast of the shofars to converge with the voice of the president.

The Coalescence of Mysteries

And it was the converging not only of the two events but of all the mysteries, prophetic threads, puzzle pieces, and streams into that one precise moment.

- The mystery of the Jubilee converged with the sounding of the trumpets in the Jubilean year of abortion's entrance into America.

- These, in turn, converged with the entrance of the plague into the land at the exact times and places in which abortion entered the land one Jubilee earlier.

- All these, in turn, converged with the mystery of the American Jehu, who set in motion the breaking down of the modern-day Temple of Baal on the White House lawn as the trumpets sounded.

- All these, in turn, converged with the mystery of the one born amidst the slaughter, the American child of the Nile, standing at the president's side when the trumpets sounded and being lifted up to fulfill the purpose for which she was born.

- All these, in turn, converged with the year of Holy Days that began on Passover and now coalesced on Shabbat Shuvah, the Day of the Turning.

- All these, in turn, converged with the Hebrew holy day of the most high court and the most high judge, and the day on which a judge was removed from the high court at the sound of the trumpets, when prayers are prayed to *revoke the evil decree*. And now another would begin rising to take her on another Hebrew high holy day. The one left her seat on the court at the sound of trumpets; the other began her rise to the same seat and to the same sound—the sound of trumpets.

- And all these would further converge with the case that had just arrived at the Supreme Court in the Jubilee of *Roe v. Wade*, the case that was sent on Sivan 23, the Day of the Decree That Revokes the Evil Decree.

To some, the Jubilee takes away. But to others, it brings restoration, return, and redemption. Now, to the ancient sound of the Jubilee, it would bring the latter.

We are now about to assemble the pieces of the puzzle to manifest the key to unlock the answer. But first, one more mystery—a mystery of trumpets.

A MYSTERY OF TRUMPETS

A ND NOW, A mystery that will connect the Jubilean ordinance to the city of Jerusalem, to a mysterious rabbi, the appointed times of Israel, an ancient vessel, an American president, and the moment when everything came together to the sound of trumpets.

The Jerusalem Jubilee

Three years before abortion on demand began on American soil, an event of biblical and prophetic proportions took place across the world. Israel, the nation to whom the Jubilee was given, was restored to the holy city of Jerusalem. It happened in 1967 on the third day of the Six Day War. It was an event long-foretold in biblical prophecy—an event connected to the last days—even required for the return of Messiah Jesus. It was also a Jubilean event—the return of the dispossessed owners to their ancestral possession.

But in the Jubilee, when one returns to one's ancestral inheritance, one's legal rights to that possession are restored. In other words, one's return is given full legal recognition. That never happened for Israel. The world refused to recognize its return to Jerusalem.

The Jubilean Declaration

Counting fifty years from that return in 1967 brings us to the year 2017. It was in that Jubilean year that the next restoration would come. It would come through the American president, Donald Trump. At the end of his first year in office, he would issue the Jerusalem Declaration. The declaration would give full legal recognition to Israel's return to its ancient capital. It was the first time a major world leader had recognized Israel's sovereignty over Jerusalem since ancient times.

The Jubilean Rabbi

At the very moment the Israeli soldiers entered the gates of Jerusalem, stood on the Temple Mount, and approached the Western Wall, the sound of the Jubilee was heard through the ancient city. Rabbi Shlomo Goren, an Israeli military chaplain, had accompanied the troops through the stone gates. And at the moment of return, he was led to sound his shofar.

Rabbi Goren was born fifty years earlier, in 1917, the year of yet another Jubilean restoration. It was then that the British Empire issued the Balfour Declaration, giving the land of Israel to the Jewish people as a national homeland.

So when Goren sounded the shofar at the moment of Israel's return to Jerusalem, it was also his own year of Jubilee. He was fifty years old—just as it was Amy Barrett's year of Jubilee when she voted on the overturning of *Roe v. Wade*.

The Horn

In the Scriptures, names, whether given at birth or later on in life, often hold great significance. The name Abraham means *father of the many*. That is exactly what he would become. The name Moses means *to draw out*. Thus he would draw out the nation of Israel from Egypt. The name Gideon means *one who cuts down*. Thus he would cut down the armies of Midian.

The name Goren, as in Rabbi Goren, in the language from which it originated, means *horn*. So the man named Horn was born to blow the Jubilean horn at the Jubilean moment. And so, the central instrument in Israel's Jubilean restoration to Jerusalem was a man bearing the name of the central instrument of the Jubilee—*Rabbi Horn*.

The Trump

The central instrument in the Jubilean year of that restoration, 2017, was President Trump. As the name Goren means *horn,* what does the name Trump mean? In English, it means *trumpet*.

The King James Bible, speaking of the trumpet of God to be sounded in the last days, calls it "the last trump."[1] So the central instrument in the Jubilean restoration of 2017 bore the name of the central instrument of the Jubilee—President Trump—two Jubilees, two instruments: a rabbi whose name means *horn* and a president whose name means *trumpet*.

I opened up such mysteries in *The Oracle*. I noted there that Trump was born on a Friday. And so there was a Scripture appointed from ages past to be read and proclaimed in the synagogues of the world. Of what did it speak? It spoke of the trumpet. On the day he was born, the appointed Scripture spoke of the making, the forming, and the preparing of the trumpet to be sounded for God's purposes.[2]

The Jubilean Trumpet

In the year of Jubilee, the trumpet is lifted up and sounded throughout the land. In the Jubilean year of Israel's return to Jerusalem, in 2017, Trump was lifted up. It was the year that began his presidency. And from that moment, the Trump began sounding throughout the land.

In the year of Jubilee, when the trumpet sounds, the owner is given possession of his ancient inheritance. So in the year of Jubilee, by issuing the Jerusalem Declaration, the Trump sounded and the owner of Jerusalem, Israel, was given possession of its ancient inheritance. But there is more to the mystery. The year 2017 was the Jubilean year for Israel. But 2020 was the Jubilean year for America with regard to abortion. The Jubilee requires a trumpet. So just as in 2017, in 2020, there was a trumpet, *Trump*, who likewise sounded throughout the land concerning the plague. The Trump presidency began in one year of Jubilee and ended in another.

Three Inaugurations

Trump's presidency began with his inauguration on January 20, 2017. His last year as president began on January 20, 2020. January 20, 2020, was also the inauguration of the plague, the day it officially entered American soil. January 20, 2020, was also the inauguration of the Jubilee, the Jubilean day of abortion's entrance into America on January 20, 1970. So the day that inaugurated the final year of the Trump presidency also inaugurated America's dark Jubilee.

The First Trumpets

The Jubilee is the Hebrew year of trumpets; the Feast of Trumpets, or Rosh Ha Shannah, is the Hebrew day of trumpets. On September 18, 2020, the two came together at sunset, and the Supreme Court justice passed from the earth. It was that sounding of those trumpets that set in motion another sounding—one week later on the Day of Turning—the sounding of Trump.

The Day the Trump Sounded

The sounding of Trump in 2020, the year of Jubilee, would set in motion the overturning and the redemption. When I stood on the stage on the Day of the Return and said, "Go!" to signal the sounding of the trumpets, I had no idea that another trumpet would be sounding as well. The trumpets sounded on the National Mall, and at the very same moment, on the White House lawn another Trump would also sound.

And yet it was all there in the mystery: it is the sounding of the trumpet in the year of Jubilee that sets in motion the reversal, the redemption, and the restoration. And so it was the sounding of the Trump in that year and on that day that would set in motion all three.

In the instant that the trumpets sounded that day, a multitude of actions, events, and mysteries converged. That convergence would, in turn, set in motion another stream of events that would unlock an ancient template. Inside that template lies the answer for our times.

It is to this that we now turn.

Part IX

THE
BROKEN
ALTAR

Chapter 40

6/24/22

IT HAPPENED ON Friday morning, June 24, 2022. The Supreme Court handed down its decision in the case of *Dobbs v. Jackson*. The ruling not only upheld the Mississippi law banning abortion after fifteen weeks but overturned the ruling that had made abortion on demand the law of the land: *Roe v. Wade*. That last ruling had come about by a vote of 5-4—the deciding vote being cast by Amy Barrett.

The Fury

Even though the leak of the Supreme Court document in the previous month had prepared the public for what was about to happen, the news still sent shock waves throughout the nation and around the world. Proabortion politicians and leaders denounced it and vowed to do everything in their power to further advance abortion in America. Angry protesters vented their fury in Washington, DC, and in city centers and town plazas across the nation.

The mainstream media overwhelmingly condemned the decision in articles that framed it as the discarding of an enshrined "constitutional right."[1] Almost none of the articles mentioned the actual heart of the issue—the killing of an unborn child.

At the same time, others rejoiced. Many cheered. Some cried tears of joy. Many gave thanks to God for the answer to years and decades of prayers, petitions, and pleas.

The Media's Witness

The ramifications of the decision were immense and far-reaching. The *New York Times* would call it

> ...a decision that will transform American life, [and] reshape the nation's politics.[2]

It then cited the two critical events that led to the overturning:

> ...Justice Ruth Bader Ginsburg died that September. Her replacement by Justice Amy Coney Barrett...changed the dynamic at the court.[3]

In doing so, the *Times* unwittingly connected the overturning of *Roe v. Wade* with the two Hebrew holy days, the two Days of Awe, and the two soundings of the trumpet. It would not be the media's only allusion to the biblical timetable. The timing of the events made it unavoidable.

"The 50-Year-Old Landmark"

Many of the articles condemning the ruling started out by noting how long it was since the ruling in *Roe v. Wade* was handed down:

> The Supreme Court on Friday overturned *Roe v. Wade*, a consequential decision that guts the nearly *50-year-old landmark* ruling that legalized...[4]

> The ruling in *Dobbs v. Jackson Women's Health Organization* abandons nearly *50 years of precedent*...[5]

> The landmark case decided nearly *50 years ago* was overturned...[6]

> The Supreme Court has voted to strike down *Roe v. Wade*, the landmark case that upheld abortion rights for *the past 50 years.*[7]

They were bearing witness to the time span of the Jubilee, the biblical year of reversal and restoration. And so it was exactly that.

The Forty-Nine and Fiftieth Years

The ancient ordinance speaks of both the *forty-nine-year* countdown and the *fiftieth* year. So in the articles decrying the end of *Roe v. Wade*, both numbers appeared:

> The US Supreme Court has overturned its *49-year-old* landmark Roe v. Wade decision that legalized abortion throughout the US.[8]

> ...after the Supreme Court overturned its *50-year-old* Roe v Wade decision...[9]

> The Supreme Court on Friday formally overturned its *49-year*-old landmark *Roe v. Wade* decision, and with it ended *a half-century*...[10]

> Roe's *50th Year* Undid Its Promise[11]

Three thousand years earlier the ordinance decreed,

> And the time...shall be to you forty-nine years....And you shall consecrate the fiftieth year..."[12]

The Jubilean Thousands

As the Jubilee brings restoration and redemption, so the Jubilee of abortion brought both—in the form of life. Most would agree that an action that causes a single life to be saved, that rescues an innocent life that would otherwise have been killed, is a decidedly moral act. What about the overturning of *Roe v. Wade*?

According to a study made by a *proabortion* coalition, in just the first two months after the Supreme Court overturned *Roe v. Wade*, the lives of over ten thousand children were saved.[13] As in ancient times, the year of Jubilee brought restoration and redemption, and gave to thousands and thousands of innocent children their lives.

Could what happened on June 24, 2022, be linked to an ancient day of broken curses?

Chapter 41

DAY OF BROKEN CURSES

WHEN THE ARMIES of Babylon destroyed the Temple of God and the city of Jerusalem, they took multitudes of the land's inhabitants captive into Babylon. The exile, known as the Babylonian Captivity, would last for several decades and only come to an end with the fall of Babylon and the rise of the Persian Empire in its place. The Persian emperor, Cyrus, would issue a proclamation allowing the Jewish people to return to their homeland and rebuild the Temple of God in Jerusalem. The Temple was Israel's center point and the center of God's purposes.

The Time of Thwarted Purposes

When the first waves of exiles returned to Jerusalem, they found their city and temple in ruins. They set out to rebuild. They laid the foundation stones of the temple, gave thanks to God, and worshipped. But soon afterward, opposition arose from the Samaritans who also dwelt in the land and brought the rebuilding to a halt.

With the passage of time, the focus of the returnees shifted to other things, their houses, their livelihoods, their comforts. Meanwhile, on the holy mountain, the foundation stones they had laid to build the temple were neglected, abandoned, and, for all practical purposes, forgotten. Thus the purposes of God were thwarted. The plans of their enemies had prevailed for a time, but the time would go on for many years.

A Curse on the Land

Then God sent them the prophet Haggai with a word of correction:

> "Is it time for you yourselves to dwell in your paneled houses, and this temple to lie in ruins?" Now therefore, thus says the LORD of hosts: "Consider your ways! You have sown much, and bring in little; you eat, but do not have enough.... Therefore, the heavens above you withhold the dew, and the earth withholds its fruit."[1]

The obstruction of God's purposes had brought a curse on the land. The curse was on everything from the fertility of their fields to the success of their plans, efforts, and endeavors.

Day of Broken Curses

The prophet's words stirred the people and led to their repentance. They set out to fulfill the charge God had given them years before. It was on that day that the years of cessation came to an end. The work on the temple resumed. The Book of Haggai reveals the date it happened:

> They came and worked on the house of the Lord of hosts,
> their God, *on the twenty-fourth day of the sixth month.*[2]

The twenty-fourth day of the sixth month was the pivotal day, the turning point, the day of breakthrough and victory, when the strategies of the enemy were nullified, when the obstructions and war against God's plans were overturned, and when the purposes of God prevailed. On the twenty-fourth day of the sixth month, the curse on the land began to break.

The Twenty-Fourth Day of the Sixth Month

Of course, the calendar of the returnees and that by which Haggai recorded the event was that of ancient Israel. But if we were to translate it into a Western or American context, what would the twenty-fourth day of the sixth month be? The sixth month of America's calendar is June. The twenty-fourth day of the sixth month would come out to June 24. Could the twenty-fourth day of the sixth month again be ordained as a day of breakthrough in the purposes—of God?

The day on which *Roe v. Wade*, the ruling that made abortion on demand the law of the land, was struck down was June 24, the twenty-fourth day of the sixth month.

The Aborting of the Aborted Purposes

So the twenty-fourth day of the sixth month became, for another people and time, the turning point, the day of victory and breakthrough. And as in ancient times, the ways and strategies of evil were nullified. On that day, that which warred against and destroyed the purposes of God as embodied in the life of a child were rolled back.

The day that had once removed the shadow that had loomed over the land of Israel had now removed a shadow that had loomed over America.

Could it be that, as in ancient times, it would also begin the breaking of a nation's curses? That would remain to be seen. But it had begun the breaking of one of them.

———————

Seven months before the Supreme Court handed down its stunning ruling, I was given a word and told of a vision.

Chapter 42

THE VISION

AFTER THE RETURN, I began praying as to the next book I was to write.

The Return of the Gods

I was led to write of a mystery originating with the ancient gods and concerning the powers and spirits the Bible says lay behind them. I wrote of the ancient warning given against opening the door to their return. The book reveals that the door has been opened, the principalities have returned, and that their workings lie behind the transformations overtaking our culture. The revelation would become *The Return of the Gods*.

It was at a Friday night worship service in early November of 2021 that I first asked the people of Beth Israel to pray for the book as I prepared to begin writing it. It was also the first announcement of the book's existence. Though I gave no details as to what the book would be about, one of those at the service that night already knew. Something strange had happened to him that morning.

A Night Vision

One of my associate ministers, a humble and godly man, had something to tell me. The day I was to announce the new book, he was awoken out of his sleep at three in the morning. Something powerful was stirring in his spirit.

He got out of bed, put on his clothes, got into his car, and drove into a nearby parking lot. There he took out his cell phone, turned on the recording function, and began giving voice to what had come over him. He had never before approached me with anything like this. It was not like him to do so. But the moment it came over him, he knew he had to tell me.

The Altars

He saw me standing in the midst of an arid landscape, turned away from his view. Before me were massive objects of light-gray and brown stone. Their tops were flat and wide. They rested on large rock bases, or pedestals. He knew he was looking at ancient altars, objects of worship and sacrifice to the gods.

The Breaking

He then heard a voice commanding me to speak or prophesy to the altars, to proclaim to them a word from God. I lifted my hand and pointed toward the altars, opened my mouth and spoke. When I finished giving the word, cracks began appearing on the tops of the altars. Then they broke in two, one side falling to the right, the other to the left. Dark, shadowy figures then began emerging from the broken altars—spirits, principalities, gods, demonic entities departing. He then saw waters pouring down from the heavens.

Interpretation of the Vision

As to the meaning of the vision, he was puzzled. He thought of ancient Israel, having turned from God and erecting altars on which to offer their sacrifices to the gods. He knew it had to do with what was now happening in America and around the world.

He had no idea that I had just begun writing a book that would speak of the gods and their altars. In fact, one of the last chapters of the book would be titled "Altars of the Gods."

And I had no idea that the vision he described to me would foretell what would happen in seven months' time.

———————————

Could a Scripture that appeared to me while waiting for a plane at an airport gate and a man named Phinehas provide the missing key to the fate of a plague?

Chapter 43

THE PHINEHAS FACTOR

I WAS IN AN airport in Chattanooga, Tennessee, when I heard the news. I was heading out to the security check on my way to catching my flight when I heard a man's voice in the distance behind me. "Wait! Wait!" It was the man who had driven me to the airport. "You have to see this!" He held up his cell phone. "It's from my wife." It was a text she had just sent him. It read: "*Roe v. Wade* has been overturned!"

As I passed through security to the gate, I pondered the news. Though it had been expected for over a month, it was still stunning. As I waited for my flight, I took out my cell phone and pressed the power button. A Scripture appeared on the screen.

Their Sons and Their Daughters

It took me a moment to realize how it had gotten onto my phone. It was because of a web search I had done earlier on in the writing of *The Return of the Gods*. Still, why it appeared at that moment remained a mystery. It was a section of Psalm 106, beginning with verse 35:

> But they got involved with the nations and learned their practices, and served their idols, which became a snare to them. They even sacrificed their sons and their daughters to the demons, and shed innocent blood, the blood of their sons and their daughters whom they sacrificed to the idols of Canaan. And the land was defiled with the blood.[1]

It was the indictment of a nation that had abandoned God and was now sacrificing their sons and daughters on the altars of the gods. It spoke of ancient Israel, but the words now stood as an indictment against America. The fact that it had appeared just then on my cell phone right after hearing the news was all the more striking.

Phinehas and the Plague

As I scrolled up to see the context of the words, I came upon another passage recounting Israel's embrace of other gods:

They joined themselves also to Baal of Peor, and ate sacrifices made to the dead. Thus they provoked Him to anger with their deeds, *and the plague broke out among them*. Then Phinehas stood up and intervened, *and the plague was stopped*.[2]

Baal of Peor was connected to child sacrifice.

They turned away from God to worship a god of child sacrifice, and a *plague broke out among them*. I thought of COVID, the plague that had come upon America.

Phinehas was a priest at the time of the Exodus, a man zealous for the ways of God. As the result of his nation's apostasy, a plague broke out among the Israelites. Phinehas intervened to stop the apostasy. Because of his act of righteousness, the plague was lifted.

The Court and the Pestilence

In the ruling that was handed down on June 24, 2022, the majority of Supreme Court justices were likewise seeking to turn back the nation's sin. Their act, like that of Phinehas, was a righteous one and would likewise lead to the saving of life.

As the words of a nation's apostasy—of child sacrifice, the coming of a plague, an act of righteousness, and the lifting of the plague—appeared on my cell phone that morning, I wondered if the court's decision could be linked to a subsiding of the plague that had overtaken America. In view of the multitude of connections between abortion and the plague, it would seem to follow that if abortion was rolled back, so too might be the plague.

Alito's Paper

In January of 2022, the plague would begin its third year on American soil. The plague was raging, as potent and as deadly as ever. In fact, from the start of the month, it was *increasing* in strength and momentum. By the end of the month, the weekly death toll had almost doubled what it had been at the start. The total number of American lives taken by the plague that January was over seventy thousand.[3] There was no end in sight.

The Supreme Court heard the case of *Dobbs v. Jackson* on December 1, 2021. The man entrusted with the task of writing the majority opinion and ruling by which *Roe v. Wade* would be struck down was Justice Samuel Alito. It is standard procedure that once a paper is finished, it is circulated in confidence among the Supreme Court justices.

Alito had been working on the paper throughout the month of January

2022—the same month in which the plague's impact was raging across America. The paper was completed in the early days of February and circulated on February 10. It was the first appearance of the opinion and ruling that would bring *Roe v. Wade* to an end. It was a major work of 98 pages, 118 footnotes, and an appendix of 31 pages.

The Question

So the question: If the Supreme Court ruling in the form of Judge Alito's paper represented the turning back of a nation's sin, an intervention, could it also, as did Phinehas' intervention, lead to the plague's subsiding? Was there any sign of a change, a turning? Was there any subsiding of the plague?

There was. And the change would be sudden and dramatic. In January of 2022, the plague's infection rate was higher than it had ever been since first entering the nation. In fact, the number of Americans infected was so high that January that it constituted a peak *over three times higher* than any other peak in the plague's time on American soil.[4]

And then something happened.

The Plunge

In January 2022, Judge Alito worked on putting together the paper on the ruling that would overturn *Roe. V. Wade* and that would constitute America's first major rolling back of abortion on a national level. The plague's infection rate had reached its peak with 5,650,933 Americans struck in one week. In comparison, when America surpassed China to become the virus' global epicenter, it did so with less than 200,000 cases.

It was then that a dramatic and sudden change took place. The numbers of those struck by the plague suddenly began to plunge. Every week saw another dramatic plunge. The descent was so dramatic that by the first half of February, the time when Alito's paper was finished and then circulated in the Supreme Court, the plague's infection rate had plunged to almost *one-eighth* of what it had been in January.[5]

"And the Plague Was Stopped"

The plague had subsided.

And it was more than that. Not only had the rate of the plague's infections dramatically plunged, but its dramatically plunged levels would continue through the spring, into the summer when the Supreme Court decision was announced, into the autumn and winter, and into the following year. It represented the plague's most pronounced, substantial, and sustained sub-siding since entering the country in January 2020. It was unprecedented.

The American Phinehas

Judge Alito had been the American Phinehas. We have noted the centrality of breath with regard to the plague. The nation's sin had taken away the first breath of its unborn children before they could draw it in. Fifty years later came the plague that took away the breath of the old. Both the sin and the plague were linked to breath. Alito sought to roll back the sin and, by so doing, rolled back the plague. The name Alito means *breath*.

Samuel

The decision that Alito drafted would represent the answer to the prayers of fifty years. The answer would bear his name. His name would be foremost in the ruling. His name, Samuel, is Hebrew. It comes from the Bible. Samuel means *God has heard*.

As in the Scripture that appeared on my cell phone the morning of the ruling, as in the days when Phinehas intervened against his nation's sin, there had been an intervention with regard to America's sin. The evil had been rolled back. And the plague had subsided. And yet there was another side to the plague's departure—and its mystery.

Chapter 44

THE JUBILEAN TWILIGHT

BEHIND THE PLAGUE's entrance into America was the ancient mystery of Jubilee. The day of patient zero was fifty years to the exact day that abortion was introduced in the New York legislature. *The day that everything changed*, when the full weight of the plague fell on the nation, was fifty years to the exact day that abortion was first legalized in the land. We have seen correlation after correlation, match after match, year to year, month to month, day to day, event to event.

What about the end?

The Marker

In the case of abortion's entrance and establishment in America, the closing, or sealing, event was, of course, the Supreme Court ruling in *Roe v. Wade*. The ruling was handed down on January 22, 1973.

Fifty years later brings us to January 22, 2023. That would be *Roe*'s Jubilean. But it was not the beginning of its Jubilean year—but the end.

The fiftieth year of *Roe v. Wade*, its year of Jubilee, would begin on January 22, 2022. That date was the marker.

Did anything of significance take place concerning it?

The answer is yes. We have already seen one part of it. The Jubilee undoes what was done. As *Roe*'s Jubilean year approached, Judge Alito was preparing the document that would represent the undoing of *Roe v. Wade*. The Jubilean year began in late January. So it was in late January that Alito was approaching the completion of the paper. As the Jubilean year of *Roe v. Wade* approached, so did the ruling that would nullify it.

The Plague's Departure

But something else happened. January of 2022 saw not only the skyrocketing of the plague's *infection rate* but one of the highest-ever peaks in its *death toll*. By the latter part of the month, its weekly death toll had reached 21,338.[1]

And then everything changed. The plague's death toll reversed its momentum and began plunging. Two weeks after that reverse, it had dropped to 18,775. The next week it had dropped to 15,332. The next week, it dropped to 11,570. The following week, it had dropped to 8,295. The week after that, it had dropped to 6,050. The week after that, it had dropped to 4,407. And the week after that, it had dropped to 3,128.[2]

In just two months, the number of those killed by the plague had gone from 21,388 to 3,128. The plunge in its death toll was so dramatic that it was now just over *14 percent of what it had been at the end of January*!

What happened to turn the plague?

We have already seen what happened in the Supreme Court.

But something else happened as well.

January 22, 2022

The Jubilee of *Roe v. Wade* began in late January 2022. The time when the plague reversed its momentum was late January 2022. So with the Jubilee of *Roe v. Wade*, the plague began to lift. It was then that it not only began to lift but continued to. The beginning of the Jubilee marked the beginning of the plague's departure.

But there was more. The National Center for Health Statistics of the Centers for Disease Control gives a date marking the peak in the January death toll and the beginning of the plague's descent.

It marks the end of the peak and the beginning of its turnaround for the week ending on *January 22, 2022.*

January 22, 2022, is the exact day that begins the fiftieth year of Roe v. Wade—the day that ushers in the Jubilee!

So the death brought in by the plague began to reverse, to descend, to plunge, and then to depart—*on the exact day that began the Jubilee of Roe v. Wade!*

The Jubilean End

The Jubilean year that was inaugurated on January 22, 2022, and that marked the beginning of the plague's departure would also see the overturning of *Roe v. Wade*. It would happen five months later. Seven months after the overturning came the end of the Jubilean year, *Roe v. Wade*'s fiftieth anniversary.

Just eight days after *Roe's fiftieth* anniversary and the completion of its Jubilean year, the president made an announcement. He would be bringing the state of emergency declared by President Trump three years earlier, on March 13, 2020, to an end. To avoid sudden disruptions, there would be a period of transition and winding down. For all intents and purposes, the national state of emergency that had been ushered in by the deadly plague was over.

The one president had declared the beginning of the emergency within days of the Jubilee of abortion's entrance onto American soil. The other president declared the end of the emergency within days of the Jubilee of *Roe v. Wade*. It was the end of the Jubilee and of the three-year window of the plague and national emergency, the three years that had paralleled the three years of the nation's darkest of sins fifty years earlier.

The Jubilean window that had begun with death in the form of a plague had ended with the revoking of death. The Jubilee had brought death. Now it brought life. It had taken life—but had now given it back.

We will now uncover the key to which the mysteries have taken us. It was all there in the vision, but I didn't realize it at the time. It will be this key that will open up the final door.

Chapter 45

THE BROKEN ALTAR

IT IS ONE of the most powerful and significant of biblical symbols. It appears throughout Scripture and has served to signal the transformation of cultures and civilizations. It will now seal the mysteries we have thus far opened and provide us with the key to unlocking the last door and the revelations it holds.

It is the sign of the broken altar.

Altars of the Promised Land

When the Israelites entered the Promised Land, it was filled with altars. They were warned to have nothing to do with the altars, the gods and idols, the rites and rituals of the Canaanites. They were told:

> You shall destroy their altars, break their sacred pillars...[1]

They were to break down the altars in the land and render them inoperable. And so their entrance into the land would be as marked by the sign of the broken altar.

Altars of Apostasy and Return

Later, when the nation turned away from God, the altars of the gods again appeared and proliferated through the land. Again, children were lifted onto their slabs as sacrifices to the gods. The difference was that now the children being sacrificed and the parents sacrificing them up were Israelites.

But the history of Israel would also see times of national repentance, reformation, revival, and return to God. These would be marked by the forsaking of the gods and the breaking of their altars.

The broken altar appears in the story of the biblical hero Gideon. It can also be seen in the reforms of the righteous kings Asa and Hezekiah. It is implicit in the account of a king we have already come across—Jehu. It appears as well in the account of Maccabees where the broken altars were central in what would become known as *Hanukkah*.

The Manuscript

In the early summer of 2022, I was speaking at a conference in Tennessee. I told my host that I believed that I would be completing *The Return of the Gods* that same night in my hotel room. As it was his birthday, he told me that he was honored by the timing. But I was unable to complete it as I had planned. I finished it the following morning. I then headed out for the airport to get back to New Jersey to speak at the Friday night worship service at Beth Israel.

My driver accompanied me into the airport to make sure there were no problems. We said goodbye, and I headed for the gate. It was then that I heard the words "Wait! Wait!" That was when I would hear the news.

The Vision Fulfilled

The Return of the Gods was finished on the morning of June 24, 2022. It was finished on the day the Supreme Court struck down *Roe v. Wade*. I remembered the vision that was shared with me. I was told to speak to the altars of the gods. When I finished bringing forth the word, the altars began breaking apart. That morning, I had finished bringing forth the word concerning the gods and their altars. And as I did, something had broken, something colossal.

And that would be the key.

The Dark and Towering Altar

What was broken on June 24, 2022, was not merely a Supreme Court ruling or even an industry or institution. It was an *altar*.

With an altar being an instrument upon which life is offered and blood is shed, there was no altar of American civilization so brazen and colossal as that of abortion. Nor had any other American institution ever shed a fraction of the blood shed by abortion. It was the dark towering altar of American civilization, the titanic slab upon which the nation had sacrificed over sixty million of its most innocent and defenseless.

On June 24, 2022, America's towering altar was broken open. It was unprecedented. It was an ancient sign—a biblical sign, the sign that had appeared again and again in the history of Israel from the days of Joshua to those of the Maccabees. But now it was manifesting in America, on the national stage, on a colossal scale.

June 24, 2022, was the day of the broken altar.

Broken Altars in the Land

The most direct and concrete counterpart to the ancient altar of sacrifice is the modern-day abortion clinic, facility, or operating room. In the wake of the Supreme Court decision, many of these began closing down throughout the country. What happened to them was what happened to the ancient altars of child sacrifice in the days of Israel's repentance—they were rendered inoperable. They were the broken altars of the modern age.

Everything we have thus far seen—all the mysteries, signs, parallels, convergences, templates, and paradigms, the appointed days, the sacred gatherings, the symbols, the trumpets—they were all leading up to an ancient biblical sign—the sign of the broken altar.

But if the broken altar is a sign, then of what? What is it revealing? Is it the key given to us in the present hour? And could it hold a secret, the answer, that which we need to know with regard to the days to come?

Sign of Hope

What did the broken altar represent to ancient Israel? The fact that it existed in the first place bore witness to a nation's fall, a nation that had once known God but now had turned to other gods. But the fact that it had now been broken signified the hope, the chance to return.

Thus the sign of the broken altar in America now bears witness to a nation that, likewise, had once known God and had likewise departed from His ways. Without that departure, America and, for that matter, the nations of the West could never have legalized the act of abortion, much less celebrated it. But the breaking of America's altar was a sign that the nation was being given a chance to return.

Sign of Revival

So the appearance of the broken altar signals the beginning, the hope, and the chance of civilizational change, cultural transformation, national repentance, reform, and renewal, the overturning of powers, the cleansing of sin and evil, and the return and consecration of a nation to God.

When one thinks of spiritual revival in the context of American culture, one might picture a church service, a gospel crusade, or a tent meeting. But the biblical sign of revival is the broken altar. And now in the overturning of abortion, the broken altar has appeared.

The Power of *If*

Will America see national revival, return, and restoration? Its future depends on it. That is the question on which the future of America hangs and that will determine whether that future will be of judgment or redemption. The chance has been given. The window has been opened.

As to which of these futures will materialize is dependent on the nation's response to the call of God. More specifically, it is dependent on the response of His people. And as in the promise of 2 Chronicles 7:14, "If My people who are called by My name…," it is dependent on the word *if*.

To the Answer

Could the broken altar be a sign from God to unlock an answer appointed for our times? This, now, is where the last key comes into play. There is more to the sign of the broken altar. It holds the key not only for America but for all who will seek to follow the ways of God and to live a life of righteousness no matter which path America or any nation chooses to follow, no matter where or when, or what the future may hold.

The last key will open up the answer for the present age and what is yet to come.

That key can be summed up in one word…

Chapter 46

JOSIAH

THE SIGN OF the broken altar points to one name more than any other—Josiah. No other name is so connected to it. It is he who will open up the revelation, the answer, the template, the blueprint, and the manifesto for our time.

For if these are the days of the broken altar, then these are the days of Josiah. We are living in the Josiah hour, the Josiah moment. Therefore, to open the revelation, we must ask the first question: Who is Josiah?

Seeker of God

Josiah was born in the royal line of the kingdom of Judah, a descendant of King David, great grandson of the righteous king Hezekiah, grandson of the evil king Manasseh, and son of another evil king, Amon. Upon the assassination of his father, Josiah, at the age of eight, ascended the throne of Judah.

According to 2 Chronicles, when Josiah was about sixteen years old, "he *began to seek the God of his father David.*"[1] At the age of twenty-six, he embarked on a campaign to repair and restore the Temple of Jerusalem. During the restoration work, a Book of the Law was found. Though the book was unnamed, it appears to have been a scroll from the books of Moses, the most likely candidate being the Book of Deuteronomy. It is Deuteronomy that warned Israel of apostasy and of the judgment it would invoke.

All His Heart and Soul

When the book was read to Josiah, he tore his garments and wept. He then convened a gathering of the nation's leaders, elders, priests, and prophets at the Temple of Jerusalem, "and all the people, both small and great."[2] There he read them the words of the book.

> Then the king stood by a pillar and made a covenant before the LORD, to follow the LORD and to keep His commandments and His testimonies and His statutes, with all his heart and all his soul, to perform the words of this covenant that were written in this book. And all the people took a stand for the covenant.[3]

Against the Gods

Josiah then set out to cleanse his nation of paganism. The cleansing began there in the temple itself:

> And the king commanded Hilkiah the high priest, the priests of the second order, and the doorkeepers, to bring out of the temple of the LORD all the articles that were made for Baal, for Asherah, and for all the host of heaven; and he burned them outside Jerusalem in the fields of Kidron, and carried their ashes to Bethel.[4]

The nation's fall from God and its worship of foreign gods was so pervasive that it had even infiltrated the Temple of God. Josiah removed the idols from the sanctuary and had them destroyed.

Josiah's reforms were not limited to the city of Jerusalem but touched all the cities and lands of his kingdom. He

> ...defiled the high places where the priests had burned incense, from Geba to Beersheba.[5]

The Breaker of Altars

Josiah not only cleansed the land of idols but broke down the altars on which his people sacrificed to the gods.

> They broke down the altars of the Baals in his presence, and the incense altars which were above them he cut down; and the wooden images, the carved images, and the molded images he broke in pieces.[6]

Nor were his reforms limited to the borders of his kingdom but spread into Samaria to the remnant of Israel's northern kingdom:

> Now Josiah also took away all the shrines of the high places that were in the cities of Samaria...[7]

Shaker of Status Quos

Josiah shook the status quo of his culture. He overturned what it had deemed sacred. Such was the intensity and depth of his campaign that he broke down and overturned even the altars, idols, shrines, and high places that had stood in the land for ages, having been erected or permitted by the kings that had preceded him, even the altars of his grandfather Manasseh:

> The altars that were on the roof, the upper chamber of
> Ahaz, which the kings of Judah had made, and the altars
> which Manasseh had made in the two courts of the house
> of the LORD, the king broke down.[8]

He even overturned the three-hundred-year-old high pagan sanctuaries built by King Solomon:

> Then the king defiled the high places that were east of
> Jerusalem, which were on the south of the Mount of
> Corruption, which Solomon king of Israel had built for
> Ashtoreth the abomination of the Sidonians, for Chemosh
> the abomination of the Moabites, and for Milcom the
> abomination of the people of Ammon.[9]

Deliverer of the Children

Josiah broke down the altars of Baal. He defiled the altars of Ashtoreth, the Canaanite incarnation of Ishtar, goddess of sexual licentiousness. He defiled the altars of Chemosh and Milcom, the gods of neighboring lands, whose altars ran with the blood of children.

The overturning of abortion in America was not merely the breaking of an altar but the breaking of an altar on which ran the blood of children. It is Josiah who, more than any other historical figure, is specifically connected to the overturning of such altars. The connection would go still deeper.

Destroyer of Hinnom

Josiah knew that his nation could never be redeemed without cleansing the central site of its most horrific of practices—the nation's unholy ground of altars, fires, idols, ashes, and children's blood—the Valley of Hinnom. So he did:

> And he defiled Topheth, which is in the Valley of the Son of
> Hinnom, that no man might make his son or his daughter
> pass through the fire to Molech.[10]

Josiah broke the altars of Hinnom by rendering them ritually unclean and thus inoperable. *Roe v. Wade* was the primary altar of the American Hinnom. When the Supreme Court struck it down on June 24, 2022, it rendered it inoperable. It was America's act of Josiah.

Josiah's Wake

What became of Josiah's nation in the wake of his acts? Did his reforms bring about real change? Did they alter the nation's direction and course? Did they avert the judgment of which the nation had been warned?

The answer is not a simple one. Josiah's acts did impact his nation and alter its course. It did bring about a return to God, a revival. It is recorded that the people followed the ways of God all the days of his reign. And during those days, the nation was blessed. And it did avert judgment—*for a time*.

But upon the end of his reign, the nation resumed its apostasy. Even Josiah's sons who reigned in his place departed from the ways of God and led the nation to do likewise. As long as Josiah lived, no judgment came upon his land. And so the life and acts of one righteous man held back the judgment of an entire nation. That, in and of itself, represented something colossal.

The Shadow of Judgment

But upon his death, the judgment commenced. Less than twenty-five years later, the armies of Babylon breached the walls of Jerusalem. The temple was razed to the ground, the city was left in ruins, and the kingdom was wiped off the face of the earth.

Josiah's reign took place against the backdrop of judgment. The very scope and magnitude of his reforms reveal the depths to which his nation had descended. It was during his kingship that the weeping prophet of judgment, Jeremiah, began uttering his prophecies. The blood of the children already shed on the altars of Hinnom and the high places would be answered. At the same time, had the nation continued in the ways of Josiah after his death, could that destruction have been averted? We will never know.

America's Future

What about America? Could the context of the broken altar be, as it was in the days of Josiah, a sign given in the context of coming judgment? Could the broken altar of *Roe v. Wade* represent the last move to righteousness on the part of a fallen nation on the way to destruction?

From my first book, *The Harbinger*, onward, I have written of the signs, warnings, and harbingers of judgment that appeared in the last days of ancient Israel, just before its destruction. I have warned that these same harbingers are now manifesting on American soil.

The kingdoms of Israel and Judah were destroyed over the blood of thousands. America's hands are covered with the blood of millions. The nation's apostasy is accelerating. Its war against God is deepening. By all biblical measures, it is a nation under judgment and heading toward calamity. The sign of the broken altar is consistent with prognosis. And so as it was in the last days of ancient Israel, America's Josiah moment carries with it a severe warning.

The Sign of Josiah

At the same time, the manifestation of the broken altar carries a hope. In the ancient case, it held back a nation's judgment. It gave a fallen kingdom a last chance to return. Had that nation's repentance and return been an enduring one, the judgment might never have fallen.

What then will happen to America? Is its fall so great, its sins so grievous, and the numbers of innocents killed so immense that its judgment is sealed? Or is there hope of averting it or, if not averting it, at least holding it back?

The sign of Josiah contains both hope and warning. It is given in the context of judgment, and yet it gives hope in the midst of that context.

The Josiah Moment

Whether such things can, at this point, be delayed or turned back will, at the very least, rest on how the nation responds to the chance it is given. Whether it uses that chance to turn away from its sins and back to God or rejects that chance—whether it heads to life and restoration or death and judgment, time will tell.

But when a nation or culture turns away from the chance God has given it, things get worse, it descends, and its descent accelerates. It is, either way, a critical time. And it is, either way, America's Josiah moment.

That is the choice confronting America and any nation so called of God. But there is another choice—that which confronts each *individual* and, in particular, every believer, every child of God. It is the choice required by God's calling. Regardless of the age or place, circumstance, culture, or civilization in which one lives, each is responsible to respond to that call. The call of God is without condition.

In every age and land, in every moment and circumstance, there is a calling. And for every generation of God's people, there is a way, a path, and an answer. In light of the present course America, the West, and much of the world are taking, it is all the more critical that the people of God stand, walk, and live in that answer. It is for them, as well, their Josiah moment.

It is now time to take the key provided by the mystery and open up the template, the blueprint, the guide, the manifesto, and the answer concerning how we are to live, to stand, and to prevail in the present hour and in the days yet to come.

MANIFESTO

THE MANIFESTO

WE NOW COME to the answer the mystery has opened. It is a template and blueprint that goes back two and a half thousand years. And yet it speaks especially to our times and to the present hour.

It centers on a man who was born into a civilization that had turned against the moral and spiritual foundation on which it stood. It had turned from the God it had once known and the ways it had once followed and was now waging war against them.

It was an age of spiritual darkness, a darkness that was corrupting and taking possession of the cultural and governmental institutions of the day. It was a time in which those who held true to God's will and purposes were seen as evil and dangerous.

This is, as well, the culture and age in which we live. It is, likewise, a time of spiritual and moral darkness and one that is taking possession of our culture. And we are fast approaching, if not already there, the day in which those who uphold the ways of God are seen as evil and dangerous.

The people of God must wake up to the gravity of the hour and, if already awakened to it, prepare. The darkness will not be content to coexist. It never is. It will seek total dominion. And there is no person, time, or space that it will not seek to bend to its will, assimilate, or destroy. There is no running from it. There is no hiding. All must and will deal with it.

But there is a way to deal with it. And there is a way to stand, to overcome, and to prevail. It comes to us from ancient times but is as relevant and new as the present moment. That is the reason for the Manifesto.

It will speak to the righteous, to the believer, to the child of God, and to all who seek to live for God, to do what is right, to not succumb to the darkness but to stand and overcome. It will speak to many realms of our lives, our culture, and our times. One may take and apply all of it at once. Or one may take and apply just one of its sections, or one of its keys or truths at a time. One may read it straight through or randomly or as led. It is for each to apply as each sees fit to apply and as it applies to each.

The template from which the manifesto springs will speak to our times. But no matter how one views the present time, the template will also speak to that which the Scriptures identify and foretell as *the end times*.

Josiah lived in a kingdom under judgment and approaching its end. The template, therefore, comes out of the *last* days of that kingdom. The manifesto will speak to days of darkness, apostasy, and persecution. It will speak to the last days. It will speak to what is and what is yet to come.

Most importantly, it will speak of hope. And for that reason it exists.

And now, the Manifesto.

I

AGE
OF
APOSTASY

Chapter 47

I

AGE OF APOSTASY

Josiah knew the civilization and times he was dealing with. Only in that could he answer it. We must likewise know the civilization and times in which we are living. So what were the days of Josiah?

An Inverted Civilization

JOSIAH was born into a kingdom that had known God but had fallen from His ways. It had come into existence for the purposes of God but had detached itself from those purposes. It became a civilization turned in upon itself and against the foundation on which it stood, an inverted kingdom, a civilization in a state of spiritual schizophrenia. It still invoked His name but lived in opposition to His ways. Josiah was born into an age of apostasy and a kingdom turned in upon itself.

We live in an inverted civilization and an age of apostasy.

SO TOO we live in an inverted civilization. As was ancient Israel, American civilization was dedicated from its inception to the purposes of God. But as did ancient Israel, it has likewise fallen from the God of its foundation. American civilization now exists in a state of spiritual schizophrenia—as does its parent, Western civilization.

The American president wars against the ways of God as contained in the Bible on which he swore his oath of presidency. The nation's currency bears the words "In God We Trust" as it is used to overturn His ways. Its highest court strikes down the Ten Commandments, the image of which is engraved on its walls.

It is a nation that takes good for evil and evil for good, the sacred for the profane and the profane for the sacred, life for death and death for life—a civilization cut off from and at war with its own foundation, with reality, and with itself.

A Civilization in Metamorphosis

JOSIAH was born into a culture in metamorphosis from the monotheism of Scripture to the paganism of the surrounding nations. Shrines, altars, and idols were everywhere. Mythology contended against God's Word, pagan values overturned biblical values, and pagan rites and rituals infiltrated the holy places.

It is a civilization in metamorphosis from monotheism to neo-paganism.

SO TOO AS American and Western civilization have turned away from God and monotheism, in its place has risen a form of revived paganism. The metamorphosis can be seen in its worship of nature, its deification of the material world, its desanctification of life, its religious syncretism, its moral relativism, its sexualization of popular culture, its abuse of life, its fragmentation of reality, its worship of images, its embrace of alternate spiritualities, and its overturning of biblical standards, values, and precepts.

A Civilization of Gods and Idols

JOSIAH was born into a civilization given to the worship of gods. Though in name it was still given to God, in reality it belonged to the gods. It was now filled with sacred groves, high places, and pagan shrines. Foremost among its gods was Baal, the spirit that embodied the nation's turn to materialism, carnality, increase and gain, and its replacement of God with idols.

It is a civilization that, having emptied itself of God's presence, that has given itself to the worship and serving of gods and idols.

A CIVILIZATION that departs from God will, in the end, give itself to other gods and idols to fill the void of His absence. It will serve and worship them, even without calling them by name, even while denying their existence. And so American civilization has become permeated with gods and idols. As in the ancient case, it has become increasingly carnal and base. In place of God's worship, it venerates profit, money, and increase. In place of the Gospel of salvation, it preaches the gospel of materialism and success. The civilization that had once been known as a beacon of Christian values has now become the world's central conduit for the promulgation of a brazenly anti-Christian morality and gospels.

A Corrupted Civilization

JOSIAH would be confronted with the worship of the goddess Ashtoreth, "the abomination of the Sidonians" whose sanctuary sat on the "Mount of Corruption" east of Jerusalem.[1] In Phoenicia, they called her Astarte; in Sumer, Inanna; and in Babylon, Ishtar. She was the goddess of sexual licentiousness and unbridled carnal passion. As the people of Israel turned away from God, they gave themselves to her worship. Sexuality was decontextualized, taken out of the bounds of marriage and poured into the mainstream culture. The culture was sexualized.

> It is a civilization that, having departed
> from God, has given itself to the principality
> of unbridled decontextualized
> and deconstructed sexuality.

SO TOO in its apostasy from God, American and Western civilization has given itself to the principality of unbridled sexual desire, the spirit of Ashtoreth. They have enshrined sexuality as an end in and of itself, a god, devoid of marriage and moral restraint. American and Western culture has become eroticized, sexualized. And as pornographic words and images filled ancient Israel in its fall from God, so they now fill our culture.

Against Truth and Reality

The faith of Israel was based on monotheism, the belief in one God. But the paganism that permeated its fall sprang from polytheism, the belief in many gods. Where there is one God, there is one truth. But where there are many gods, there are many truths. And where there are many truths, truth becomes subjective, anything and everything, and nothing. The culture into which Josiah was born was saturated with gods and idols, and truth had vanished.

> It is a civilization devoid of truth,
> opposed to the concept of truth,
> and at war with reality.

In the turning away of our culture from God has come the turning from truth. The absolute has become subjective, and the subjective has become the new absolute before which all must pay homage. If a man believes he is no longer a man but a child, or a tree, or a squirrel, it is now his authentic truth—all is true and nothing is true but what the culture says it is. And when truth disappears, so does reality. We now live in a civilization that wars not only against truth but against reality.

Against Nature

The paganism of Josiah's age bent and broke the distinctions of nature and reality, God and creation, man and animal, male and female. The goddess, Ashtoreth or Ishtar, whose idols and altars marked the land, was especially known for the bending and altering of gender. In her priesthood were men who dressed in the clothing of women. She was praised for *turning* men into women and women into men.[2] And among her priests were those who had been physically transitioned, surgically altered.

Josiah's culture was given to the worship of the goddess and thus to the confusion and alteration of gender that filled her sanctuaries. Having turned from God, it had no defense against such things. The Book of 2 Kings indicates that it even made its way into the precincts of God's Temple.[3]

> It is a civilization that wars against nature
> and thus against human nature
> and so seeks the alteration
> and destruction of gender.

When one departs from the Creator, one will depart from the creation. So as our culture has fallen from God, it has set itself against nature and the natural order. So as in the days of Josiah, it has set itself against the order and distinction of gender. It celebrates the bending, merging, and destruction of male and female.

The nation whose teachers once led its schoolchildren in the Lord's Prayer now confuses them as to their sexuality and leads them into a process that ends with the removal of their organs on the operating table. It was not safe to be a child in the paganism of Josiah's day. It is no less dangerous now in its revival.

Against Life

JOSIAH's culture was indwelt by a spirit of death. God had called Israel to choose life and abstain from the practices of death that characterized the surrounding pagan nations. Among the darkest acts of those nations was the offering up of children as sacrifices. And so when Israel departed from God, it began sacrificing its children to the gods. Josiah could have only been horrified by the altars that covered his land and dripped of children's blood.

> It is a civilization, having departed from God,
> that has desanctified and degraded life
> and terminated the lives of its most innocent.
>
> It is a civilization of death.

AMERICA and the West, in their departure from God, have desanctified, devalued, and degraded life. This has resulted in the killing of its unborn children and also in the abuse of life—sexual abuse, self-abuse, addiction, suicide, mutilation, and self-destruction. It is a civilization impelled by and drawn to death and self-destruction.

Against God

Josiah was born into a civilization that not only had fallen from the ways of God but was now engaged in war against them. What had begun as a departure had turned into enmity and hatred.

> It is a civilization that not only
> has departed from the ways of God
> but now wars against them.
>
> The war is increasingly being waged
> from the highest levels of culture.

Our culture's departure from the ways of God has increasingly turned into open hostility and warfare against them. As it was in the days of Josiah, so now those who war against God can be found in the highest realms of culture. They are increasingly directing its course.

And as it was in Josiah's day, the civilization that once knew God is now rivaling in its descent and, increasingly, surpassing those that never did. And so it is with the once Christian-based Western civilization that now leads the world in the ways of apostasy. As it was in the days of Josiah, so now—it is a most dangerous thing to have known God and then to have turned away.

Against the Good

King Manasseh, Josiah's grandfather, had embarked on a campaign to further the worship of foreign gods, to erect pagan shrines and altars, and to bring the practices of the pagan world into the land. In its initial stages it could be championed in the name of tolerance, acceptance, freedom, and openness to the new.

But once such things were legitimized, established, and enshrined, the banner of openness and tolerance was withdrawn and replaced by an iron rod of coercion, oppression, persecution, and cultural totalitarianism. It is no accident that Manasseh is recorded as having "shed very much innocent blood, till he had filled Jerusalem from one end to another."[4] It was the inevitable flip side of the coin. It was inevitable that the same culture that called evil *good* would call what was good *evil*. If one embraces evil, one must end up waging war against the good. Of the great quantities of blood shed by Manasseh was the blood of the innocent, even the blood of the prophets and the righteous.

Those who in former times would have been revered as exemplars of virtue and godliness were now viewed as intolerant, troublemakers, and enemies of the state. They would now be marginalized, vilified, persecuted, prosecuted, silenced, canceled, imprisoned, and eliminated.

The enshrinement of evil and the war against the good continued long after Manasseh's reign had ended. It was now woven into the nation's cultural and political fabric. So the royal descendants of Manasseh would persecute the prophet Jeremiah and throw him into prison, where he would remain until the day of the nation's judgment that he, himself, had prophesied.

> It is a civilization that calls what is
> evil *good* and what is good *evil*.
>
> Thus it seeks to marginalize, vilify,
> silence, cancel, and destroy
> those who uphold the ways of God
> and who resist the apostasy.

In our day, it began as it did in the days of Josiah. First came the acceptance of evil, the legitimizing of what had always been judged as sin. The new morality, values, and practices entered the culture under the banner of tolerance, openness, acceptance, and freedom, the calling of evil *good*—the first phase.

But once legitimized and established, the banner of tolerance and openness was withdrawn and good was called *evil*—the second stage. In place of tolerance came judgment, condemnation, and cancellation. In place of freedom came the demand for absolute ideological conformity in action, speech, and thought—a cultural totalitarianism.

The values that had always defined American and Western civilization or Christian civilization were overturned and condemned as oppressive, hateful, and evil. They had to be delegitimized and eradicated. The war was waged in the public school system, in the workplace, in corporate boardrooms, on television, in the movies, on the web, in children's cartoons, in houses of government, even in the army.

Those who resisted the new values and practices, the new ideologies and pseudo-religions, those who would not comply or join in their celebration, would be increasingly marginalized. In the name of inclusivity, they would be excluded. In the name of self-expression, they would be silenced. In the name of acceptance, they would be condemned. And in the name of love, they would be vilified, railed against, and hated.

As it was in the days of Manasseh, those who upheld the ways of God became the enemies of state and culture. They would be deplatformed, demonetized, blacklisted, denied admission, expelled, fired, boycotted, compelled to undergo corrective reeducation, forced to publicly confess their sins, censored, banned, silenced, prosecuted, persecuted, canceled, eliminated.

Thus is the civilization in which we live.

Thus was the civilization in which Josiah was born.

But he would not accept it.

II

AGAINST THE FLOW

Chapter 48

II

AGAINST THE FLOW

Against Evil

Josiah was unique in that he did not accept what most of his generation accepted. He did not go along with the status quo, the majority, the tradition of his fathers, or the prevailing norms of his culture. He knew he was living in an age of darkness and in a culture given to evil. But instead of accepting the dark and the evil, he set himself against it. He would not go along with it; he would resist; he would fight against it. And he would do so no matter what it would cost him. This would be his life and his greatness.

When a civilization sets itself
against the ways of God,
the people of God must set themselves
against the evil of that civilization.

They must draw a line in the sand
and stand against that which is evil
even when it is praised,
supported, established, enshrined, and enforced
by the culture and state in which they live.

They must take their stand,
no matter what the price of that stand.
The good can only be good
inasmuch as it opposes evil.

And the greater the evil,
the more powerfully must the
righteous stand against it.

Those who allow for evil, those who are at peace with it, who collaborate with it, who do nothing to fight or stop it are not good but ultimately evil. When evil takes over a culture, most do nothing to oppose it. Most Germans did not oppose Hitler, most Russians did not oppose Stalin, and most of those who lived in a culture that practiced slavery did nothing to stop it. But believers do not have that luxury. It is the requirement of good to stand against evil. So they have no choice but to oppose it.

So the great men and women of God have always stood and fought against evil, from Moses in the court of Pharaoh to the apostle Paul in the prisons of Rome. And in an age of increasing evil, they must all the more strongly draw the line, take up their stand, and fight.

Against the Flow

From the age of eight, Josiah reigned as king of Judah. Yet his life and actions were not representative of the society or status quo into which he was born. He lived in opposition to his nation's mainstream culture. He lived against the flow of its apostasy. Though he sat on the throne, his life did not embody his culture. Rather, it was a countercultural force and an instrument for the overturning of the status quo.

> The people of God must increasingly live
> against the flow of culture.
>
> The church must, likewise,
> operate less and less
> as a cultural institution
> and increasingly
> as a countercultural phenomenon.

The people of God are called to live against the flow of the world. But it is now all the more critical that they do so. Since the establishment of Christianity in Western civilization, much of what has been known as "the church" has existed in a state of union with or as part of the culture that surrounded it. But except for a spiritual revival, that time is drawing to an end.

As the mainstream of Western culture grows increasingly hostile to God and the Christian faith, the church can no longer operate in unity with that culture. If it retains its former position in a now apostate culture, it will itself become apostate. Thus it will either hold on to its place and lose the presence and power of God, or it will let go of that place and retain God's presence and power. It must choose the latter.

So it is for each believer. One cannot follow the ways of God and, at the same time, the ways of a culture that wars against Him. It will, in the days to come, become increasingly crucial that each commits to living decidedly, actively, and unashamedly against the flow of the world and of any culture, civilization, or entity that sets itself against the ways of God.

Against the Majority

Josiah could never have accomplished what he accomplished had he sought the approval of man or feared the wrath of the majority. Josiah was committed to doing what was right in the sight of God even if it was unpopular and scorned, even if the majority hated him for doing so. So too he committed himself to refrain from what was popular or championed by the majority if it was against the will of God. He needed the approval of only One.

> In times of evil, the righteous will stand in the
> minority. They must not fear the majority,
> conform to it, be silenced by it,
> be intimidated by it, or in any way
> be moved because of it.
> They must neither seek its approval
> nor fear its reproach.
>
> The greatest of man's evils have been committed
> or made possible by the majority.
> The majority has no moral authority.
>
> But the ways of God are true and right.
> And the one who stands in them
> will be greater than the majority.

The majority came against the prophets. The majority were at peace with a culture that sacrificed children. The majority are most often wrong. The wrath of the majority, even in the form of persecution, often means the approval of God. The righteous are to take strength in that. And it is for that reason that Yeshua, Jesus, told those who would follow Him:

> Blessed are you when they revile and persecute you, and
> say all kinds of evil against you falsely for My sake. Rejoice
> and be exceedingly glad, for great is your reward in heaven,
> for so they persecuted the prophets who were before you.[1]

The one who seeks the approval of the many or fears their judgment will never be able to stand for God. Therefore, the righteous must renounce the pursuit of man's acceptance and the fear of his rejection.

They are not on earth to gain the acceptance of man but to bring others into the acceptance of God. And therein is the antidote to the fear of man with which the righteous must be filled—the acceptance, the approval, the blessing, and love of God.

Against Fear

Josiah was not only righteous but bold and courageous. He was not afraid or intimidated by the evil that had taken possession of his culture. He knew that the power of God was far greater. Without that he never would have accomplished what he did. He was not only godly but powerful in goodness, bold in righteousness.

> To fear evil is to empower it and weaken the good.
> The one who fears evil will be more apt
> to surrender to it and be mastered by it.
>
> Therefore, the righteous must never
> be shaken by the power of evil no matter how great
> that power appears to be
> or how weak the power of the good appears to be.
>
> They must remember that in the end
> evil is powerless and good is almighty,
> as the Almighty is good.
>
> The righteous must fear no evil.

In a culture and age in which power is increasingly allied with evil and evil with power, the righteous may be tempted to fear. But they must choose to not fear. As it is written, "I will fear no evil."[2]

The answer to fear is not the absence of evil but the presence of God. It was the presence of God that caused David to overcome an evil giant. It is that same dynamic that has enabled the righteous to overcome their fears and stand strong against giants, kingdoms, empires, all evil, and all odds. The presence of God is the antidote to fear.

The darker the evil and the greater the odds against them, the more the righteous must fix their eyes on the Almighty, who is for them. In that they must rise above their fears and become courageous for the good, as it is written, "The righteous are as bold as a lion."[3] For they must remember that their God is also a lion.

Against the Night

There had been other righteous kings of Judah before Josiah, but none of them had reigned over a nation of such advanced and profound apostasy. And yet the spiritual darkness of his times did not discourage Josiah from acting. Rather it inspired him. It was because of the darkness that he embarked on a campaign of national repentance, cleansing, and redemption. Josiah is listed among the greatest of kings on the throne of David, if not *the* greatest. The darkness of his times did not lessen his greatness but enabled it.

> A candle in the daylight can hardly be seen,
> but the candle that shines at night
> lights up the dark.

> The righteous of this hour
> must shine as a candle
> in the night against the darkness
> to light up the night.

As Josiah, we are not to be intimidated by the darkness of our age but to embrace its challenge. To those who will stand, these will be the days that produce greatness. To stand for God in a Judeo-Christian culture is to shine as a candle in the daylight. But to stand for God in a post-Christian or anti-Christian culture is to shine as a candle in the night.

The light that shines at night does not blend into its surroundings but stands apart from them and against them. It is the contrary light, the light of contradistinction. And it is that contrast and distinction that magnifies its radiance. The greater the contrast between the light and the surrounding darkness, the greater will be its power and impact.

The people of God must now become the light in the night.

Against the Gray

For Josiah to bring his nation back to God required the removal of evil from good—the removal of compromise, apathy, and impurity from God's people. He had to remove the gray in all its forms and traces that the light would become wholly light.

In an age of polarization, when the
darkness is purging itself
of its grayness
to become wholly dark,
the light must, likewise,
purge itself
of its own grayness
to become wholly light.

If the darkness is to become darker,
the lights must shine all the more bright.

We are living in a time of moral, spiritual, and civilization polarization. Western civilization is decoupling itself from the faith and worldview to which it has been joined for nearly two thousand years. Its mainstream culture is purging itself of Judeo-Christian values, beliefs, laws, practices, worship, ways, and culture.

If, therefore, the dark is purging itself of grayness to become totally dark, then the light must do likewise and purge itself of its own grayness that it might become totally light.

Against the Odds

The odds were against Josiah. It was, in effect, one man against a civilization. But the odds didn't matter to him. The only thing that mattered was the will of God. That was all. And in that he overcame.

No matter what the circumstances,
no matter what the culture, no matter what the odds,
there's always a way to fulfill the will of God;
there's always a way to overcome;

there's always a way to glorify Him;
there's always a way to live victoriously and prevail.

As it was for Josiah, so now the circumstances and odds do not have the last word. God's will and purposes are not bound by circumstances. And so there is always a way to fulfill them.

It was in the midst of persecution that the prophet Jeremiah fulfilled the purposes of God and in the midst of a prison cell that the apostle Paul completed the will of God. In the end nothing will stop the purposes of God. Therefore nothing will stop the one who walks in them.

Radical Goodness

It was not only that the light of Josiah's witness *appeared* brighter by contrast—but that it *was* brighter. Confronted with the evil of his age, Josiah committed himself all the more strongly to the ways of righteousness, holiness, and godliness. The evil of Josiah's day produced its counterweight in the greatness of his witness.

The believer must act as a counterweight
and counterforce to an apostate
and darkened civilization.

In the face of a radically evil culture,
the believer must become radically good.

Believers are called to respond to the darkness of their age by becoming its antithesis, its counterforce. Moses was a counterforce to Egypt, Elijah to Ahab and Jezebel, the apostle Paul to Rome.

The believer who lives in an age of apostasy must become a counterforce of faithfulness. Those who live in a culture of immorality must become a counterforce of purity and moral virtue. Those who live in a godless culture must become a counterforce of God's presence.

And those who live in a culture of radical evil must become radically good.

Revolutionary

Most of those born to the throne or of royal houses have a vested interest in protecting the status quo. Josiah was different. He sought to overturn it. Though he was king, he was a revolutionary. He overturned the status quo of his culture and age. It was because of that he would be remembered as among the greatest of his nation's kings. He was revolutionary for God.

The people of God are called
to be revolutionary.
In the days to come,
it is all the more critical
that they become so.

Their witness and their light will require it.

The more a culture departs
from the ways of God,
the more revolutionary
it will be to walk in them.

Every godly act will become a revolutionary act.

Every godly word will become a revolutionary word.

And every godly life will become a revolutionary life.

The people of God must increasingly live
as a revolutionary people.

Those who follow the Messiah
must increasingly return
to their first of all states,
the state of revolution.

Western civilization is returning to its original and ancient state—that of paganism. Thus the church must do likewise and return to its original and ancient state—its first and most powerful state—that of the Book of Acts.

It was in the Book of Acts that the Christian faith existed in its purest of forms, not as an established institution, not as a cultural fixture, and not as a worldly power—but as a life-changing, revolutionary, and world-changing movement.

So too each believer must return to the first of states, to that of the first believers, the disciples, the apostles, the messengers of the New Covenant—those who transform the course of culture, civilization, and human history.

III

SEPARATION AND RESISTANCE

Chapter 49

SEPARATION AND RESISTANCE

Separate

Josiah had to decide early in life to separate himself from the practice that had infiltrated not only his nation but the royal precincts, even his own house. He had to separate himself from the ways of his fathers. He had to separate from the ways of his culture. He had to not be afraid to be different and to stand apart. Only then could he fulfill his calling to bring restoration to his nation.

> When a culture increasingly
> separates itself from God,
> the people of God must increasingly
> separate themselves
> from that culture.
>
> In an age of darkness the righteous
> must not be afraid
> to separate from darkness.
>
> Only those willing to be different
> will make a difference.

The righteous cannot live in the present time as they did in earlier times. The culture that once upheld and supported Christian values and a biblical worldview is gone. It is increasingly anti-Christian and anti-God.

The farther the culture turns against the ways of God, the more critical it is that God's people begin the process of separation. Failure to do so is not only unwise but, with regard to one's spiritual life, can be fatal. If one does not separate, one will end up partaking of evil. If one is dealing with a flood, one must get out of the waters before one is swept away by them.

The righteous who lived in ancient Israel in the days of its apostasy could not partake in the entertainments of paganism or the rituals of Baal; they could not allow their children to play games designed by the sacred prostitutes of Ashtoreth, or entrust the priests of Molech to babysit or educate their children.

One must thus resist the natural temptation to conform. One must not be afraid to stand out, apart, and alone. The first Christians had to stand apart from the paganism of Rome; the believers of Germany had to be willing to stand apart from the evil of the Third Reich. In such cultures and ages, to be different is the requirement of righteousness.

An apostate and defiled culture will create apostate and defiled literature, movies, songs, television shows, school curriculums, internet content, library events, and other content unfathomable to an earlier generation. Those who would walk in the ways of God must now separate from such things.

Parents must now guard their children against children's media and programming, education and entertainment designed to indoctrinate, sexualize, sow confusion, or destroy. They must guard against such things as they would against the priests of Baal, Ashtoreth, and Molech.

Believers must establish clear and immovable lines and boundaries between the darkness of the surrounding culture and their lives, their homes, their communities, and all that they value and cherish. They must build strong and even stronger hedges, safeguards, parameters as to what they will and will not do and what they will and will not allow or entertain.

What specifically must the righteous separate from and to what degree? Each believer must seek the answer from God. In some cases this will mean separating from entire realms of culture; in other cases, from parts of those realms, specific functions, participations, activities, matters, content, and aspects of such realms. The goal must be to protect oneself against any defilement, compromise, hindrance, sin, or evil. The more apostate and evil the culture, the greater must be the separation of the righteous.

And if a nation or civilization comes to the point of declaring all-out war against God, His ways, and His people, what then? Then, as have the great and mighty of former ages, the righteous must rise to the moment and stand for God and what is right, regardless of the price, come what may.

Do Not Bow Down

Josiah's faith and life in God is summed up in 2 Kings 23:25:

Now before him there was no king like him, who turned to the LORD with all his heart, with all his soul, and with all his might, according to all the Law of Moses; nor after him did any arise like him.

To follow the Lord with all his heart meant taking a stand against the gods. He would not bow down or submit to them, nor would he pay them any homage or show them any reverence.

> **The righteous must not bow down to,**
> **submit to, obey, or pay any respect,**
> **or reverence in any way,**
> **the gods of their age.**
>
> **They must not accept any authority above,**
> **against, or in place of the authority of God.**

In the absence of God, all things become hallowed, deified, worshipped, served, and sacrificed to. Man-made objects, structures, and systems become idols. Political ideologies are venerated as sacred truth. Newly constructed values are proclaimed moral absolutes. And those who question or refuse to revere the new idols and gods are condemned as heretics to be punished.

And thus believers will always present an obstacle for every ism, idea, and ideology, every institution and system, every organization, every government, state, culture, ruler, nation, or power that attempts to assume the mantle and authority of godhood. They have done so from the days of imperial Rome to those of modern totalitarianism. And now, in the midst of a rising post-Christian world order, they must do so again.

They must not bow down or show any reverence to anything that claims to be God or to possess His authority, no matter how hallowed and enshrined it may be. They must, as did Josiah, see it for what it is, an idol, a false god that enslaves and, in the end, brings destruction. They must not bow down before any other god.

Remove Your Altars

The apostasy of Josiah's time had touched Jerusalem. So the king's acts of cleansing would likewise touch the holy city. The gods and their altars had made their way into the royal precincts and into the temple. Josiah could not cleanse the apostasy from his nation without cleansing them from his own backyard.

> Before the people of God can overcome the gods,
> the idols, and the altars of their world,
> they must first overcome them in their lives.

Even the righteous may have altars—strongholds in their lives, compromises, corruptions, that which has been placed above God, or served in place of God, that which stands in conflict with God's will. The righteous must break them down. They must render them permanently inoperable. They must rid them from their lives.

They must remove from their lives the altars of Baal—any idol of increase, gain, success, anything they have honored above God.

They must remove from their lives the altars of Ashtoreth—any indulgence or partaking in sexual immorality, whether of promiscuity, pornography, adultery, perversity, any form of sexuality outside the bounds of marriage and gender.

They must remove from their lives the altars of Molech—any practice that devalues or leads to the destruction of life, whether abortion, abuse, defilement, or degradation.

Houses of Darkness

The apostasy of Josiah's time was represented not only by individuals but by houses, institutions. The worship of Baal and most other gods involved organized cults, temples, priesthoods, and officiants. Josiah had to separate himself from the houses of the gods, of darkness, and immorality.

> Inasmuch as one's participation in any institution
> or in any part, function, or aspect of that institution
> would constitute participation in evil
> or the compromising of one's walk with God,
> then one must separate from that institution
> or from that part thereof.

Many institutions that once served the purposes of God now war against them. Countless believers send their children to public schools to be indoctrinated against everything they have taught them about faith and God. Those same parents will then spend their life savings to send their children to colleges to receive years of intensive indoctrination aimed at undermining and undoing everything they have spent all the previous years accomplishing.

It is one thing to deal with apostasy when it manifests informally—it is something else when the apostasy takes the form of an institution or takes one over. Resisting ungodliness at one's workplace can lead to suspension, reeducation sessions, or firing. Resisting it in one's school can lead to expulsion. Resisting it in one's profession can lead to the revoking of one's credentials or license. Such things are not hypothetical in American or Western culture—but are already taking place. Nevertheless, one must resist—and separate.

As time goes on, the issue of separation will become even more critical. Believing parents will have to make the choice as to whether it is right and of God to send their children to public schools and colleges to be indoctrinated against their faith and to risk their relationship with God—or to seek another course.

The principle applies to every realm of society. Any participation in any institution that would hinder or compromise one's faith and obedience to God or constitute the participating in ungodliness—must be foregone and separated from. One must separate from such institutions even if doing so means sacrifice; hardship; the loss of one's privileges, position, or opportunity; or the wrath of that institution. One must do so remembering that one's future is not ultimately in the hands of that institution but of God.

Break the Spell

Josiah did not wait for others to resist the evils of his age. He was first. He was the groundbreaker. He broke customs, conventions, and the status quo. He did what others had thought to do, had felt to do, and believed to do—but, because of fear, did not do.

But once he resisted, the consensus was shattered. The sacred cows of his culture lost their aura, the gods lost their authority, and the houses of cards began to crumble. It only took one man and one act of courage, and the spell was broken.

The gods, the sacred cows, and falsehoods
of any age only remain standing
as long as they stand unchallenged,
as long as their commandments
remain unquestioned
and their taboos unbroken.

The righteous must challenge
the unchallengeable.

Question the unquestionable.

Think the unthinkable.

Speak the unspeakable.

And break the unbreakable.

They must be willing to do
what no one before has dared to do.

They must be willing to be the first,
the breaker of the spell.

The story is told of the emperor deceived into believing that he was wearing invisible garments. He paraded himself naked before his people. Everyone went along with the deception and praised the emperor's new garments until a little child blurted out, "The emperor has no clothes!" And the spell was broken.

It is human nature to follow the status quo. But when evil and falsehood take over a culture, the tendency to follow becomes an instrument of darkness. Without the many who followed the status quo, who went along with falsehood and evil, who did and said nothing to resist, the darkest powers of modern times, from the totalitarianism of the Soviet Union to that of the Third Reich, could never have risen.

The righteous must be willing to be first in breaking the taboos of falsehood and dogmas of evil. They must be children who dare to say, "The emperor has no clothes!"

The Underpinnings

The civilization into which Josiah was born had once been filled with governmental, cultural, and societal underpinnings and supports to encourage the people to live, practice, and transmit their faith. But the apostasy had removed them. In their place were now impediments to faith and obedience to God. The culture now created new props and supports to encourage idolatry, immorality, apostasy, evil, and the worship of foreign gods. Josiah overturned those props and restored the underpinnings of righteousness.

When a civilization turns away from God,
it removes the supports, props, and underpinnings

that once encouraged its people to follow
the ways of God, to spread His Word,
and to transmit their faith to the next generation.

It replaces those supports and props with impediments,
disincentives, obstacles, and opposition
against their faith.

Therefore, the people of God can no longer presume
or rely on the support of their culture.

They must begin building their own vessels,
underpinnings—channels, networks, organizations,
subcultures, countercultures, and, if needed,
an underground to allow, enable, support,
and empower the living, the practicing,
the spreading, and transmission of their faith.

American and Western culture were once filled with governmental, societal, and cultural infrastructure and underpinnings that encouraged faith and worship, upheld biblical values, fostered godly practices, and facilitated the transmission of the faith to the next generation. But they have overwhelmingly been removed.

Believers can no longer rely on the surrounding culture to encourage faith and biblical values but rather to discourage and nullify them. They can no longer presume that a cultural code of moral standards will safeguard their families against a flood of immorality pouring into their homes and saturating their loved ones. Therefore, they must increasingly develop and apply their own code of standards and put into effect their own hedges of protection.

The civilization that once encouraged worship and prayer will now seek to eliminate them. The state that once expected and encouraged its people to transmit their faith to the next generation will now seek to prevent them from doing so and will instead seek to baptize them into its own ungodly and anti-biblical religion. The society that once honored the Word of God will now seek to prevent its proclamation and spread.

Believers must do everything in their power to replace the supports and channels the culture has removed. They must compensate for what no longer exists within the larger culture and counter the influence of what does. They must establish and support networks, systems, programs, organizations, schools, functions, or whatever channels and supports are needed. The role of churches and faith-based organizations in providing what has been lost will become increasingly vital.

Individually, each believer must now establish his or her own personal supports, practices, ways, and means needed to compensate for what the surrounding culture has removed or forbidden—and to counter what it now champions or compels.

With regard to their children, they must take full charge and the authority that God has given to them and not to the government, not to the state, not to the media, not to the culture, and not to the educational system. If they have ceded that responsibility, they must take it back. They must all the more strongly impart to their children biblical faith, values, and practices. They must protect them against any influence that would endanger, weaken, or compromise them. And they must exemplify such faith, values, and practices in their homes and houses of worship.

The people of God can expect that a civilization at war with God will ultimately seek to bar them from its support, its services, its employment, its functions. They must therefore be ready for that day by establishing alternate ways and means to fulfill the will and purposes of God. They must do what they must do, knowing that God will always provide a way to fulfill His purposes.

Do Not Obey

When Josiah broke down the altars, idols, and high places, he was transgressing against the norms, standards, and conventions of his day. But Josiah knew that when the law of man breaks the law of God, then that law of man must be broken that the law of God be upheld.

When a civilization enacts wars against God,
so too will its laws,

When such a law is enacted
that would force the righteous to disobey
the ways of God or obey the ways of evil,
it is then that the line has been crossed.

And it is then the righteous must disobey that law.

Such a law has no legitimacy or authority.

Obedience to a law of disobedience is disobedience.
And disobedience to a law of disobedience is obedience.

When a law of man breaks the law of God,
it is then that the former must be broken
that the latter can be upheld.

It is then that the righteous must not comply.
It is then they must resist—
they must disobey.

Under normal circumstances believers are to follow the laws of the land in which they live. Under normal circumstances they are to be the most lawful and exemplary of citizens. But there are circumstances and times that are not normal. In such circumstances and times, believers must do otherwise. When an authority or government enacts a law that stands in direct conflict with the laws and will of God, when submission to such a law would mean disobedience to God—then the line has been crossed.

The Book of Daniel records that the Babylonian king Nebuchadnezzar erected an idol of gold and commanded all to bow down before it. The Jewish exiles, Shadrach, Meshach, and Abednego, refused to obey the king's command. They were brought to the king and threatened with death in a burning furnace. They responded,

> Let it be known to you, O king, that we do not serve your
> gods, nor will we worship the gold image which you have
> set up.[4]

To obey the king's command was to break the command of God. Even if it meant their execution, they would not obey.

In the Book of Acts, it is recorded that the governing council of the Sanhedrin commanded the disciples "not to speak at all nor teach in the name of Jesus."[5] But Jesus had specifically commanded them to proclaim the Gospel to all creation and to make disciples of all nations. Thus the commandment of the Sanhedrin was in direct conflict with the commandment of the Messiah. The disciples answered,

> Whether it is right in the sight of God to listen to you more
> than to God, you judge. For we cannot but speak the things
> which we have seen and heard.[6]

They were drawing a line in the sand; when the laws of man clearly contradict the laws of God, the righteous have no choice but to obey the latter and disobey the former.

The early Christians were confronted with the same ultimatum. By imperial decree they were to offer sacrifices to the gods of Rome or an offering of incense in worship to the emperor. To disobey the command was to risk imprisonment and execution. And yet the righteous chose to follow the commandments of God over the emperor's command.

Believers in the Soviet Union faced a similar choice. They were now to celebrate and praise the new gods of Marxist ideology. They were to cease spreading their faith to others, even to their own children. Obedience to such commands meant disobedience to God. They could only obey the laws of God by breaking the laws of Communism.

In Nazi Germany, it was a crime to smuggle Jewish children to safety or to hide them in one's home. To break those laws was to follow the law of God. And many believers risked their lives to do so.

In an age of evil, obedience is disobedience, and disobedience, obedience.

The righteous must prepare for the days ahead in which an apostate culture will increasingly enact laws that will directly and brazenly war against the laws of God. They must prepare to make the same choice made by the righteous of past ages. When confronted with a command that would force them to disobey the ways of God, they must prepare to disobey it.

They must do so soberly, wisely, and judiciously, as the breaking of a law is a serious matter. It must be done according to God's Word and leading and only with regard to a law that clearly forces the violation of God's laws, when there is no other way, and when not doing it would transgress the will and law of God. When that is the case, the righteous have no choice.

A law prohibiting the use of a sound system to preach into a residential area at two in the morning does not contradict the commands of God. But a law that prohibits all preaching and spreading of the Gospel does. So too would any command to silence the righteous from speaking the truth, as God has ordained the truth to be spoken. So too would any law that prohibited them from imparting the ways of God to their children or that would direct their children away from faith and into darkness. And so too would any law or command that would compel them to advance, celebrate, or participate in sin.

The passing of a Christian age into a post-Christian age will create increasingly brazen anti-Christian laws, directives, and orders. This will result in persecution. Persecution, in turn, may result in suffering, imprisonment, or martyrdom. Nevertheless, confronted with the choice to obey the laws of man that transgress the ways of God or to follow the ways of God that transgress the laws of man—the righteous have no choice. They must stand as did Josiah, knowing that the ways of man are transient, but the ways of God are eternal.

They must transgress the transgression, defy the defiance, and obey not the commands of darkness.

IV

POWERS

Chapter 50

IV

POWERS

Weaned

The more dependent Josiah was on his culture, the less able he would be to impact it. He could not be dependent on anything connected to the idols, gods, and pagan rites of his culture. He had to wean himself of any such dependency. At the same time, he had to strengthen his dependency and connection to God. The stronger that connection, the more able he would be to impact his world.

> The righteous must do everything in their power
> to wean themselves from any dependency
> that would weaken their ability to do the will of God.
>
> At the same time, they must become
> all the more strongly connected to God.
>
> To live unplugged from the world,
> they must live all the more plugged in to God.

Those who would stand against the evil of their culture, who would impact their world for God, must wean themselves from any dependency on such things. In order to do so, they must become more strongly connected to that which is greater than the world—God. The two are commensurate; the stronger one's connection to God, the greater one's independence from the world.

The prophet Elijah stood against the evil of his culture and the corruption of the king and queen that ruled it. In order to do so, he had to become all the more dependent on God. The Bible records that in the midst of famine, he sat by a stream of water, fed by ravens sent by God. The image embodies both his dependence on God and his independence of the world. As the culture darkens, it is all the more critical that the righteous wean themselves

223

from it. The way to be unplugged from the world is to become all the more strongly plugged in to God.

The Inner Power

Josiah had to maintain a strong inner life with God. He could not have stood so powerfully against all the outer forces arrayed against him and overcome them without doing so. He was undoubtedly a man of a strong inner life, a man of prayer. It was his inner life that overcame his outer world.

> The inner realm is the counterbalance,
> and the antidote to the outer realm.

> The darker the outer realm,
> the more vital and powerful
> must be one's inner realm.

> Those who would be great and powerful
> in times of evil must become great
> and powerful in prayer—great and powerful in the presence of God.

> The inner realm is the ground from which
> the roots of the righteous draw life
> and the fruits of righteousness are brought forth.

Without a strong inner life with God, one becomes more vulnerable to the fluctuations, corruptions, and temptations of the world. But the most powerful and effectual figures of Scripture were men and women of prayer. Moses subdued an empire, performed miracles, and delivered a nation from slavery. David slew Goliath, put foreign armies to flight, and established a kingdom. Elijah stood unmoved by persecution, withstood an evil government, opened up the heavens, and turned a nation back to God. The apostle Paul pressed on against all odds and obstacles, even in prison, and changed the course of world history. Each was a man of prayer. In view of the days ahead, a strong prayer life is not optional but critical. Those who will stand immovable in the days of darkness will be those who stand immovable in the presence of God. They must do so every day of their lives. It is their privilege, their joy, and the antidote to the world.

The Unreframed

Josiah's culture had redefined what was acceptable and what was not, what was right and wrong, what was holy and profane. Josiah had to reject the reframing and affirm and stand by what he had always known to be true and right.

> An apostate civilization, a fallen culture,
> will seek to bend, to alter, to reframe,
> and to redefine reality to align with its fall.
>
> But the righteous must reject it.
>
> They must uphold, affirm, and reaffirm
> the unchanging and the true.
>
> They must uphold the uncorrupted, unaltered,
> unfallen state of man, of woman, of marriage,
> of family, of fatherhood, of motherhood,
> of childhood, of humanity, of life.
>
> They must uphold and manifest it
> not only in their culture but in their homes,
> their families, and their lives.

A culture that has fallen from God will always seek to justify its altered state by altering standards, redefining values, and reframing reality. The reframing is corrosive and works to corrupt even those who seek to resist it. That which provoked shock from nonbelievers of past days now fails to provoke even a raised eyebrow from believers of the present day. When one is continually exposed to darkness, one is in danger of having one's sensibilities numbed and one's conscience desensitized.

The righteous must reject their culture's altered standards, its redefined words, its modified language, its mutated values, and its inversion of good and evil. They must not let it alter in any way what they have known to be true. They must purify themselves from its corrupting influence and renew themselves in the truth.

The apostate king Ahab sought to reframe the prophet Elijah by calling him a "troubler of Israel."[1] But Elijah refused to be redefined and responded by telling the king that it was he who was the troubler of Israel by forsaking God for Baal. So, as it was with Elijah, it is the faithful and unchanging stand of the righteous that testifies against the changed standards of the apostate culture in which they live. Their culture will hate them for it. Nevertheless, they must bear witness and uphold the truth. It was by so doing that Elijah and Josiah turned their nations back to God. Without truth such civilizations have no hope. But with truth there is hope and the righteous are endowed with power.

The Word

Josiah lived in a culture that had departed from the Word of God. Thus he had to hold all the more strongly to the Word of God. So seriously did Josiah take the Word that when he realized how far his nation had fallen from it, he set in motion a spiritual revolution. His most important acts were birthed by the Word. He would not attempt to change or reinterpret it in order to align with his culture or life. Rather, he would change his life and his culture to align with the Word of God.

> And apostate civilization will depart from the Word.
> The righteous must do the opposite
> and *hold* to the Word all the more strongly.
>
> An apostate culture bends the Word
> or the truth to conform to its ways.
> The righteous must bend their ways
> to conform to the Word.

The most evil of governments in the modern age have waged war against God's Word. The Third Reich attempted to subvert and redefine it. The regimes of Communism attempted to suppress, ban, or abolish it.

In modern American and Western culture, the war against the Word is now waged through its disparagement, its marginalization, its reinterpretation, and its progressive removal from mainstream culture and life. The farther a culture departs from God, the more it must undermine or redefine His Word. At the same time, the more in need of the Word it becomes.

The greater a culture's apostasy from the Word, the more strongly must the righteous hold to the Word—the more strongly they must receive it, treasure it, share it, proclaim it, act upon it, live by it, and bring their lives into conformity with it. They must never soften or dilute it, add to, or in any way take away from it.

They must treat the Word as the true bread of their lives and every day partake of it. They must remember that before the world was the Word—and so shall it be after the world is no more. The Word is more powerful than the world.

Emunah

Josiah was a man of faith. It was his faith in that which was beyond and greater than his world that gave him the power to overcome it. So it was the power of faith that enabled the righteous in biblical times to overcome all things. Of these the Book of Hebrews records:

> …who by faith conquered kingdoms, performed acts of righteousness, obtained promises, shut the mouths of lions, quenched the power of fire, escaped the edge of the sword, from weakness were made strong, became mighty in war, put foreign armies to flight.[2]

Faith sees through and beyond the world.

The darker the world, the more must the righteous live by faith and the greater must their faith be.

The power of faith overcomes the world.

One cannot overcome the world or escape its temptations and fears if the world is one's only and ultimate reality. It is faith that gives the power to transcend the boundaries of one's world and one's life.

It is no accident that the Hebrew word for *faith*, *emunah*, is also the word for *steadfastness*. And both words are connected to the Hebrew word for *truth*. It is faith that connects righteous to the truth, which is steadfast and unchanging. And it is faith that gives the righteous the power to become steadfast and unshakeable.

It was faith that enabled the first Christians to stand against the most powerful empire on earth. It was faith that enabled the righteous of the modern age to stand against the most oppressive of totalitarian governments. It was faith that enabled them to do what was right, to transcend themselves, and to save the lives of others even when it meant risking their own. Greater darkness will require greater faith.

The Eternal

Most of Josiah's contemporaries believed that the kingdom in which they lived would go on indefinitely. But Josiah knew differently. He knew that the kingdom was temporary, its days numbered—but that God and His Word were forever. Thus Josiah would not live his life by the dictates of a world he knew was passing away—but in the light of eternity.

> The righteous must see the culture and world
> in which they live and the darkness they face
> as temporary, as passing away.
>
> They must set their eyes on the eternal
> and see all things in its light, and live accordingly.

For those who have lived under the weight of totalitarian evil, the darkness often appears unstoppable, unbreakable, and unending. Resistance appears futile and hopeless. And yet, in the end, all such powers have crumbled or will crumble into nothingness.

It is the nature of nations, kingdoms, cultures, and civilizations to assume the mantle and aura of permanency. But each will, in the end, pass into dust. In light of the eternal, the most powerful and enduring of kingdoms are but vapors that appear for a moment and are swept away by the wind.

The righteous must never be awed, intimidated, or shaken by what is passing away. They must remember the prophets, the desert wanderers, the ragged preachers who stood in the margins of such empires, those whose voices echoed against the walls of Babylon, Nineveh, and Rome. In contrast to the kingdoms and empires of their day, they appeared small, insignificant, hopeless, and on the wrong side of history. And yet the empires that towered above them now lie in ruins. But the words of the prophets endure to this day. The darkness can only exist for a time and then must fade into the light.

The children of God must set their eyes and their hope on that which never fades but is forever—the eternal. They must see and judge all things by its light and live their lives in its light. Those who see and live by the eternal will overcome the temporal.

AGENTS OF
HEAVEN
ON EARTH

Chapter 51

V

AGENTS OF HEAVEN ON EARTH

Agents of Heaven

It was not enough that Josiah separated himself from the spiritual darkness of his times. Had he done only that, though he would not have been listed among the many evil kings of Judah—he would not have been numbered among its greatest. It was not enough to separate himself from evil—he had to overcome it.

The darkness of his age was not passive but active. The blood of the children shed in the Valley of Hinnom testified to that fact. Josiah knew that a passive righteousness would be of little effect in the face of such potently active darkness. He would not be impacted by the apostasy of his day; he would impact it. He would not be defined by his culture; he would define it. And he would not be conformed to his age; he would transform it. Josiah would become an active agent of light in the midst of the surrounding darkness.

The children of God are not to live in the world
as passive inhabitants but as active agents.

They are not *of* earth but heaven.
Thus they are not to live *from* the world.
They are to live *to* the world,
to their culture, and *to* their age.

They are not to be defined by their times.
They are to define them.

They are not to be changed by the world.
They are to change it.

They are to live as agents of heaven on earth.

Messiah told His disciples that they were to be the salt of the earth and the light of the world.[1] Both salt and light function as active agents upon their circumstances. Salt acts as a preservative, and light acts to transform the darkness. So too the believer is not to be in the world or in any circumstance without, in some way, impacting and transforming it.

The light that does not shine ceases to be a light. And the light that does shine *against* the darkness ceases to be the light. And so the righteous who do not act *against* evil and impact the world for the good cease to be the righteous.

Those who do not overcome evil will be overcome by it. The Scripture charges the righteous to be not overcome by evil but to overcome evil with the good.[2] So it was for the first believers who, against all odds, prevailed against all opposition and persecution and overcame an empire.

The people of God are to live as agents of heaven on earth—because they are.

The Advancing

Josiah did not live defensively. Nor did he seek only to hold his ground against evil. Rather, he fought it in the public square. He fought it in the realm of government. He fought it throughout his land. He lived on the offensive and on the advance. He did not wait for the darkness to come to his doorstep. He brought the battle to the doorstep of evil.

**If the righteous do not live on the offense,
they will live on the defense.**

**They must fight the darkness in the public square,
or they will end up fighting it at their doorstep.**

They must live always advancing.

When a government or culture launches a war against a people, it is natural for those on the receiving end of that war to live in a state of defensiveness and self-protection. But the people of God are not to live as such. When Messiah gave His disciples the Great Commission, he said, "Go."[3] *Go* requires a motion of advance. So the righteous must always go forward and advance. Even in the midst of attack and opposition, they are never to stop moving forward or advancing. They are to fulfill their prime directive, which is to go and to take new ground.

When Messiah spoke to His disciples of the kingdom of hell, He did not say that its armies would fail in its attacks—but that its *gates* would not prevail against them.[4] The people of God are not to live in fear of gates—but to fight them, to break through them, and to prevail against them. The word *go* does not allow for a life of defensiveness or of reaction—but only for advance.

All Things

Josiah used everything in his power, every means and resource, every skill and talent, every instrument of state and authority, everything at his disposal to touch every part of his land and kingdom.

> The righteous must make the most
> of every opportunity and moment.
> There is no time or place, no hour,
> situation, or state that cannot
> be used to impact the world.
>
> They must use all means, all resources,
> all that is at their disposal,
> all that is in keeping with the will,
> the ways, and the love of God
> to accomplish His purposes.

The people of God must make the most of every moment and circumstance to impact their world—in their homes, their workplaces, their schools, in their positions of power and influence, their skills and abilities, their experiences, and resources, their coming and their going, in all times and places.

They must use all means and resources at their disposal to fulfill the purposes of God. The apostle Paul wrote, "I have become all things to all men, that I might *by all means* save some."[5] Thus there was no limiting on that which could be used for God's purposes except that it be consistent with the ways of God. All such means and actions must be measured by the words given by Messiah and of the New Covenant Scriptures. All things must be done in love and for life and redemption.

In other words, one cannot overcome the world *by* the world, or evil by evil means. One cannot use ungodly means to accomplish godly ends. One cannot, by the devil, cast the devil out. On the other hand, there are many means and strategies that do not conflict with the ways of God. And the fact that they may have been used for worldly or ungodly purposes does not prohibit their being employed for God. The apostle Paul used Roman law to advance the Gospel, even the words of pagan writings to share the Gospel to Athens from Mars Hill. He used all things for God that *by all means* he could save some. So the righteous must do likewise.

And they must always remember that their most powerful of means are not of this world but spiritual—that of prayer, the Word, the presence and power of God. In times of repression or persecution, there may be no other power. If then, their only means are spiritual, it will be enough. For no instrument of man, no force of government, no power on earth is strong enough to stop the means given by the Spirit of God.

State of Mission

Josiah did not live for himself, his comfort, or his own advantage. Rather, he lived to do what was right, regardless of what it required or meant. He lived beyond himself, beyond his life. He did not live to survive. He lived as one on mission. And so the life he lived was one of purpose and greatness.

**The righteous are not on earth to live their lives
in a state of survival but in a state of mission.**

**Only then can they live lives of righteousness
and fulfill their calling.**

They must live beyond their lives and rise above them.

**They must live as those on mission
as if sent into the world by God.**

The dictates of self-interest and survival will ultimately come into conflict with the dictates of what is right and of God. It was in view of survival and self-interest that millions of Germans followed the evil of Nazism. But those who did what was right did so by transcending their self-interest. It was by living beyond and above themselves that they were able to live lives of righteousness and greatness.

The people of God must free themselves from living by the dictates of self-interest and survival. They must live for what is greater. Only then can they live a life worth living, a life of greatness.

They must resolve to pay whatever price must be paid, to offer whatever sacrifice must be sacrificed, and to let all chips fall where they may to live a life of righteousness. For only those who let go of their lives for the sake of righteousness will end up finding them and the purpose for which their lives were given.

Breaking the Altars of the Age

It was not enough that Josiah paid no homage to the gods. It was not enough that he broke down their altars in the royal precincts, his own backyard. He knew that if he was to turn his nation back to God, he would have to break, render inoperable, and remove the altars of the gods from his land. As long as they stood, the gods would be served, and on their slabs, the nation's children would be sacrificed. So Josiah would come against the altars of his land.

It is not enough for the righteous
to not bow down to the gods of their age,
their culture, and their world.
They must actively stand against them.

They must oppose their altars.
And as much as it is in their power,
they must overturn them.

It is not enough that the righteous do not bow down or pay homage to the gods. It is not enough that they overturn the altars in their lives. They must actively stand against the gods of their age and culture and seek the overturning of the altars in their land.

When a culture enshrines an ideology, an ism, a movement, a "truth"—a god—on its high and holy places, the righteous must stand against that god and its altar. They must not be silent or do nothing in the face of evil and falsehood.

How do they identify the altar of a god? An altar is any vessel or instrument by which evil is served and sacrificed to. The altar manifests as a system, an institution, an organization, a practice, a custom, an industry, any vessel by which the purposes of evil are served and the purposes of God warred against.

When believers entered pagan lands with the purpose of bringing the Gospel, they were confronted with altars—the infanticide of Rome, the cannibalism of the South Pacific, the widow burning of India, the human sacrifices of pagan Europe, the involuntary mutilation of eunuchs and priests, and the forced prostitution of young women and girls, the sex trafficking of the ancient world. Confronted with such altars, they sought to nullify them, render them inoperable. It was no accident that the movement to bring slavery to an end, abolition, was inspired by faith, motivated by Scripture, begun and propelled by Christians seeking to fulfill God's purposes.

The righteous cannot be at peace with any system that indoctrinates, confuses, mutilates, or kills millions of their children, or that which enslaves, corrupts, poisons, oppresses, defiles, abuses, and degrades or destroys human life—whether of the innocent in the womb or the feeble, the infirm, and the aged. Nor can they be at peace with any system that wars against God's ways and laws, His creation, His image, and His purposes—whether of life, of sexuality and gender, of marriage and family, of humanity. They must uphold each of these and stand against the modern-day altars of Baal, Ashtoreth, and Molech in all their manifestations.

And as much as it is in their power to do so, they must seek, as did Josiah, for their overturning and their abolition. They must use every means in their power to do, whether political, legislative, judicial, or economic, by speaking and not being silent, by organized campaign, by protest, by media, and by any other means that are consistent with the ways and love of God and to the touching of hearts. And they must do so always by prayer, the Word, and the power of God. By these they must seek to nullify, remove, or render inoperable the vessels of death and destruction their culture has erected—they must overturn the altars of the gods.

VI

KINGDOM OF THE LAMB

Chapter 52

VI

KINGDOM OF THE LAMB

The Good

Josiah sealed his campaign of cleansing and reformation by calling his people to convene in Jerusalem for a national assembly and celebration:

> Then the king commanded all the people, saying, "Keep the Passover to the LORD your God, as it is written in this Book of the Covenant." Such a Passover surely had never been held since the days of the judges who judged Israel, nor in all the days of the kings of Israel and the kings of Judah. But in the eighteenth year of King Josiah this Passover was held before the LORD in Jerusalem.[1]

Though the Passover was to be celebrated every year, the implication here is that it had *not* been celebrated for some time or not as had been commanded. Josiah's Passover was an act of restoration. Though the breaking down of the altars, idols, and shrines epitomized his reign, it was the Passover that sealed his campaign and more accurately defined his life. His life was not about destruction but restoration. He was not ultimately a destroyer of worship but its restorer. His life was not defined by the altars and idols he fought against but by the God he affirmed. His campaign against evil was waged only to bring his people back to the good. His kingdom was heading to destruction. Josiah sought to turn it back.

To desecrate the altars of desecration was an act of sanctification. To destroy the altars on which children were murdered was an act of life. And to overturn that which had overturned his nation was to bring restoration. The impact of his life was positive.

**The righteous must not ultimately be defined
by that which they stand against
but by that for which they stand.**

Their lives must bring forth life healing,
restoration, salvation, and redemption.

Their impact on the world must be positive.

They must love in the face of hatred,
bless in the face of persecution,
return good for evil,
and manifest heaven
in the face of hell.

Their lives must be lived as gifts to the world.

The danger of living in an especially darkened culture and of fighting evil, as one must, is to become defined by that against which one is fighting, to let evil become one's focus, to live in reaction to it, and become its reflection. The righteous must guard against that. They must not be defined by what they stand against but by what they stand for.

They must stand against the ways of death because they are people of life. They must oppose sin as much as they would oppose a life-threatening disease. When confronted by hate, they must respond with love. And as their faith is based on the blessing and gift of God, their lives must reflect and manifest that. Each must become a living vessel of blessing, each, a gift as given by God to the world.

Hearts and Stone

Josiah knew that if he only overturned the altars of pagan worship without overturning hearts, his campaign would fail. He had to change their hearts. To that end, he called his people to Jerusalem to celebrate the Passover, to worship the Lord, and to stand in His presence. Only if the people came to know God for themselves would there be lasting change.

If the righteous seek only to change
the outward structures of culture, laws,
institutions, and systems, their efforts will be undone.

If one changes laws without changing hearts,
the changed laws will be changed back
by the unchanged hearts.

In order to revolutionize the world,
one must revolutionize the heart.
And to revolutionize the heart
requires the power of God.

Change the heart,
and the world will follow.

The people of God *are* called to seek the changing of laws, of institutions, of systems and frameworks, of establishments and outward structures in impacting the world for good. But if they transform such things without transforming the inside, the heart, their efforts will, in the end, be undone.

While seeking to impact the world around them, their ultimate goal must be spiritual. They must seek to change the hearts of their generation. They must do all that is possible and everything in their power to bring those of their generation to God—that they might come to *know* God, to receive His salvation, and to have His presence fill their hearts and lives.

The Prime Directive

Passover was the festival of deliverance and salvation. It celebrated God's salvation of Israel from Egypt. It focused on the Passover lamb. So when Josiah called the nation to Jerusalem to observe Passover, he was calling them to celebrate their salvation. Thus the celebration of salvation was the sealing and crowning event of his campaign.

The first priority and prime directive
of God's people as touching the world is salvation.

Each generation of believers is charged to do all
in its power to reach and save as many
of their generation for God as is possible.

They must share the message of the Lamb,
the good news, the Gospel, by any and all means,
and to as many as possible.

That charge does not abate in times of tribulation
or persecution or under godless powers
that war against its sharing. To the contrary,

it is then all the more vital to share it.

Josiah's celebration focused on the Passover lamb and specifically on its blood, the substance that saved Israel out of judgment and bondage. Yeshua of Nazareth, Jesus, is called the Passover Lamb. The Lamb is Jesus. So the prophet Isaiah foretold the Jewish Messiah in the imagery of a sacrificial lamb,

> He was led as a *lamb* to the slaughter.[2]

So John the Baptist heralded his coming with these words:

> Behold! The *Lamb of God* who takes away the sin of the world...[3]

So the apostle Paul, writing in 1 Corinthians, says,

> For Messiah, our *Passover Lamb,* has been sacrificed.[4]

If one had to sum up the message of Passover in a single statement, it could read, "We were saved from bondage, judgment, and death, by the blood of the Passover lamb." If one had to sum up the message of the Gospel, it could read, "We were saved from bondage, judgment, and death by the blood of Messiah, the Passover Lamb." The Christian faith is a Passover faith, and the Gospel message is the message of Passover.

As Josiah summoned his people to partake of the lamb, every believer is called to bring all people to salvation in the Lamb. They must seek to do this by all means possible, by the spoken word, the written word, by image and media, by action, by example, and by their lives.

This is the prime directive for every believer. It is for all times and places. Paul, even in his imprisonment, even in chains, shared the Gospel, even to his captors. To possess the cure to a deadly disease and not share it with those dying of that disease is an immoral act. So to possess the Gospel, the cure, and antidote to a dying world, the answer, salvation, and to refrain from sharing it, is an even greater act of immorality.

As for a civilization that seeks to prohibit the sharing of the Gospel, believers must follow the command of a higher authority. The very fact that the Gospel has been prohibited bears witness to the fact that the need to share it with that civilization is even greater.

So Josiah led his people to the celebration of salvation, the feast of the Lamb. So Jesus is the Lamb, and his name, Jesus, or Yeshua, means "salvation."

Unto the Lamb

All that Josiah did to cleanse and save his nation was leading up to the Passover. The connection with Passover and the lamb is so strong that the Hebrew word for the feast, Pesach, actually means *the Passover lamb*. It was all leading up to the lamb.

> The Word of God reveals the Lamb as the mystery,
> the alpha and omega, the beginning and end,
> the center and aim, and the reason
> and purpose of all things.
>
> So it must be for the people of God.
> They must make the Lamb the alpha and omega,
> the beginning and end, the reason
> and the goal of their lives.
>
> They are to fix their eyes on the Lamb,
> speak the name of the Lamb,
> glorify the Lamb in all they do,
> and walk in the footsteps of the Lamb.
>
> They are to live their lives from the Lamb,
> for the Lamb, in the Lamb, through the Lamb,
> of the Lamb, and to the Lamb.

The acts and lives of the believer must likewise be to the Lamb, to Messiah, to Yeshua. His love and sacrifice as embodied by the cross must be the foundation and center of their lives. They must not be moved away from it, and if they are, they must always come back to it.

They must, each day, seek His leading and His ways and follow in His footsteps. They must seek to know Him more each day than they knew Him the day before. They must aspire to fully live in His presence and allow His presence to fully live in them.

They must live in His living, move in His moving, love in His loving, and overcome in His overcoming.

And in an age when His name is warred against, they must all the more boldly proclaim it. They must make Him the beginning and end, the reason and purpose, of and for all they do and are.

The Radical Love

Josiah's life was ultimately led by love. He gave himself to the saving of his kingdom, of his people, of their children, of their future. His campaign was ultimately driven by love, his love for God and his love for his people.

Those who would follow the Lamb
must live as He lived, a life of radical love.

Their love as His must have no conditions,
no limits, no earthly reason,
and no natural cause.

They must love the unloving,
the unlovely, and the unlovable.

They must manifest their love
in the sharing of salvation to the lost
and in compassion to the needy
in feeding the hungry,
clothing the naked,
healing the sick,
and setting the captives free.

Their love must not, in any way,
weaken their stand against evil.
Nor must their stand against evil
in any way weaken their love.

They must live a life of love
that confounds the world.

The lambs of Josiah's Passover epitomized sacrifice. The Lamb of God, Messiah, epitomizes self-sacrifice, the giving of one's life to save others—total love. The one who follows the Lamb must live likewise.

Their love does not, in any way, lessen their calling to stand against evil. Rather, it requires it. Parents who do not seek with all their strength to fight against the disease that ravages the life of their child do not love their child. So the righteous who do not fight against the evil that destroys their world and those in their lives do not love. At the same time, the fight against evil must never compromise the command to love. The people of God must love their enemies, bless those who curse them, and pray for those who persecute them—and by so doing, confound and overcome the world.

The Weaponry of Praise

The Passover to which Josiah called his people was more than an observance. In Hebrew, Passover was called Khag Pesach. The word *Khag* means feast or festival. It comes from a Hebrew root word that can be translated as "to dance in a dance of circles." The Passover was filled not only with lambs but worship and praise. Josiah knew the power of praise and that a people who worshipped in God's presence would be less likely to worship at the altars of Hinnom. The power of worship and praise would overcome the darkness of the gods that had once overcome his people.

> Worship and praise are not only
> necessities for God's people
> but powers and weapons.
>
> They endow the righteous
> with the power to do His will,
> to stand against darkness,
> to fight their battles
> and become victorious.

It is written that God *inhabits the praises of His people.*[5] Praise and worship are the portals of God's presence. In His presence His people are filled, purified, and empowered. Thus praise and worship give power to the righteous—all the more so in the midst of their warfare and trials, and times of adversity and evil.

The army of King Jehoshaphat was led by worshippers. The Bible records that when "they began to sing and to praise," their enemies turned against each other until they were defeated.[6] Praise is also a weapon, a shield, and an armor by which the righteous are to fight and win their battles.

Joy

The festivals of Israel were characterized not only by holiness and worship—but great joy. The Israelites were to rejoice in their festivals. So in leading his nation to the festival, Josiah led his people to joy.

Joy is of God. Joy is holy.
Righteousness leads to joy.

Thus the righteous must
be a people of joy.

The joy of the righteous is not of the world
but of heaven.

It transcends the world
and is without condition.

And so the righteous
can apprehend it at all times
and in all circumstances.

It is a contrary joy,
a chosen joy,
a radical joy.

The more it is practiced,
the stronger it becomes.

The joy of the Lord is the strength
and safeguard of the righteous,
empowering them to resist evil.

For it is the joy of the Lord also
that lights up
and overcomes the world.

Joy is a fruit of the Spirit. In the Book of Nehemiah, the people of Israel are told "the joy of the LORD is your strength."[7] The joy of the Lord is a source of power. It is a safeguard. For one will be drawn to that which one rejoices in. On the other hand, one will be drawn away from that in which one does not rejoice. So in times of evil, temptation, and darkness, believers must grow all the stronger in the practice of joy.

The most pivotal generation in the history of the Gospel is that which is recorded in the Book of Acts. Though small and unlikely, though birthed in the fires of persecution, it was the generation that most changed the course of history. How did the believers in the Book of Acts withstand all that was waged against them and overcome against all odds?

They did so by joy. Joy permeates the account of the first believers. They rejoiced in good news, in bad news, in persecution, and tribulation. They rejoiced for the honor of being persecuted for Messiah. Their joy defied and transcended their circumstances. And they prevailed. So will the generation of the last days if it will likewise live in the same unconditional, unexplainable, and unstoppable joy.

COMPLETION

Chapter 53

VII

COMPLETION

Beth El

After cleansing Jerusalem and the land of Judah of its altars and shrines, Josiah set out for Beth El. The name Beth El is Hebrew for *the house of God*. It held a special place in the nation's history. It was there that the patriarch Jacob received a dream from God in which a ladder that stretched from heaven to earth—*Jacob's Ladder*.

But centuries later, when Israel turned from God, Beth El was converted into a pagan high place with a massive altar and idol. For centuries it stood as a pagan sanctuary. Josiah was now led to go there to cleanse it. And so he did:

> ...both that altar and the high place he broke down; and he burned the high place and crushed it to powder, and burned the wooden image.[1]

Then, to render the altar inoperable, he desecrated it:

> As Josiah turned, he saw the tombs that were there on the mountain. And he sent and took the bones out of the tombs and burned them on the altar, and defiled it.[2]

And then something happened. An object caught his attention:

> Then he said, "What gravestone is this that I see?"[3]

The gravestone was the key that would unlock a mystery ages in the making.

Jeroboam's Altar

Three centuries before Josiah came to Beth El, another king went there, Jeroboam. Jeroboam had led the rebellion that split the kingdom of David, and formed the northern kingdom known alternately as Israel and Samaria.

In fear that his subjects would journey to Jerusalem in the southern kingdom of Judah to worship God, he set up two sanctuaries of worship, each with an idol, a golden calf, and each with an altar on which he decreed that his people should offer sacrifices. The one, he erected along the northern border in the land of Dan, and the other, along his southern border at Beth El. They were the shrines of national apostasy.

Jeroboam was standing beside the altar at Beth El about to offer incense on it when a man of God from the kingdom of Judah appeared with a prophecy. It was a word for the apostate king and his nation but directed at the altar.

A Prophecy for an Altar

Then he cried out against the altar by the word of the LORD, and said, "O altar, altar! Thus says the LORD: 'Behold, a child, Josiah by name, shall be born to the house of David; and on you he shall sacrifice the priests of the high places who burn incense on you, and men's bones shall be burned on you.'"[4]

The prophecy spoke of an event that would take place three hundred years into the future. It revealed the name of the one who would fulfill it ages before that one was given his name or conceived in his mother's womb. And it came with a sign:

> And he gave a sign the same day, saying, "This is the sign which the LORD has spoken: Surely the altar shall split apart, and the ashes on it shall be poured out."[5]

Josiah's Foreshadow

The king ordered the prophet's arrest. But as he did, his hand suddenly withered and the sign spoken of in the prophecy was manifested:

> The altar also was split apart, and the ashes poured out from the altar, according to the sign which the man of God had given by the word of the LORD.[6]

The sign of the broken altar was the sign given to mark the very first mention of the man who would be known as Josiah. It would symbolize his mission of cleansing the land of idols, of turning his nation back to God, and breaking down the altars of the gods. So the broken altar appeared as the sign of Josiah ages before he was born.

Those alive at the time of the prophecy's giving would be long gone at the time of its fulfillment. And the one who fulfilled it had no idea of its existence. Its remembrance was kept alive by the people of Beth El to be revealed on that day:

> So the men of the city told him, "It is the tomb of the man of God who came from Judah and proclaimed these things which you have done against the altar of Bethel."[7]

And that was when it all came together for Josiah, the fulfillment of his calling, the purpose of his existence, and the mystery of his life. Everything in his life was leading up to that place, that event, and that moment. And now, for the first time, he could see it.

What does it reveal to us?

The Appointed Destiny

There was an appointed destiny to Josiah's life. It was there ages before his birth. The fact that he lived in an age of apostasy and a civilization of god-lessness did not in any way lessen his calling or nullify his destiny. Rather, it made it possible.

> ### To each child of God and each generation of God's people there is a calling, a purpose, and an appointed destiny.
>
> ### It is for each generation to seek it and fulfill it.

In the Book of Psalms, David wrote:

> Your eyes saw my substance, being yet unformed. And in Your book they all were written, the days fashioned for me, when as yet there were none of them.[8]

Before he was born, all the days of David's life were written in God's book, his becoming a shepherd, a hero, a warrior, and a king. So too God spoke to the prophet Jeremiah and said,

> Before I formed you in the womb I knew you; Before you were born I sanctified you; I ordained you a prophet to the nations.[9]

So too the apostle Paul could write,

> But when it pleased God, who separated me from my mother's womb and called me through His grace...[10]

It is not only for them but for all of God's children. There is a calling, a purpose, and a destiny—for the famous and the obscure, the powerful and the weak, and those of every age and land.

Josiah, Jeremiah, and Paul each lived in an age of evil, apostasy, or persecution. And yet none of those things stopped the purposes of God from coming to pass in their lives. So too for the believer who lives in a culture and age at war with God's purposes. Nothing will stop their calling or their appointed destiny from coming to pass—as long as they don't stop in following God's will.

The Josiah Stratagem

Josiah only knew of his destiny when it was revealed at Beth El. How then did he know to go to that exact place at that exact time? He simply followed the will of God.

It began with the temple's restoration and the discovery of the Book of the Law. It was that which impelled him to bring his nation back to God. In other words, he sought to obey God's will as revealed in Scripture. That included turning away from the gods, repenting from idolatry, and overturning the altars. By simply obeying the will of God he knew, it would lead him into the will of God he did not know—and, specifically, to Beth El. It was by that alone, he would be directed to the fulfillment of the prophecy given three centuries before his birth.

In God, the revealed leads to the unrevealed.

As the righteous follow
the revealed will of God,
it will lead them
into the unrevealed
will of God
and to the revealing
of their appointed destiny.

How does a child of God or a generation of believers know the destiny to which they are called? Josiah holds the answer. They must simply follow the will of God already revealed to them as given in the Scriptures. By following the revealed will, they will be led into the unrevealed.

The will of God as revealed in the Scriptures would lead one generation of believers to end the practice of infanticide. It would lead another to abolish slavery. It would lead still another to stand against the killing of the unborn. It would lead all generations of believers to share the Gospel and to bring as many people as possible to salvation. The will of God as revealed in the Scriptures will lead each child of God and each generation of believer to their exact and appointed destiny.

The Mountaintop Principle

Beth El was situated on the mountains of Samaria. In order to go there, Josiah had to ascend. And there on the pinnacle, he would come into his destiny. In Josiah's journey to Beth El is contained a crucial principle and key into entering one's destiny.

> The most important direction
> in the lives and callings of God's people is up.
>
> It is the upward path that brings every road,
> pathway, and footstep into perfect convergence
> in the exact place and at the exact time.

If one is standing at the bottom of a mountain to begin a journey to its peak, and one has to choose between a multitude of mountain paths by which to get there, which one does one take? The answer is, in the end, it doesn't matter. All one has to do is continually choose the higher step and ground—the upward path. And no matter where one starts from, one will end up on the pinnacle.

So it is with one's calling. One does not need to know exactly what it is or which of a multitude of paths and steps one must take to get there. All one has to do is to go continually higher, to choose the step of God's highest will—upward. And in the end one will be brought to the pinnacle of a mountaintop. One's footsteps will converge at the very center of God's perfect will and destiny. It is true for every child of God and for every generation of His people.

The Invisible Hand

Though Josiah's decisions and acts were central in the fulfillment of the prophecy concerning his life, there was no way he could have brought it about by his own efforts alone. The fulfillment required the orchestration and coalescence of countless events. Many of those events were beyond his control. Many did not even directly involve him. And none of them took place in the awareness of what had been foretold. It was the hand of God that moved all things to their appointed end.

God is sovereign over all events and all things.
His invisible hand will guide every action,
reaction, and interaction,
every event and moment,
into the outworking of His purposes.

And He will work all things,
the good and the bad,
together for the good
of those who follow Him.

The righteous must trust in His sovereignty
and rest in the workings of His hand
to fulfill His purposes in their lives.

The purposes of God do come about through the actions of the righteous. But they also come about apart from them. Inasmuch as they are able, the righteous must seek to fulfill His purposes. Inasmuch as they are not able, they must trust in His power to do so. In days of evil, when it seems as if everything is out of their control and moving against the purposes of God, they must all the more trust in His power to bring them to pass.

Each to One's Age

Josiah's life was appointed for his age. And his age was appointed for his life. In other words, the age of apostasy into which he was born required his life. And his life of righteousness was given as an answer to his age.

The children of God are appointed
for the age into which they were born.

And the age into which they were born
is appointed to them.

Each is to live his or her life
as an answer to that age.

Moses was born into an Egypt that worshipped idols, oppressed God's people, and sought to end his life in infancy. Elijah was born into an age where the prophets of God were hunted down and where he would be branded an enemy of the state. Jeremiah was born into an apostate kingdom that would imprison him, Esther was born into an empire that would order the destruction of her people. Paul was born into a pagan empire that would persecute and imprison him.

But all these—Moses, Elijah, Jeremiah, Esther, and Paul—were appointed for the ages in which they were born. Their ages required them.

So the children of God are not only born but appointed for the age of their birth. The timing of their births is not a matter of chance or accident but of destiny. And if they are born into a brazenly godless, apostate, or anti-Christian age, they are not out of place. They are not to fear their age or be intimidated by it. They were born for it. Their age requires them. As it was said of Esther, so too of them, they came to their position "for such a time as this."[11]

The children of God must live their lives as an answer to the ages in which they were born. And their lives must manifest to their age Him who is the answer to all ages.

One

Why was Josiah's life so greatly used of God? The answer is in the account. It is written that Josiah "turned to the LORD with all his heart, with all his soul, and with all his might."[12] It was Josiah's single-minded, focused, and total commitment to God and His will that enabled him to live a life of greatness, to accomplish that which others could not, to alter the history of his nation.

One person, wholly consecrated to God,
can change the course of a nation.

One people, wholly consecrated to God,
can change the course of the world.

The children of God must seek
to become that generation.

The child of God must seek
to become that one.

The Scriptures are filled with accounts of individuals who changed the courses of nations, even civilizations. They had this in common: they turned to God with all their heart and lived lives wholly consecrated to His will and purposes.

One such person is more powerful than the many. One such people is more powerful than the world. One prophet Elijah was more powerful than the entire kingdom of Ahab and Jezebel. One apostle Paul was more powerful than the entire Roman Empire. And twelve unlikely disciples were more powerful than the world.

The same book that speaks of Josiah's consecration to God says this:

> ...the eyes of the LORD move to and fro throughout the earth that He may strongly support those whose heart is completely His.[13]

Those who are wholly given to the will of God will manifest His power. They are the ones who will move mountains, part seas, overturn kingdoms, and change history.

We are the generation of the broken altar,
the sign of Josiah.

If we will each commit to live as he lived,
to seek God as he sought God
and to become as he became,
a totally consecrated vessel
for God's purposes and glory,
then God will greatly manifest His power.

For there is no limit and no end
to what God will do
through the one
whose heart is completely His.

We must become that generation.

We must each become that one.

THE LAST MYSTERY

Chapter 54

THE LAST MYSTERY

Return to the Island

We began on an island of mysteries. What we found there, the first of all mysteries, the Jubilee, opened the door to all the others. These, in turn, led us to the manifesto, a guide for the present hour, the days to come, and the end times. The manifesto and guide will now lead us back to the island for one last revelation. It is, likewise, for the end times and one that will serve as the last word and the sealing of the guide.

We now return to the island where it all began—and to that very first day on which the Jubilee was ushered in. It was on that same day that something else happened. The Jubilee was inaugurated in the morning. But it was that night that something else began. Word of it would spread across the island and be told and retold over and over again.

If someone were to tell me what I am now about to relay, I don't know that I would have believed them unless I knew them well enough not to doubt their veracity. But I was there to see it with my own eyes, as were many others.

The Night of Joel

It was the evening of the first day of the monthlong Cuban Jubilee. Earlier, in the morning, the inaugural event, the first mass gathering, was held in the city of Moa. I had heralded it with the sounding of the shofar to a passage of Scripture proclaimed from the stage.

The Scripture was from the Book of Joel—the same that was appointed to be read on Shabbat Shuvah and that I would recite on the National Mall years later on the day of The Return. It called for a sacred assembly of prayer and repentance and promised blessing and the breaking of a curse. So The Return opened up with its reciting and would lead to blessing, the breaking of a curse.

But there was more to the Scripture. And that night would reveal it. Another gathering, linked to the first, would convene in Moa that night. It would likewise take place outdoors but under the night skies. I was asked to go there and give them a message. When I prayed about what to speak, I was led to the Book of Joel. I would give a message based on Joel and then call for

261

prayer and intercession for Cuba. Then, as in the Book of Joel and the Jubilee, I would sound the shofar and pray for the power of God to be released.

The Swarming Plague

I arrived with my team at the site of the event as the sky began to darken into night. In my hand was a Bible, a binder with my notes, a shofar, and the Hebrew prayer shawl. Soon after I arrived, one of our translators told me that the people were saying to each other, "Look, Moses is here!" They had apparently never before seen a bearded Jewish man with a prayer shawl.

The Book of Joel opens up with a plague of insects, the swarming and devouring locusts. It was the sign of the curse that darkened a land that had turned from God. I had planned to open my message speaking about the plague of insects and the curse that darkened the land of Cuba. But before I could, something happened.

"Has Anything Like This Happened?"

Suddenly, a massive swarm descended on the event, a plague of insects. I had never seen anything like it, nor had any of my team. Nor, apparently, had the people at the event, as they were all panicking. But then the Book of Joel opens up to that same effect:

> Has anything like this happened in your days, or even in the days of your fathers? Tell your children … and their children another generation.[1]

Insects were everywhere, filling the sky, raining down on the people, creating a dark haze in the air. The event came to a sudden stop. Many in the crowd were trying to ward off the swarm; others were crying out in prayer; others were on their knees and faces.

One of the plagues that Moses called down on Egypt was that of locusts. Those who had joked, "Moses is here!" were no longer joking. Of course, I was as amazed as anyone. But I had come there to speak on the Book of Joel, and I knew that both the book and my message opened up with a swarm of insects. So too now did the event. I reached for my Bible and opened it up to Joel and to the chapter that speaks of the different locusts that will come on the land:

> What the devouring locust has left, the swarming locust has eaten; what the swarming locust has left, the young locust has eaten; and what the young locust has left, the destroying locust has eaten.[2]

As I opened to that page, insects from the swarm began descending from the sky and landing on that page—and on the verses that spoke of the swarming insects.

"Day of Darkness"

I had not yet shared a word of my message, but God was manifesting it before our eyes. After the plague, the Book of Joel goes on to speak of "a day of darkness."

> A day of darkness and gloominess, a day of clouds and thick darkness.[3]

After speaking of the plague, I had planned to share of the darkness from the book and on the land of Cuba. The plague had manifested in real time and space. Now it was time for the darkness.

Suddenly everything went dark. The electricity powering the lights that illumined the event suddenly cut off. Everyone was still interceding and crying out over the plague. Now they did so in the dark.

Light in the Dark

The Book of Joel then moves on to speak of the answer, the hope, the way to redemption, the call to the nation to return to God in prayer and repentance, and the promise of restoration. It was then that a sign of hope appeared.

It was a light shining in the darkness. But it was not a normal light. It was a ball of radiance moving back and forth over the multitude. Everyone's eyes were fixed on it. It took some time before we realized what it was—it was some sort of luminescent insect, but with a light that appeared to be at least two inches in diameter and even more dramatic against the blackness of the night. It was unlike any insect we had ever seen and apparently much more anointed.

An Incandescent Hand

At that point, I could not help but laugh. But in the midst of my laughing I spread out my hands in prayer and worship, seeking some discernment as to what was happening. As I prayed, I felt something fall into my hands.

It was the light, the glowing ball of light that had hovered over the people. Of all the places it could have fallen that night, it fell into my hand. Beyond that, it had apparently been stunned in the midst of its flight and landed in my hands upside down. The end result was that my hand was now radiating with light—and all eyes were fixed on it.

In the Book of Joel, it is written that the sons of Aaron, the priests, were to minister in the nation's repentance, in prayer and intercession. I was a son of Aaron, and I had planned to minister in prayer and intercession on behalf of the nation that night. The people who had assembled had no idea what I was doing there and certainly no idea that the message I had planned to give them concerned a swarm of insects, a time of darkness, and a hope. But after that light landed in my hand, they were all ears.

The Intercession

And then the lights returned. The swarm of insects had vanished. They called me up to the stage to speak. At that point, had I given them a lecture on the joys of tomato farming, they would have repented. I began speaking to them from The Book of Joel, of the cursed land, the plague of insects, the darkness, and the light of hope. Everything I shared they had just witnessed with their eyes.

Then I called for prayer and intercession on behalf of their nation. And so they prayed and interceded for Cuba. I was leading them in prayer over the sound system, but they didn't need much leading. Their prayers and intercessions were accompanied by tears of repentance as they cried out to God for their land—just as in the Book of Joel.

"Blow the Trumpet"

Then, as it had been sounded in the Book of Joel and in the Jubilee, I prepared to sound the shofar. I asked them to pray for God's blessings to pour out from heaven upon the land. I declared the coming of those blessings, then sounded the first blast of the shofar.

I was about to move on to the second blast when my translator stopped me, touching my shoulder to get my attention. "Did you feel it?" he asked. "What?" I replied. I had sounded the shofar with the prayer shawl over my head. It stopped me from knowing. I took it off. That's when I felt it.

"He Will Cause the Rain to Come Down"

It was the next event in the Book of Joel. The promise of Joel is that after the nation turns back to God in prayer and repentance, God will turn their curse into blessing and will restore them. He will open up the heavens,

and He will cause the rain to come down for you.[4]

Rain was crucial to Israel. Without it the blessings of God would disappear. Rain was life and revival. When I prayed for God's blessings on the

The Last Mystery

land and sounded the shofar, the heavens opened it. And the blessing promised in the Book of Joel came down upon the land—rain.

They felt the raindrops sprinkling their heads and shoulders, and a wave of revival came over them. They began crying out to God all the more for His blessings on their land.

I was then led to speak of God's power, His outpouring, and revival—that these would come to them in the same way—first as a sprinkling, then as a rain, then as a downpour, and then as a deluge.

I finished ministering and stepped down from the stage. The people resumed their worshipping. But the Book of Joel wasn't finished.

The Latter Rain

It speaks not of just one rain—but of another.

> And He will cause the rain to come down for you—the former rain, *and the latter rain*...[5]

The one rain came in the spring, the other in the autumn. One was called the *moreh*, and the other, the *malkosh*. So on the night of Joel, the first rain had come. Now it was time for the latter rain—and then it came.

It came, as did the first, gently. In the midst of their worshipping, a gentle sprinkling of rain came upon the people. But this one did not stay a sprinkling. What I had just told them of God's power and blessings now manifested in the rain. About a minute after it began, it had become a light pouring. About a minute later, it had become a full rain. About a minute later, it was a downpour. And about a minute after that, it was a deluge.

One would have expected the people to have run for cover and the event to have ended—but they didn't, and it didn't. Because of everything they had witnessed that night, they didn't run for cover, and they didn't stop worshipping. Instead, something else happened.

"I Will Pour Out My Spirit"

In the Book of Joel, after God promises the outpouring of rain, He promises to pour out something else.

> And it shall come to pass afterward that I will pour out My Spirit on all flesh; Your sons and your daughters shall prophesy.[6]

And that is what happened. As the deluge of rain poured down upon the people, there was an explosion—an explosion of worship, of praise, of the

Spirit of God. Whatever their worship was before, it was nothing compared to what now happened in the midst of the downpour.

They were singing, praising, worshipping, dancing, shouting, celebrating, dripping wet, and swept up in the joy of God's presence. The outpouring of rain is given in the Scriptures as a symbol of the outpouring of God's Spirit. That night, one could not tell where the one outpouring ended and the other began. The two downpours became as one.

It is written in Joel that when the Spirit is poured out, it will be poured out on the old and young together. That night, old men and women, young boys and girls were all swept up together, in the joy of that outpouring of the rain and the Spirit.

The Unforgettable Night

It was about midnight when we left. But the people were still there worshipping in the middle of the downpour. Neither the rain nor the Spirit showed any sign of abating.

Word of what happened that evening would spread across the region and the island. It would be known as the Unforgettable Night. It was the night that ushered in the month of Jubilee and revival for the believers of Cuba. The rains of God's Spirit would go on long after the celebration had officially ended.

And it all began with the locusts, the darkness, a light, a word, a prayer, a shofar, a rain, a second rain, and the outpouring of God's Spirit. It all began with a vision of Joel in the heavens and earth. And even that had a parallel in the book itself. After the words "I will pour out My Spirit," it is written, "and I will show wonders in the heavens and in the earth."[7]

———

I have long pondered the events of the Unforgettable Night. It was a manifestation of the Book of Joel in real time, the same book from which the apostle Peter quoted on the Day of Pentecost, when the Spirit was poured out on the first believers.

As Joel speaks of two rains, the two rains of the Hebrew year, and as rain is a biblical symbol of the outpouring of the Spirit, so the Bible speaks of two outpourings of the Spirit. The first took place on the Day of Pentecost, as was summed with the disciple's quoting of Joel. But the second is yet to come. The first was appointed for the beginning of the age, the second, for its end.

———

It is this last outpouring as prophesied in the Book of Joel that will yield the last words of this book, words for the righteous, words for God's children, words for the end times, and words for all times and ages of darkness. These now are for the encouragement, the strengthening, the overcoming, and the prevailing of all who would walk in the ways of God.

Never

The fact that biblical end-time prophecy speaks of evil on one hand and the outpouring of God's Spirit on the other is a word in and of itself—God is never finished. And so, the people of God are never finished. So they must always take hope. In God there is always hope. Josiah lived in the midst of a civilization under judgment. Yet he still did everything in his power to save his people. Josiah was moved by hope, persevered by hope, and, by hope, never gave up.

So the righteous of the present hour and of the end times are living in a civilization under judgment. But God is never finished. His purposes are never voided even in days of judgment. His power of redemption will still be manifested.

The first believers lived in the midst of persecution and against all odds. But they were people of hope. They never gave up. And so too those who will prevail in the present hour and the end times, even in the darkest hour, must be committed to hope. They must never give up. For in God the darkest of hours always leads to light.

God is never finished.
He is never out of plans.
He is never not able.

Even in times of judgment,
even in the most hopeless of times
and darkest of ages,
He still has a purpose and a way.

Therefore, no matter what happens
in the world,
His people must always take hope,
always press on,
and never give up.

The Great

According to biblical prophecy, the end times will be marked by the increase of evil but also by the outpouring of God's Spirit. Thus it will be marked both by great good and great evil. Thus the end-time believers must aspire not only to goodness—but to greatness. They must seek to become great in faith, great in love, great in righteousness, great in prayer, great in purity, great in worship, great in zeal, great in hope, great in joy, great in goodness, great in God.

> The end times will not only
> be marked by great evil
> but great good.
>
> As evil moves from bad to worse,
> the righteous must move from goodness
> to greatness.

The Spirit and the Outpouring

When the Spirit fell on the Day of the Pentecost, it was for a purpose. It was vital; it was essential. The Spirit would give power to that first generation of believers. By the power of that outpouring, they would overcome all opposition, all obstacles, and all persecution to fulfill the Great Commission to proclaim the Gospel to all nations.

So if there is to be a second outpouring of the Spirit appointed for the end times, it must also be for a purpose, just as essential and just as vital. The challenges facing the believer at the end of the age will be even greater than that which faced those at the beginning. Thus they will need the power of the Spirit all the more so.

The people of God must pray for that outpouring. And they must remember that the outpouring spoken of in Joel is ushered in through prayer and repentance. And the people of God must all the more seek that power for their own lives. They must live and move by the Spirit. By the power of His Spirit, they will stand as they never otherwise could stand, overcome what they could never otherwise overcome, and live and do the life and works they never otherwise could live or do.

> If the Spirit and power of God
> are to be poured out in the end times,

then it is because the end times
will require it.

There is no force more powerful
than the Spirit of God.

By the Spirit the righteous are enabled
to overcome all powers
and the world.

They must pray for its outpouring
upon the world
and upon their own lives.

They must seek to live by the Spirit,
move by the Spirit,
overcome by the Spirit,
and do all things by the Spirit.

Apart from the Spirit
they cannot succeed.
But by the Spirit,
they cannot fail.

It Will Have Begun

As the broken altar is linked to revival, so is the outpouring of God's Spirit. And so if there is to be an end-time outpouring, there must also be an end-time revival. The people of God must all the more fervently pray for, believe for, work for, and spread the Gospel of salvation for revival. And they must do something else as well. Though alive in the Spirit, they must seek to become more alive. They must seek first their own revival. They must not only pray for revival—they must choose revival. They must choose to live in revival.

Where the Spirit is,
there is revival.
If the Spirit is given in the end times,
then revival must also come.

The people of God must never lose hope in that.
They must never give up praying for revival.
And they must not only pray for revival;
they must actually begin
living in revival.

If they do that,
revival will have begun.

As in the Book of Acts

The Spirit of God ushers in the Book of Acts. And while it is commonly called the Acts of the Apostles, it has also been known as the Acts of the Spirit. In either case, it is the outpouring of the Spirit that produces the acts of the apostles—the Book of Acts.

It is not only that the church and every believer must now return to their first states, to the Book of Acts. But the end-time outpouring is even more than that. It is the will and power of God to actually *cause* that state to come to pass. The first outpouring gave birth the Book of Acts. To what will the second give birth? If there is to be another outpouring, then there must be a return to Acts, to its power, to its people, and to its miracles.

The end-time believer must seek to rise to the mantle of those in the Book of Acts.

The first outpouring of the Spirit
produced the Book of Acts.

If there is to be a second outpouring,
then it is for the purpose of producing
an effect comparable to that of Acts.

Then it must be for the purpose
of imparting at the end of the age
the power of the beginning.

And thus the end-time believer
is to be given the power to live as did
the first disciples and messengers
of the Gospel in the Book of Acts.

The end-time believer is therefore to rise
to the mantle of the first believers,
to live as they lived,
to stand as they stood,
to believe as they believed,
and to overcome
as they overcame the world.

The Impossible

It is impossible for a universe to come forth out of nothing, for a sea to part in two, for a man to shut up the heavens, for a virgin to conceive a child, for the dead to rise to life, for a weak and broken band of disciples to change the world, and for a nation that has been dead for two thousand years to come back to life. But God is the God of the impossible. And those who follow Him, especially in times of adversity and impossibilities, must live against the odds, above the laws of the natural, and by the power of the impossible.

With God, all things are possible
and nothing will be impossible.

The outpouring of the Spirit is a sign of that.

The Spirit imparts the power to do
what is impossible to be done.

The end times will present the people of God
with impossibilities.
But the Spirit of God will give them
the power to do the impossible.

Therefore, they must commit
to believing the impossible,
praying for the impossible,
living in the impossible,
moving in the impossible,
doing the impossible,

and overcoming
in the impossible.

The Prevailing

God is called the Almighty—the all-powerful. There is no greater power. God is also good. Therefore, the good will, in the end, prevail.

Evil, therefore, cannot endure or prevail in the end—but only for a moment. It is in that moment when evil appears to thrive and reign and prevail and when the purposes of God do not, it is then that the righteous must stand strong and hold on to the fact that they surely will.

It is for the moment when they appear to be on the losing side that they hold fast and in confidence that they are in reality on the winning side and on the right side of eternity. They live not for the moment—but to the eternal.

When Moses stood before Pharaoh, he did not look as if he was on the winning side—but he was. When Elijah stood before King Ahab, he did not look as if he was on the winning side—but he was. When Jeremiah stood in his prison cell, he did not look as if he was on the winning side—but he was. And when Paul stood in chains and on trial for his life, he did not look as if he was on the winning side—but he was.

So it has been for the righteous of God in every age. And so it will be all the more so for the righteous in the end times. And so they must all the more stand strong, confident, bold, and assured in knowing that the good will prevail and with God they are, without question, on the winning side.

In an age at war against the purposes of God,
His people will appear as weak,
as the few and the hopeless.

But it is an illusion.

The will of God will, in the end, prevail.

The purposes of God will come to pass.

The Word of God will be fulfilled.

The light of God will overcome the darkness.

The love of God will overcome all things.
And the one who lives in these things
will prevail.

The people of God must hold to that truth
and live in that confidence
that they were on the winning side—
because they are.

In the End

When God created the world,
first came night and then the day.

So too the purposes of God lead always
from darkness to light, from sorrow to joy,
from death to life.

So the night of the end times
will lead to the dawn of heaven.

And the path of the righteous will lead to glory.

The children of God go
from glory to glory
and then to a glory
in which all their sacrifices
will be redeemed
and all their tears wiped away
and all their hardships
and sorrows
transformed into joy.

And all the good
they upheld,
and the darkness
they resisted,
and the love
they manifested,

and the blessings
they brought forth,
and the warfare
they waged,
and the stands
they held to,
and the truth they
stayed faithful to,
and the prices
they paid

will all then be illuminated
in the radiance of heaven
and then appear as what,
in reality, they always were,
the good, the beautiful,
and the glorious,

when the night
gives way to morning
and the darkness
to the breaking of dawn,

when the righteous
lay down their armor

and the child of God
at last comes home.

NOTES

Chapter 3

1. Leviticus 25:8–10.
2. Leviticus 25:10.
3. Leviticus 25:10.
4. Leviticus 25:11.
5. Leviticus 25:28.
6. "The Liberty Bell," National Park Service, accessed July 2, 2023, https://www.nps.gov/inde/learn/historyculture/stories-libertybell.htm.
7. Leviticus 25:39, 54.

Chapter 4

1. Joel 2:1.

Chapter 5

1. Leviticus 25:10.
2. Leviticus 25:10, author's translation.
3. Leviticus 25:10, author's translation.

Chapter 7

1. Leviticus 25:8.
2. Leviticus 25:8.

Chapter 9

1. 1 Kings 11.5.
2. Jeremiah 32:35.
3. Jeremiah 19:1–2.
4. Jeremiah 19:4, MEV.
5. Jeremiah 7:32, author's translation.
6. Jeremiah 21:6, NASB, emphasis added.

Chapter 10

1. Abraham Lincoln, "Second Inaugural Address of Abraham Lincoln" (speech, Washington, DC, March 4, 1865), https://avalon.law.yale.edu/19th_century/lincoln2.asp.
2. "Data Center: Number of Abortions, Average Annual No. of Abortions Among Women Aged 15–49, 2015-2019," Guttmacher Institute, accessed June 2, 2023, https://data.guttmacher.org/countries/table?country=AF+AL+DZ+AO+AR+AM+AU+AZ+BD+BB+BY+BE+BZ+BJ+BT+BO+BA+BW+BR+BG+BF+BI+CV+KH+CM+CA+CF+TD+CL+CN+CO+KM+CG+CR+CI+HR+CU+CZ+KP+CD+DK+DJ+DO+EC+EG+SV+GQ+ER+EE+SZ

+ET+FJ+FI+FR+GF+GA+GM+GE+DE+GH+GR+GD+GP+GT+GN+GW
+GY+HT+HN+HK+HU+IS+IN+ID+IR+IQ+IT+JM+JP+JO+KZ+KE+KI+
KG+LA+LV+LB+LS+LR+LY+LT+MG+MW+MY+MV+ML+MQ+MR+M
U+YT+MX+FM+MN+ME+MA+MZ+MM+NA+NP+NL+NZ+NI+NE+N
G+MK+NO+PK+PA+PG+PY+PE+PH+PL+PT+PR+MD+KR+RE+RO+RU
+RW+LC+VC+WS+ST+SN+RS+SL+SG+SK+SI+SB+SO+ZA+SS+ES+LK+
PS+SD+SR+SE+CH+SY+TJ+TH+TL+TG+TO+TT+TN+TR+TM+UG+UA
+GB+TZ+US+UY+UZ+VU+VE+VN+YE+ZM+ZW&topics=406&dataset
=data; "Abortion Worldwide Report: 100 Countries, 1 Century, 1 Billion
Babies," Family Research Council, January 25, 2017, https://www.frc.org/
events/abortion-worldwide-report-100-countries-1-century-1-billion-
babies.

3. Marie Gallagher, "As 45th Anniversary Approaches, Roe v. Wade Is
Losing Steam and Support," National Right to Life News, January 2018,
https://www.nrlc.org/uploads/NRLNews/Jan2018NRLNews.pdf.

4. "WHO Coronavirus (COVID-19) Dashboard: Global Situation," WHO,
accessed June 2, 2023, https://covid19.who.int/; " WHO Coronavirus
(COVID-19) Dashboard: United States of America Situation," WHO,
accessed June 2, 2023, https://covid19.who.int/region/amro/country/us.

Chapter 11

1. Alan F. Guttmacher, "The Genesis of Liberalized Abortion in New York:
A Personal Insight," *Case Western Law Review* 23, no. 4 (1972): 764,
https://scholarlycommons.law.case.edu/cgi/viewcontent.cgi?article=2899
&context=caselrev.

2. Peter Robison, Dina Bass, and Robert Langreth, "Seattle's Patient
Zero Spread Coronavirus Despite Ebola-Style Lockdown," Bloomberg,
updated March 9, 2020, https://www.bloomberg.com/news/
features/2020-03-09/how-coronavirus-spread-from-patient-zero-in-
seattle.

Chapter 12

1. Exodus 13:12.

Chapter 13

1. "WHO Coronavirus (COVID-19) Dashboard: United States of America
Situation," WHO.

2. "WHO Director-General's Opening Remarks at the Media Briefing on
COVID-19—11 March 2020," WHO, March 11, 2020, https://www.who.
int/director-general/speeches/detail/who-director-general-s-opening-
remarks-at-the-media-briefing-on-covid-19---11-march-2020.

3. John Burns, quoted in A. A. Smyser, "Hawaii's Abortion Law 30 Years Old," *Honolulu Star-Bulletin*, March 21, 2000, https://archives.starbulletin.com/2000/03/21/editorial/smyser.html.

4. Laurel Wamsley, "March 11, 2020: The Day Everything Changed," NPR, March 11, 2021, https://www.npr.org/2021/03/11/975663437/march-11-2020-the-day-everything-changed.

5. Joey Schneider, "TIMELINE: March 11, 2020—What Happened When COVID-19 Was Declared a Pandemic Two Years Ago," KY3, updated March 11, 2022, https://www.ky3.com/2022/03/11/timeline-march-11-2020-what-happened-when-covid-19-was-declared-pandemic-two-years-ago/.

6. Danielle Abreu, "The Day Everything Changed: A Timeline of March 11, 2020," NBC San Diego, updated March 11, 2021, https://www.nbcsandiego.com/news/coronavirus/the-day-everything-changed-a-timeline-of-march-11-2020/2545558/.

7. "Tom Hanks, The NBA, and COVID's Day of Reckoning in the US: An Oral History," BuzzFeed News, March 11, 2021, https://www.buzzfeednews.com/article/buzzfeednews/march-11-covid-tom-hanks-nba-who.

8. Amanda Aguilar, "World Health Organization to Vote on Ending COVID-19 Pandemic Declaration," ABC30, January 27, 2023, https://abc30.com/coronavirus-covid-19-pandemic-declaration-world-health-organization/12742403/.

9. "WATCH: 'Things Will Get Worse' in COVID-19 Outbreak, Fauci Testifies," PBS, updated March 11, 2020, https://www.pbs.org/newshour/health/watch-live-nih-cdc-officials-testify-on-u-s-coronavirus-response.

10. Catherine Thorbecke, "Dow Plunges Into Bear Market After Selloff From Coronavirus Fears," ABC News, March 11, 2020, https://abcnews.go.com/Business/dow-plunges-bear-market-selloff-coronavirus-fears/story?id=69529962.

11. Tim Reynolds, "March 11, 2020: The Night Sports, as We Knew Them, Ended," AP News, March 11, 2021, https://apnews.com/article/march-11-2020-sports-coronavirus-1-year-1294b56341d5605c9ce3f9cc68fcc4fe.

Chapter 14

1. Jeremiah 19:4–6.

2. Bobby Allyn and Joe Neel, "U.S. Surpasses China in Cases of Coronavirus," NPR, March 26, 2020, https://www.npr.org/sections/coronavirus-live-updates/2020/03/26/822248693/u-s-surpasses-china-in-cases-of-coronavirus; PIX11 Web Team, "Latest Coronavirus Updates in New York: Thursday March 26, 2020," PIX 11, updated March 26, 2020,

https://pix11.com/news/coronavirus/latest-coronavirus-updates-in-new-york-thursday-march-26-2020/.

3. Yelena Dzhanova, "New York State Now Has More Coronavirus Cases Than Any Country Outside the US," CNBC, updated April 10, 2020, https://www.cnbc.com/2020/04/10/new-york-state-now-has-more-coronavirus-cases-than-any-country-outside-the-us.html.

Chapter 15

1. Wm. Robert Johnston, "Historical Abortion Statistics, United States," Johnston's Archive, updated April 26, 2023, https://www.johnstonsarchive.net/policy/abortion/ab-unitedstates.html; Wm. Robert Johnston, "Historical Abortion Statistics, New York (USA)," Johnston's Archive, updated January 15, 2023, https://www.johnstonsarchive.net/policy/abortion/usa/ab-usa-NY.html.

2. Benedict Carey and James Glanz, "Travel From New York City Seeded Wave of U.S. Outbreaks," *New York Times*, updated May 7, 2021, https://www.nytimes.com/2020/05/07/us/new-york-city-coronavirus-outbreak.html.

3. Carey and Glanz, "Travel From New York City Seeded Wave of U.S. Outbreaks."

4. Carey and Glanz, "Travel From New York City Seeded Wave of U.S. Outbreaks."

5. Carey and Glanz, "Travel From New York City Seeded Wave of U.S. Outbreaks."

6. Carey and Glanz, "Travel From New York City Seeded Wave of U.S. Outbreaks."

7. Benedict Carey and James Glanz, "Travel From New York City Seeded Wave of U.S. Outbreaks," *New York Times*, updated May 7, 2021, https://www.nytimes.com/2020/05/07/us/new-york-city-coronavirus-outbreak.html#:~:text=The%20research%20indicates%20that%20a,away%20as%20the%20West%20Coast.

Chapter 16

1. Johnston, "Historical Abortion Statistics, United States."

2. "Excess Deaths Associated With COVID-19: National and State Estimates of Excess Deaths," CDC, accessed February 15, 2023, https://www.cdc.gov/nchs/nvss/vsrr/covid19/excess_deaths.htm#data-tables.

3. "Excess Deaths Associated With COVID-19," CDC.

4. "Tracking Covid-19 Excess Deaths Across Countries," *The Economist*, accessed June 4, 2023, https://www.economist.com/graphic-detail/coronavirus-excess-deaths-tracker.

Chapter 17

1. 1 Corinthians 10:11.

Chapter 18

1. 2 Kings 10:31.
2. 2 Kings 9:20, CSB, MSG

Chapter 19

1. 2 Kings 10:27–28.

Chapter 20

1. "Quotations," Architect of the Capitol, accessed June 5, 2023, https://www.aoc.gov/explore-capitol-campus/art/quotations.
2. "House of Representatives," *Congressional Record* 167, no. 1 (January 3, 2021), H1, https://www.congress.gov/117/crec/2021/01/03/CREC-2021-01-03-pt1-PgH1.pdf.
3. 2 Kings 10:25, author's translation.
4. "READ: Chuck Schumer's Statement to the Senate on the Storming of the Capitol," *U.S. News and World Report*, January 6, 2021, https://www.usnews.com/news/elections/articles/2021-01-06/read-chuck-schumers-statement-to-the-senate-on-the-storming-of-the-capitol, emphasis added.
5. "Durbin Speaks on Senate Floor About Violence at the U.S. Capitol & 2020 Election Certification," US Senate Committee on the Judiciary, January 8, 2021, https://www.judiciary.senate.gov/press/dem/releases/durbin-speaks-on-senate-floor-about-violence-at-the-us-capitol-and-2020-election-certification.
6. Elena Moore, "Pelosi Reconvenes the U.S. House: 'Our Purpose Will Be Accomplished,'" NPR, January 6, 2021, https://www.npr.org/sections/congress-electoral-college-tally-live-updates/2021/01/06/954244836/pelosi-reconvenes-the-u-s-house-our-purpose-will-be-accomplished.
7. Michael O'Connell, "80 Arrested for Civil Unrest at US Capitol and Around DC," Patch, January 8, 2021, https://patch.com/district-columbia/washingtondc/80-arrested-civil-unrest-us-capitol-around-dc.
8. 2 Kings 10:24, author's translation.

Chapter 21

1. 2 Kings 17:16–17.
2. 2 Kings 10:28, emphasis added.

Chapter 22

1. "Affidavit of Norma McCorvey," Civil Action No. 3-3690-B and 3-3691-C, June 11, 2003, https://thejusticefoundation.org/wp-content/uploads/2020/05/Norma_McCorvey_Affidavit.pdf.

Chapter 24

1. Esther 8:5.
2. Esther 8:8.
3. Esther 8:9.
4. "Special Prayer for the 23rd of Sivan," Atzmut, accessed June 6, 2023, https://www.atzmut.org/sivan23/.
5. "Special Prayer for the 23rd of Sivan," Atzmut.
6. Esther 3:13, CSB.
7. Esther 3:12.
8. Esther 8:9.
9. Esther 3:12.
10. Esther 8:9.
11. Esther 3:12.
12. Esther 8:9.
13. Esther 3:12.
14. Esther 8:10.
15. Esther 3:15.
16. Esther 8:10.

Chapter 25

1. "Sarah Weddington and Jay Floyd: Roe V. Wade Oral Arguments Before the USSC," American Rhetoric, December 13, 1971, https://www.americanrhetoric.com/speeches/roevwadeoralarguments.htm.
2. "Thomas E. Dobbs, State Health Officer of the Mississippi Department of Health, Et Al., Petitioners, V. Jackson Women's Health Organization, Et Al., Respondents," Supreme Court of the United States, December 1, 2021, https://www.supremecourt.gov/oral_arguments/argument_transcripts/2021/19-1392_4425.pdf.

Chapter 26

1. "WOMEN'S MARCH CALLS FOR A SUMMER OF RAGE AFTER SCOTUS DECISION TO OVERTURN ROE V. WADE," Women's March, accessed June 6, 2023, https://www.womensmarch.com/newsroom/womens-march-calls-for-a-summer-of-rage-after-scotus-decision-to-overturn.

Chapter 27

1. Leviticus 25:8, 10.

Chapter 29

1. Exodus 12:13, emphasis added.

Chapter 30

1. Leviticus 23:15–16.
2. John 20:22.
3. Acts 1:1, 3–4, emphasis added.
4. Matthew 3:11, emphasis added.
5. Exodus 19:18, emphasis added.

Chapter 31

1. Leviticus 23:24.
2. Rabbi Yitzchak Schwartz, "Part 3: Chapter 1, Verse 6 Commentary," Torah.org, accessed July 4, 2023, https://torah.org/learning/iyov-iyov3/?printversion=1&print-posts=print.
3. Psalm 82:1, isv.
4. Rosh Hashanah 17a:15, https://www.sefaria.org/Rosh_Hashanah.17a.15?lang=bi&with=Sheets&lang2=en.
5. Schwartz, "Part 3: Chapter 1, Verse 6 Commentary."
6. Schwartz, "Part 3: Chapter 1, Verse 6 Commentary."

Chapter 32

1. Exodus 1:22.
2. Exodus 2:3.

Chapter 35

1. Joel 2:12–13.
2. Joel 2:25.
3. Joel 2:15–16.
4. Jonathan Cahn, *The Harbinger* (Lake Mary, FL: FrontLine, 2011), 223, emphasis added.
5. Cahn, *The Harbinger*, 215, emphasis added.
6. Cahn, *The Harbinger*, 215, emphasis added.
7. 2 Chronicles 7:13–14, niv, emphasis added.

Chapter 36

1. in:ciite, "The Return Live Stream," Vimeo, July 6, 2022, https://vimeo.com/727437096.
2. in:ciite, "The Return Live Stream."

3. in:ciite, "The Return Live Stream."
4. in:ciite, "The Return Live Stream."
5. Psalm 18:13, author's translation.
6. in:ciite, "The Return Live Stream."
7. Hosea 14:1–2, author's translation, emphasis added.
8. Joel 2:15–16.

Chapter 38

1. in:ciite, "The Return Live Stream."
2. in:ciite, "The Return Live Stream."
3. in:ciite, "The Return Live Stream."
4. in:ciite, "The Return Live Stream."
5. Psalm 47:5, author's translation.
6. Adam Shaw, "Trump Announces Amy Coney Barrett as Nominee for Supreme Court Seat," Fox News, September 26, 2020, https://www.foxnews.com/politics/trump-amy-coney-barrett-supreme-court-pick.

Chapter 39

1. 1 Corinthians 15:52, kjv.
2. Numbers 10:1–10.

Chapter 40

1. See, for example, Remy Tumin, "Special Edition: Roe v. Wade Is Overturned," *New York Times*, updated June 26, 2022, https://www.nytimes.com/2022/06/24/briefing/roe-v-wade-abortion-supreme-court-guns.html.
2. Adam Liptak, "In 6-to-3 Ruling, Supreme Court Ends Nearly 50 Years of Abortion Rights," *New York Times*, updated November 2, 2022, https://www.nytimes.com/2022/06/24/us/roe-wade-overturned-supreme-court.html.
3. Liptak, "In 6-to-3 Ruling, Supreme Court Ends Nearly 50 Years of Abortion Rights."
4. Talia Lakritz, "The Supreme Court Overturned Roe v. Wade. Here's What That Means for Abortion Access in Your State," Insider, June 24, 2022, https://www.insider.com/roe-v-wade-overturned-states-ban-abortion-2022-6, emphasis added.
5. "Roe v. Wade," Center for Reproductive Rights, accessed June 7, 2023, https://reproductiverights.org/roe-v-wade/, emphasis added.
6. Devin Dwyer, "Supreme Court Overturns Roe v. Wade in Landmark Case on Abortion Rights," ABC News, June 24, 2022, https://abcnews.go.com/Politics/supreme-court-overturns-roe-wade-landmark-case-abortion/story?id=85160781, emphasis added.

7. Josh Gerstein et al., "Supreme Court Gives States Green Light to Ban Abortion, Overturning Roe," Politico, June 24, 2022, https://www.politico.com/news/2022/06/24/supreme-court-overturns-roe-v-wade-00042244, emphasis added.

8. Callie Patterson and Samuel Chamberlain, "Supreme Court Overturns Roe v. Wade, Leaves Issue up to States," *New York Post*, June 24, 2022, https://nypost.com/2022/06/24/supreme-court-overturns-roe-v-wade/, emphasis added.

9. "Roe v Wade: US Supreme Court Ends Constitutional Right to Abortion," BBC, June 24, 2022, https://www.bbc.com/news/world-us-canada-61928898, emphasis added.

10. Julie Rovner, "Supreme Court Overturns Roe in Landmark Abortion Ruling," *Hoptown Chronicle*, June 24, 2022, https://hoptownchronicle.org/supreme-court-overturns-roe-in-landmark-abortion-ruling/, emphasis added.

11. "Roe's 50th Year Undid Its Promise," *At Liberty* (podcast), January 19, 2023, https://www.aclu.org/podcast/the-50th-anniversary-of-roe-that-well-never-see, emphasis added.

12. Leviticus 25:8, 10.

13. "#WeCount Report," Society of Family Planning, October 28, 2022, https://doi.org/10.46621/UKAI6324.

Chapter 41

1. Haggai 1:4–6, 10.

2. Haggai 1:15, emphasis added.

Chapter 43

1. Psalm 106:35–38, NASB.

2. Psalm 106:28–30, emphasis added.

3. "Daily Updates of Totals by Week and State: Provisional Death Counts for Coronavirus Disease 2019 (COVID-19)," CDC, accessed June 7, 2023, https://www.cdc.gov/nchs/nvss/vsrr/COVID19/index.htm.

4. "United States of America Situation," WHO.

5. "United States of America Situation," WHO.

Chapter 44

1. "Daily Updates of Totals by Week and State," CDC.

2. "Daily Updates of Totals by Week and State," CDC.

Chapter 45

1. Exodus 34:13.

Chapter 46

1. 2 Chronicles 34:3.
2. 2 Kings 23:2.
3. 2 Kings 23:3.
4. 2 Kings 23:4.
5. 2 Kings 23:8.
6. 2 Chronicles 34:4.
7. 2 Kings 23:19.
8. 2 Kings 23:12.
9. 2 Kings 23:13.
10. 2 Kings 23:10.

I: Age of Apostasy

1. 2 Kings 23:13.
2. "A Hymn to Inana for Išme-Dagan (Išme-Dagan K), 19–31," Electronic Text Corpus of Sumerian Literature, accessed June 8, 2023, https://etcsl. orinst.ox.ac.uk/cgi-bin/etcsl.cgi?text=t.2.5.4.11#.
3. 2 Kings 21:7; 23:4, 7.
4. 2 Chronicles 21:16, author's translation.

II: Against the Flow

1. Matthew 5:11–12.
2. Psalm 23:4.
3. Proverbs 28:1, NIV.
4. Daniel 3:18.
5. Acts 4:18.
6. Acts 4:19–20.

IV: Powers

1. 1 Kings 18:17.
2. Hebrews 11:33–34, NASB.

V: Agents of Heaven on Earth

1. Matthew 5:13–14.
2. Romans 12:21.
3. Matthew 28:19.
4. Matthew 16:18.
5. 1 Corinthians 9:22, emphasis added.

VI: Messengers of Light

1. 2 Kings 23:21–23.
2. Isaiah 53:7, emphasis added.

3. John 1:29, emphasis added.
4. 1 Corinthians 5:7, TLV, emphasis added.
5. Psalm 22:3.
6. 2 Chronicles 20:22.
7. Nehemiah 8:10.

VII: Completion

1. 2 Kings 23:15.
2. 2 Kings 23:16.
3. 2 Kings 23:17.
4. 1 Kings 13:2.
5. 1 Kings 13:3.
6. 1 Kings 13:5.
7. 2 Kings 23:17.
8. Psalm 139:16.
9. Jeremiah 1:5.
10. Galatians 1:15.
11. Esther 4:14.
12. 2 Kings 23:25.
13. 2 Chronicles 16:9, NASB.

Chapter 47

1. Joel 1:2–3.
2. Joel 1:4, CSB.
3. Joel 2:2.
4. Joel 2:23.
5. Joel 2:23, emphasis added.
6. Joel 2:28.
7. Joel 2:28; Joel 2:30.

ABOUT JONATHAN CAHN

Jonathan Cahn caused a worldwide stir with the release of the *New York Times* best seller *The Harbinger* and his subsequent *New York Times* best sellers. He has addressed members of Congress and spoken at the United Nations. He was named, along with Billy Graham and Keith Green, one of the top forty spiritual leaders of the last forty years "who radically changed our world." He is known as a prophetic voice to our times and for the opening up of the deep mysteries of God. Jonathan leads Hope of the World, a ministry of getting the Word to the world and sponsoring projects of compassion to the world's most needy; and Beth Israel/the Jerusalem Center, his ministry base and worship center in Wayne, New Jersey, just outside New York City. He is a much-sought-after speaker and appears throughout America and the world.

To get in touch, to receive prophetic updates, to receive free gifts from his ministry (special messages and much more), to find out about his over two thousand messages and mysteries, for more information, to contact him, or to have a part in the Great Commission, use the following contacts.

Check out:	Write direct to:
HopeoftheWorld.org	Hope of the World
	Box 1111
	Lodi, NJ 07644 USA

To be kept up to date and see what's happening:

Facebook:	Jonathan Cahn (official site)
YouTube:	Jonathan Cahn Official
Twitter:	@Jonathan_Cahn
Instagram:	jonathan.cahn

Email:	contact@hopeoftheworld.org

To find out how you can go to the Holy Land with Jonathan on one of his upcoming Israel Super Tours, write to: contact@hopeoftheworld.org or check online for the coming Super Tours.

OUR <u>FREE GIFT</u> TO YOU

Dear Reader,

We hope you found **The Josiah Manifesto** to be as dramatic and mind-blowing as all of Jonathan Cahn's other books.

If you're ready to unlock more ancient mysteries with Jonathan Cahn, we have a **FREE GIFT** for you.

SCAN THIS CODE

Stream **The Harbingers of Things to Come:**

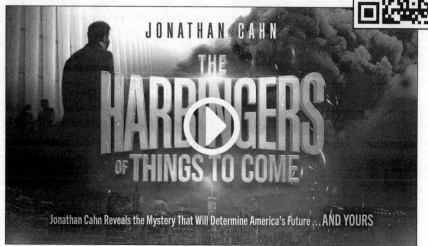

18141

Scan the code above to get this **FREE GIFT**, or go to **www.booksbyjonathancahn.com/movie2023**.

Thank you again, and God bless you.

—Publisher of FrontLine books